GW00501595

HITLER'S LAST ARMY

HITLER'S LAST ARMY

GERMAN POWs IN BRITAIN

ROBIN QUINN

The History Press

For my grandson, Louis

First published 2015

The History Press
The Mill, Brimscombe Port
Stroud, Gloucestershire, GL5 2QG
www.thehistorypress.co.uk

© Robin Quinn 2015

The right of Robin Quinn to be identified as the Author
of this work has been asserted in accordance with the
Copyright, Designs and Patents Act 1988.

British Library Cataloguing in Publication Data.
A catalogue record for this book is available from the British Library.

ISBN 978 0 7524 8275 0

Typesetting and origination by The History Press
Printed in Great Britain

Contents

Acknowledgements

I was sure from the very beginning that this book had to be based on the first-hand testimony of the former prisoners of war themselves. I'm therefore grateful to those who kindly allowed me to interview them – often at some considerable length. They have not only provided the information which forms the backbone of this book, but have also extended their hospitality, friendship and encouragement to me over the last two years. So I must begin by thanking them, together with their spouses and partners, as follows: Karl-Heinz Decker and Dorothy Masterman; Theo Dengel and his late wife, Joan; Bruno Liebich; Peter Roth; Werner and Iris Völkner; and Eberhard and Kathleen Wendler. I feel honoured to have met them all and to have been allowed to share their memories.

The following individuals have provided me with indispensable information, help and advice: John Andrews; Raymond Blackman; Arno Christiansen; Keith Ennis; Phil Fairclough; John Glanfield; Harry Grenville; Ingeborg Hellen; Mark Hickman; Mary Ingham; David Martin; Andrew Mitchell; Peter Osborne; Veronica Parker; Winston G. Ramsey; Maureen Small; Anne Smith; Sven Urbanski; Peter Venner; Malcolm Whitaker.

I am deeply indebted to the writers whose works I have consulted: the background information in their books has provided a solid foundation for this present volume.

Special thanks go to Stephen Walton (Senior Curator, Documents and Sound Section, The Imperial War Museum), whose help has been above and beyond the call of duty; likewise the kind assistance provided by his colleagues at the IWM's London Research Room. I am also grateful to the courteous and ever-resourceful staff at the British Library; the London Metropolitan Archives; the National Archives and the former Newspaper Library at Colindale; and to those at the many local libraries and archives I have contacted around the country.

Mark Beynon, my editor at The History Press, has been attentive and helpful throughout the whole process; I have had no hesitation in entrusting this work to him and his team of colleagues to work their magic on it before it finally makes its public debut.

Last but not least, a very big thank you to Jacqui, without whose love and support I could not even have considered embarking on this project.

Prologue

As the hop-pickers clambered into the back of the lorry none of them imagined that within minutes they would be fighting for their lives.

Every year the same families came down from London to the Sussex village of Bodiam for a working holiday, a good get-together, a breath of fresh air, and the chance to earn some welcome cash. It was mainly the women and children who went 'hopping': the men of the family could seldom get time off from their regular jobs, and only visited at weekends, if at all. During the war a hop-picking holiday had been especially prized as a respite from the bombing, a couple of weeks away from it all. But this was September 1947 – more than two years since VE Day – and people were slowly adapting to peacetime.

With thirty people on board, the lorry was hopelessly overloaded. Yet none of the passengers seem to have given a second thought to the short journey ahead. It was, after all, only a ten-minute ride and they'd soon be back in camp after a glorious summer's day in the sunshine. Some of the older women used to bring wooden chairs from home, and sat on them whenever they took a quick break from hop-picking. Now they put the chairs in the back of the truck and perched on them in relative comfort while the younger ones sat on the floor, all squashed together, wherever they could find a space.

From year to year the routine seldom varied, peacetime, wartime, rain or shine. 'There were about twenty in our group who went together with a family called the Moneys,' says Maureen Blackman, who was just 7 years old at the time. 'We all shared two wooden huts, numbers 51 and 52 – every year the same ones.'

George Middleton started the engine and drove off. Everyone knew George would take it nice and steady – his wife and their two young children were in the lorry. Minutes later they reached Bodiam village and approached the humpbacked bridge across the river. Back in 1940 a pillbox with a two-pounder gun had been installed close by to defend against the feared German invasion. Then the Home Guard found that the solid brick-built parapets on either side of the bridge blocked their line of fire: workmen had been sent to remove the masonry and some flimsy, makeshift railings were put in its place. And since the war no one had quite got around to putting the bridge back as it once was.

The hop-pickers are uncertain what happened next. There were some indistinct recollections of a car coming the other way at speed, but from the back of the lorry most of them simply couldn't see.

'One moment we were going along, all singing in the back,' Raymond Blackman remembers, 'then suddenly we were in the water.' The lorry had crashed through the railings, falling 10ft into the river and turning on to its side. The passengers were all thrown into a heap. For a few moments everyone was stunned, immobile, confused. Some were unconscious, a few seriously injured or gasping for air, trapped by the lorry's canvas cover.

Fifteen-year-old Donald Money had just left school and taken a job as a messenger with the Southern Railway. He'd recently taught himself to swim at the local pool. Freeing himself from the wreckage he spotted a small child whom he rescued from the water. But he knew he couldn't save the rest of them, not on his own: instead he ran 200 yards to a small encampment of tents in a field by the river. He had passed this way many times before and remembered seeing the soldiers there. When he arrived, the camp was almost empty, but he found four men preparing dinner for their comrades.

Out of breath, Donald tried to explain to the cooks what had happened. There was something of a language barrier, for these were not British soldiers.

They were German prisoners of war.

Somehow Donald made them understand. One of the men seized a sharp cooking knife and they all rushed back to the scene of the accident. The Germans dived into the river and started to rescue the crash victims. One slashed the canvas cover at the rear of the truck with the knife he had brought from the camp, freeing those trapped inside.

'They were brilliant,' says Raymond Blackman. 'They pulled us out and wrapped us in blankets. If it hadn't been for them, people would definitely have died.'

Though several people were hurt, all seemed to be accounted for, at first. One of the injured was Ellen Blackman – mother of Maureen and Raymond – who had sustained a broken arm and 'a terrible gash' to the head. When she looked around, she realised that Maureen was missing. According to her son, the late Terry Blackman, Ellen was 'a powerful, stocky woman, very strong.' But the news that Maureen was nowhere to be seen was too much even for her to bear, and she passed out.

'All the others were found close to where the accident happened,' recalls Maureen, 'but I was only 7 and small for my age. I was carried downstream, unconscious, and washed up against some reeds and rushes.' One of the Germans must have realised what had happened: he immediately ran along the riverbank until he found Maureen, dived into the water and lifted her out. Despite her ordeal she was, incredibly, uninjured and soon regained consciousness.

An account of the accident found its way into most of the national newspapers: the *Daily Herald* quoted a witness who summed up the incident in four words, 'The prisoners were wonderful.'

'My Dad bought the German prisoner a silver lighter to say thank-you, but a big regret was that we never got his name,' says Maureen. 'I would have loved to have tracked him down to let him know how grateful I was that he saved my life.' But it seems that the Germans were never publicly named.

Today – decades later – it seems extraordinary that German prisoners were still being held captive in Britain two years after the end of hostilities. Indeed, to quote

Professor Terry Charman of the Imperial War Museum, 'The entire POW experience for the British revolved around Colditz and the Great Escape. I think many young people would be surprised to learn there were German POWs living here at all.'

The fact is that as many as 400,000 Germans were detained as prisoners in the UK during and after the war – some until 1948.

This is their extraordinary story.

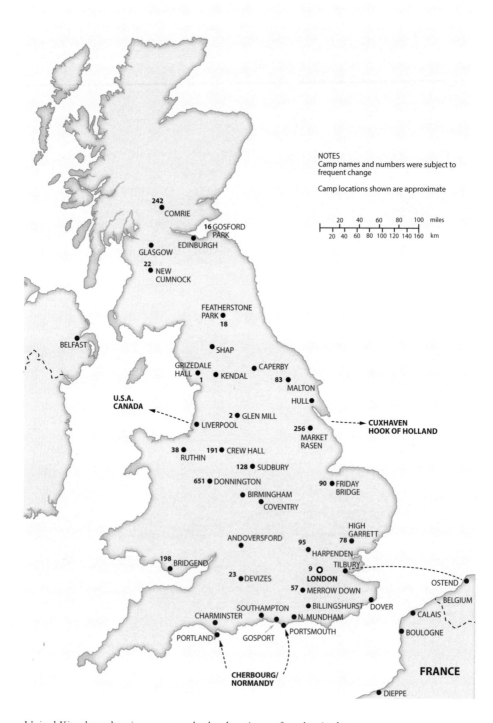

242 COMRIE

16 GOSFORD PARK
EDINBURGH
GLASGOW
22 NEW CUMNOCK

FEATHERSTONE PARK 18

BELFAST

SHAP

GRIZEDALE HALL 1 KENDAL CAPERBY 83

U.S.A. CANADA

MALTON
HULL

2 GLEN MILL
LIVERPOOL

256 MARKET RASEN

CUXHAVEN HOOK OF HOLLAND

38 RUTHIN 191 CREW HALL

128 SUDBURY

651 DONNINGTON

90 FRIDAY BRIDGE

BIRMINGHAM
COVENTRY

HIGH GARRETT

ANDOVERSFORD 95 78
HARPENDEN

198 BRIDGEND

23 DEVIZES

9 TILBURY
LONDON

OSTEND

57 MERROW DOWN

BELGIUM

SOUTHAMPTON BILLINGSHURST DOVER
CHARMINSTER N. MUNDHAM
PORTLAND GOSPORT PORTSMOUTH

CALAIS

BOULOGNE

CHERBOURG/ NORMANDY

FRANCE

DIEPPE

20 40 60 80 100 miles
20 40 60 80 100 120 140 160 km

United Kingdom, showing camps and other locations referred to in the text.

1

'Let's Go, Let's Go!'

It was towards the end of 2011 when I decided to write this book. I knew I'd need to interview people who'd actually been there – eyewitnesses to an almost forgotten chapter in our history. But *how* do you go about finding a former enemy who fought in the Second World War and was taken prisoner and held captive in Britain?

The answer came sooner than expected. That same evening BBC television carried a short piece about German ex-POWs who had stayed on in this country after the war: one of them, Bruno Liebich, talked about his experiences. Next morning I was speaking with him on the phone.

'I'd be glad to help,' he says, 'but I wouldn't be able to see you for several months. I'm busy writing my life story.' We chat for a few minutes. Bruno relents and I visit him at his home in St Albans soon afterwards. A framed oil painting of Field-Marshall Erwin Rommel stares down at us. 'One of the ex-prisoners gave that to me,' he says, almost apologetically. 'It's not a *very* good picture but it is a fair likeness, so I decided to keep it.

'I met Rommel once, you know …' In his thoughts Bruno is back in France, in Normandy, almost seventy years ago, standing to attention with his comrades as the great *General-Feldmarschall* inspects the troops. 'I come from Weißfurt, Lower Silesia,' Bruno says:

> It's a very small village with about thirty families, that's all. I was born on the 21 July 1926 in a *Gasthaus* [inn] which my grandfather built in 1846. There was a farm with it as well. My father was one of ten children – five boys and five girls. He died very young and so my branch of the family didn't inherit a share of the business. I attended *Volksschule* [people's school] from the age of 6 and, shortly before my 14th birthday, I was taken on as an apprentice at a savings bank. After almost three years I became a full employee. I was called up for the army on my 17th birthday, which was normal at the time. I did a bit of training in Germany, and then we moved to France before Christmas 1943. I was 17½.'

He was posted to Normandy. Very few of the soldiers there could be classed as 'crack troops'. Bruno's unit included many older men, some of whom had been wounded in Russia, and teenagers like Bruno himself. The average age was 37. They were stationed near the coast for three or four months at Vierville – listed in one pre-war guidebook as a *station balnéaire* – a sea-bathing resort with just 270 inhabitants. The main task of the German troops was to keep an eye on the French population, and after five years of occupation the two sides had settled down to a reasonably trouble-free coexistence.

> We were told to treat the French with respect. As I was one of the youngest, the sergeant would send me to get butter from the farm. I took my rifle – we had to *pretend* to be armed, but I don't remember whether we had any ammunition or not. I'd go alone, although we were supposed to go in pairs. And I'd say, '*Avez-vous du beurre, si'l vous plait?*' And I'd pay for the butter – we *always* paid – and take it back.

One winter's night in November 1943, just after they arrived, Bruno's sergeant sent him out for kindling wood so that they could light a fire and keep warm. 'We were living in the garage of a house, and the owner lived in the house itself. I went out and it was cold and dark, and I saw a fence outside and just broke off two of the wooden slats. We used it as kindling and the fire was going like mad and everybody was happy.' He adds, 'Next morning at 7.00 – "Everybody out!" and we all lined up outside. The commandant said, "Madame So-and-so has complained that two slats are missing from her fence. Who has taken them?" They all looked at one another. Bruno didn't say a word. "We'll soon find out who did it. Now, dismiss!"'

'Just two bits of wood and I could have finished up on the Eastern Front! Specially if they'd found out later and I'd told a lie. But that's how strict they were with us.'

Near the village, extending about 8km eastwards, was a sandy beach, which the writers of the *Guide Michelin* didn't even consider worthy of a mention. Yet it would soon become one of the most talked-about beaches in the world and have a name of its own – Omaha Beach.

'Rommel came up one day in March or maybe April 1944 and inspected the coast. He was my supreme commander, you see. Above him was only von Rundstedt for the whole of France. He said, "This is where they're going to land. We'll put some defences here to stop them." He was right, of course, but he was too late.' Soon after Rommel's visit, Bruno's unit was moved about 20km inland and they made camp in an orchard where apple trees were grown for the local tipple, Calvados. By this stage in the war the German army was overstretched and poorly equipped – fuel and spare parts were in short supply and soldiers frequently had to travel to their posts using farm carts or bicycles.

A few minutes before midnight on 5 June, sounds of gunfire reached Bruno and his comrades from the direction of the coast. 'We didn't take it seriously at first but when it didn't stop we realised something was happening. At about 4 a.m. the commandant said, "Get ready to move", so we left between five and six o'clock towards the coast.'

It was a cold, windy, overcast morning. They set off on the new black bicycles which had been delivered to them only a week or two earlier, with their personal belongings following on behind in a horse-drawn cart. Halfway to the coast they heard more intense gunfire as the first Allied troops landed on Omaha Beach. The largest combined sea, air and land operation of all time was just beginning.

Abandoning their cycles they cautiously moved forward on foot. At about midday they arrived at the coastal village of Colleville and looked toward the horizon. Before them an armada of almost 7,000 ships, landing craft and other vessels stretched as far as the horizon. One of the defenders later likened it to a 'gigantic town on the sea'.

At Omaha Beach alone, 34,000 Allied troops had landed, or were about to land, on that first day. Bruno recalls:

> It was something exceptional that we'd never seen before and we were simply lost for words. We could see hundreds of ships and balloons, lots of aeroplanes, guns firing, troops, tanks, machine guns, noise, landing craft. We said, 'Oh, my God!' We realised we'd never beat that lot; there was a massive superiority there. We'd been expecting the invasion, expecting it all the time, but nobody knew when and where. We carried on as long as we could. Later in the day we took an American prisoner so we realised it was the Americans against us and we were then driven back.
>
> Next morning we were trying desperately to get out because we were surrounded, and our little unit was getting smaller and smaller. Some must have disappeared or gone their own way or whatever.

The American prisoner had also slipped away. Bruno and his comrades considered this to be a problem solved, for they had been wondering quite what to do with him.

> There were only about fifty or sixty of us left now. We were lying in this ditch in the Normandy fields – they always have ditches and hedges to keep the cows in, not fences – and a small unit of ten or twelve men were coming towards us. We saw them but they couldn't see us. Our sergeant said, 'Don't shoot, let them come a bit closer.' So we waited till they were about 80m away, and he said 'Shoot!' After we'd fired one maybe two shots, he said, 'Now, *run! Get out of it!*'

'It was my one-shot, twenty-four-hour war.'

They ran this way and that. Bruno found himself at one end of the column – at its head or its tail, depending on their direction at any given moment. 'I was in front when we ran over this little field path into the hedge on the other side. We jumped, we crawled, whatever. There was a hell of a noise behind us. They'd spotted us. All those behind us were shot to pieces, wounded or killed. There were five or six of us – not more – in this hedge looking out and we saw fifty men standing there with rifles ready and a tank behind them. Our sergeant said, "We can't fight all this lot, we're caught. We'll have to give ourselves up."'

From the moment he surrendered, Bruno's future was to be irrevocably changed. And the same would be true for thousands of other soldiers as the invasion proceeded. 'That moment was the first time I'd ever thought about being taken prisoner. It had never entered my mind. But for this one step … it could have been a completely different life.'

Was Bruno afraid? 'Not really. Personally I was never frightened – I don't know why, I *should* have been. We didn't have time to think, just to look after yourself. I was hoping they were decent people like me.' It was only later that reports surfaced of Allied troops killing prisoners in retaliation for their own losses. At Omaha Beach alone, some 2,000 American soldiers had already died under withering machine gun fire from German defensive positions overlooking the beach. The blood of the fallen invaders tinted the water red. Those who had witnessed the slaughter were often in no mood to take prisoners. According to one American officer, paratroopers in particular were 'apt in going along the road with prisoners and seeing one of their own men killed, to turn around and shoot a prisoner to make up for it'. Some units, it is claimed, had actually been ordered to shoot any enemy soldiers they captured rather than be hindered by the burden of guarding them. 'There was no way we could take prisoners because there was no place to put them,' one Allied soldier explained.

Bruno and what was left of his unit came out of hiding and made a show of throwing their guns away, so that the enemy could plainly see they were unarmed. 'We put our hands up – as high as they'll go – and walked toward them very slowly and they told us to stop, then they searched us.' The Americans took away their gas masks and any other surplus equipment, and frisked them for hidden weapons. They also took advantage of the situation to collect some spoils of war. Swastika emblems were highly prized as mementoes. Most of the prisoners lost theirs. Many had their watches stolen too – but not Bruno. 'To have a wristwatch in the 1940s was *something*, not just an everyday thing. I'd managed to buy one in France with my soldier's pay, and I was very proud of it.' Somehow he managed to remove it from his wrist and slip it inside his sock. Rings, too, were 'confiscated'. Aside from that, Bruno says, 'They didn't treat us roughly at all. No pushing or kicking, they just wanted souvenirs.'

Many conflicting thoughts swirled in his mind. 'It wasn't a good feeling to give up what we were here for. And you worry about what's going to happen.' His concerns were no longer for the bigger picture. 'It was all over in such a short time and, being taken prisoner, you've got to worry about what's happening next. So we just took one day at a time.'

Another German soldier, Josef Kox, captured later that year in Holland, told a researcher, 'Being taken prisoner is quite traumatic. You don't know what's going to happen. There are a thousand thoughts going through your mind, all in a split second.' Günther Mauff, on the other hand, had just a single preoccupation: 'What's going to happen to me? What will they do to me? That was all.' Franz Kriesch took a philosophical view: 'What you have to do to survive [is] you put up your hands. If you don't you're a hero – but a dead one.'

'A strange new existence was about to begin,' another German recalls. '[We were] in a kind of limbo, a vacuum between the old life and whatever the future held.'

Having frisked the prisoners, the Americans gestured with their rifles and yelled the words that tens of thousands of prisoners would hear repeated over the next weeks and months: 'Let's go, let's go!'

Plucked from the highly structured world of army life into the unknown, the prisoners clutched at the smallest of straws. Minor details assumed massive proportions and stayed fixed in the memory like a photographic image. 'The first building we passed there was a farmer standing at the gate with a big tub of cider,' Bruno recalls. 'We hadn't had anything to eat or drink for a couple of days. He gave me a cup of cider – it was heavenly, lovely – and I remember that so clearly.'

'We were just herded together in a field. There was no barbed wire, and only a couple of guards. They knew we wouldn't run away. We spent a couple of nights just lying on the grass. It was bitter cold during the night because we had no blankets – they'd been thrown away, left behind.' Around this nucleus of a few men hundreds more captured German soldiers clustered as the hours went by.

Allied deception plans had led the German high command to believe that the attack in Normandy was only a feint: in other parts of France men were kept on standby for the time being, while their commanders waited to see where the *real* invasion would take place.

Just to the south of St Nazaire, 250km from Omaha Beach, a slightly-built 18-year-old soldier named Eberhard Wendler was on duty. From a fortified bunker near the shore he could look out on to the windswept Atlantic Ocean. By his own admission he was a reluctant participant in the war. Given the choice, he would much rather have stayed at home and begun a career as a precision engineer – a vocation for which he'd just completed an apprenticeship back home. But home was a long, long way to the east, close to Germany's border with Czechoslovakia.

I lived in a little village in the *Erzgebirge* – the Ore Mountains. It was beautiful. We knew all the neighbours – it was like a big family. We had no cinema, nothing, but we were very happy. We weren't well-off but my parents had work. I'd never been away from home – I must have been 16 before I went to the next town. I was always shy and retiring and never mixed much.

My father was called up first and my mother went to work spinning yarn to make cloth. Every night after she came home from work she cooked for me and my brother Gert, who was three or four years younger than me. And about 10 p.m. she would sit and write a letter to my Dad. *Every night!* And she'd go out in the dark and post it.

Before being called up into the army, Eberhard was conscripted to do compulsory duty in the *Reichsarbeitsdienst* – the National Labour Corps – a quasi-military organisation which served to prepare Hitler Youth members for the full-time military. 'I had to go to Borkum, an island in the North Sea,' he explains. 'We were always marching and singing. When you got to the coast there was a promenade and the beach a long way below. We had to jump down. I was afraid but you counted for nothing in the German army – you just jumped. Then we had exercises on the beach – *every morning.*'

Eberhard returned home from his stint in the Labour Corps and awaited his call-up papers, which arrived in the post on 20 January 1944. He was so flustered that he inadvertently dropped them into a bucket of water. His mother went with him to the barracks. Within a few days he and his new comrades had been issued with their uniforms, gas mask, gas cape, Karabiner 98 rifle and sidearm. Strictly against all the rules, Eberhard had begun to keep a secret diary on scraps of paper, which he hid in his gas cape. The recruits boarded a train to their posting and as they passed through towns and cities he noted details of the journey – a gazetteer of exotic places he had scarcely even heard of before:

> **4 February 1944**: left Plauen in goods wagons (40 men to each wagon). We went via Reichenbach, Zwickau, Glauchau, Leipzig, Marburg, Koblenz, Trier, Metz, Paris, Le Mans, Nantes, Pont Château – where it snowed for the first time.

Even at that stage in the war, the shops in France still offered luxury goods which would have been difficult or impossible to buy in Germany:

> **14 March 1944**: sent two 1-kilogram packages to home. Contents: one silk scarf (350 *francs*), one pair stockings (160 *francs*), pudding, baking powder, one jar of soap, and one bottle of liqueur (160 *francs*).

News of the invasion seems to have momentarily disrupted the normal routine:

> **6 June 1944**: alarm and move out. We had to take our vehicles and horses and everything and go under cover in the little wood by the château. At 14.00 hours we could go back to our quarters.

'Everybody expected the Allies to come, but they didn't come where *we* were,' he says with a flicker of a smile. 'When the Allies landed in Normandy it was apparent *that* was the place, and that Germany was being beaten, and so it was decided to move us. We'd heard that they'd landed, but we hadn't a clue where we were being marched to. All that way, hundreds of miles we marched at night – only at night – [to avoid daytime aerial attack]. There were hundreds, thousands of men. They wouldn't have told us where we were going and we wouldn't have dared to ask.' They avoided towns and used only country lanes:

> The blisters! When you stopped, ah! That was a relief. But when you started again … we had jackboots on and in the army they said, 'If they don't fit it's not the boots, it's your feet.' I was a little chap then, one of the smallest. The big tall ones marched in front, and when they make one step you make about two, and we marched like that. And we were *absolutely* worn out.

It was 20 July – six weeks after D-Day – when Eberhard's unit arrived in the village of La Chapelle near St Lô. They were immediately given five days leave to recover from the long march, but had to move camp twice because of artillery fire and aerial attacks. Although the Allied forces had gained a foothold in France, they had failed from the beginning to achieve their objectives on schedule. General George S. Patton's Third Army was given the objective of breaking out and advancing further inland. Patton (whose motto was 'In case of doubt, attack') arranged for the air force to drop thousands of bombs on the defending German troops before his men moved in to finish off the enemy. Eberhard wrote:

> **25 July 1944**: in the morning the carpet-bombing of St Lô took place. I immediately left with *Oberleutnant* Spieß and others to look for new quarters. At 20.00 hours the order came to make ready and we advanced in an armoured personnel carrier. At 22.00 came the order to advance on foot. We suffered heavy artillery fire on the march. Houses were burning and on the streets stood blazing tanks in which the ammunition kept blowing up. Our group was attached to the first company and we lost contact in a little wood. We could go no further on the road because it was under artillery fire and there was a burning tank with exploding ammunition. I was sent forward alone to try to make contact and lost my way repeatedly. After I had joined the group we took up position in a trench on the front line and dug in.

> **26 July 1944**: in the morning we were continually attacked by fighter-bombers and came under attack from heavy artillery, grenade-launchers and automatic weapons. I was slightly wounded by a piece of shrapnel in the upper left arm.

'The noise was deafening,' he adds, the scene as vivid to him today it was then. 'The fighter planes came over so low they almost touched you. The worst was the trench mortars, you don't see them come, you don't hear them. And they hardly need touch a leaf and they explode.' The ground shook 'like an earthquake' as the bombs fell, he remembers, and for weeks afterwards he could hear gunfire and explosions in his sleep. 'It was hopeless to do anything, and in any case I was wounded. The Yanks shouted, "Come out, come out!" But you were afraid to come out. You don't know if they'll shoot you. Nobody wanted to move. Then they start firing again and so it goes on.'

Finally, around midday, Eberhard and his comrades emerged from their defences and surrendered. 'They checked us all, and they were very keen to take our watches and everything, and handle you roughly. And they took some of our men to interrogate … and then one by one march them back, all the time hands-up.' This initial interrogation served to identify the men's unit and deal with any urgent matters, such as the number of troops remaining. The soldiers' pay-books, together with any other documents they carried, including letters and photographs, were taken from them. These would provide useful intelligence and serve as the basis for a more detailed interrogation a few days later.

Eberhard and the others were forced to climb into a truck. 'There were one or two Americans in the back with rifles ready,' he remembers. What many POWs recall is that most of the drivers were black. In the racially segregated US Army, African-Americans were often employed in support roles such as transport: but for almost all the Germans it was the first time they had ever seen a black man except in pictures.

To prevent the prisoners from escaping, the drivers had been ordered not to slow down under any circumstances. 'They drove like devils,' says Henry Metelmann describing his own experiences a little later in the war. 'One lorry overturned, and was lying at the bottom of an embankment. We could hear the shouts and the cries and saw the prisoners crawl out from underneath like eels – those who could still crawl. What a way to die, a day or so after having escaped the war alive!'

'There were sixty to a hundred prisoners of war in each lorry,' Heinz Matthias told a German TV interviewer. 'We had to shout [a warning] whenever there was an overhanging apple tree with a low branch. The man standing in front of me was too slow to react and the branch hit him in the face at 60km an hour. He collapsed and slid down – he couldn't fall over because the men were so tightly packed – and his head was between my legs and blood spurted out. His skull was smashed and he was finished.'

They were taken to a succession of temporary camps, none of which provided shelter of any kind for the captives. 'We were just in the open, there was no accommodation and we didn't know where we were,' says Eberhard Wendler. For a long time they received no food or drink, then finally they were given American ration packs. 'That was wonderful! One packet had got some stuff in it, we hadn't a clue what it was.' (It was in fact a mixture of powdered tea, artificial sweetener and powdered milk which, with the addition of boiling water, made an instant hot drink.)

Eberhard and his comrades ate it straight from the packet: 'It was lovely. We were hungry. We'd have eaten anything.'

2

In the Land of the Enemy

Planning for D-Day had started months beforehand: 65,000 copies of the meticulously prepared operation manual – each one as thick as a phone directory – were printed. Every contingency was covered, including the procedure for dealing with POWs. The Geneva Convention required that prisoners should be removed from the battle zone to a place of safety as soon as possible. To this end, captured troops would be transported to England until conditions on the Continent were suitable for them to be kept in camps there.

A small fleet comprising sixteen LST (Landing Ships, Tank) was set aside to transport prisoners across the Channel, and operated a shuttle service between Normandy and the British Channel ports. In their usual role, these 400ft-long ships could carry twenty medium tanks; as POW-carriers they could take up to 800 prisoners at a time to English ports – a total of up to 2,000 a day. When this scheme was unveiled to the High Command before the invasion, the planners had admitted that they may have been somewhat optimistic in planning for so many prisoners: but, in the event, daily totals were occasionally twice as high as predicted.

The Channel crossing was estimated to take twenty-four hours: in bad weather, though, it might last for up to four days. The LSTs came right in to the Normandy beaches at right-angles to the shoreline, their bow doors open 'like gigantic whales'. The German prisoners marched down the beach and into the surf until the water reached their knees, then up the ramp and into the landing ship.

For its size, Germany has relatively few kilometres of coastline and consequently the Germans as a whole are not a seafaring nation. Most of the prisoners had never been on a ship of any kind and some had never seen the sea. Bruno Liebich remembers being swallowed up in 'a plain, empty hull, totally empty, and on the side were two huge ropes'. By lying on the deck around the outside of this vast space, they could rest their heads on these great hawsers and use them as a pillow. Beyond that, the craft offered no comfort: another POW describes the LST:

an enormous, square, iron box, with floors, walls and ceiling of steel. It had no windows, only very small round portholes very high up so that no one was able to see out of them, and they would only let in the minimal amount of fresh air. Slowly the boarding ramp was winched up and every vestige of daylight, and every sound faded from eye and ear … as the last crack of daylight disappeared from the top of the boarding ramp, a little rustle of panic rippled fitfully among [the POWs].

'When the tanks come off the ship,' Fritz Jeltsch explains, 'the big ramp comes down and the tanks roll over it. The ships come as far up the beach as possible but water gets in. When we were on the high seas the ship was swinging and the deck was awash with rusty water. It sloshed about over our feet and soaked our uniforms.'

John Andrews was a crew member on board one of the LST's smaller counterparts, the LCT (Landing Craft, Tank). These flat-bottomed craft were nicknamed 'kipper boxes' by all who sailed in them, and were notorious for the unreliability of their engines. On those occasions when they could be persuaded to function at all they had a maximum speed of 10 knots and carried eleven tanks.

In the latter part of D-Day, Andrews noticed 'cruisers, destroyers, troopships, LSTs, LCTs as far as the eye could see'. They crossed in mid-Channel with other craft which had already unloaded their precious cargo of men, munitions and machines, and arrived at Gold Beach late at night. When a rope became entangled with their propeller, the beach-master ordered some of the waiting POWs to help free it.

While the ships would soon be leaving densely packed with prisoners, some of these earlier sailings were almost empty. 'It wasn't really crowded, so we could lie down and have a little rest,' Bruno Liebich says. On each vessel twelve armed guards watched over the POWs. 'They were standing at one end and bartering with chocolate for souvenirs – swastikas, rings and things like that – and they were having a lovely time, I think. We were cooped in there; we didn't know whether it was day or night.' Under such conditions, and having hidden his watch, Bruno quickly lost track of the time. But he believes the crossing took two days, and this is consistent with other prisoners' accounts.

Many former POWs speak of a sense of helplessness, a complete inability to control their own destiny. 'Every second a fresh decision was being taken [about us] which we ourselves couldn't influence.' Although they had no idea what lay in store for them, their fate for the next few years, possibly for the rest of their lives, was already determined – by as trivial a factor as the initial letter of their surname. Britain and the United States had agreed to share responsibility for the prisoners. From now on, the general rule was that those whose surnames began with a letter in the first half of the alphabet were to be imprisoned in the United States, and the remainder in Britain.* Prisoners chosen to stay in Britain generally made the 'short sea crossing', as it was known in official circles, to either Southampton or Gosport. Newhaven and, on occasion, other ports were also used.

Those bound for the United States were shipped to Portland in Dorset, then onwards to Le Marchant Camp at Devizes, Wiltshire, for further processing. They

---

* A man whose name began with the letter Z was sent to Canada; his belief was that all those with this initial went to the same destination, but this has not been verified.

usually spent a week or two in Britain before being transported on troopships – usually via Liverpool – to America, where most would stay for many months.

At Portland harbour Bruno set foot in the land of the enemy for the first time. But the significance of this event affected him only slightly:

> I can't remember that I was overwhelmed by anything. I think at the time the five steps in front of you are important – the rest you can't absorb. There's a group of you – you're among your own men, that's reassuring. You listen for orders and you haven't got time to absorb the situation, the fact that you're now in England. It was just land – people, houses – very similar to the other side, really, so it wasn't a momentous occasion. No, it was minute by minute, day by day. You don't even tell yourself what to do – it's automatic that you don't make any mistakes, don't say anything wrong.

On disembarkation from the landing ship, the POWs were marched a short distance to a railway platform. When they saw the train that would take them to their next destination, they were astonished. '[As soldiers] in Germany and France you were put in a cattle wagon. The doors shut, you may not see anything. But here we were sitting on seats, with a table. It was lovely, the difference, you know.'

Their destination was unknown to them; what would happen to them on arrival they couldn't guess. But any apprehension that Bruno and his comrades felt was balanced by their relief at being out of the war. There was an unexpected sense of exhilaration, too. 'Strange as it sounds, it was an exciting sort of experience.' He smiles. 'Yet it could have been deadly, couldn't it? At the time, though, because we were young and innocent, perhaps, we didn't perceive it in that way.'

On arrival in Devizes they were subdivided into still smaller groups.* After two or three days they travelled by rail to Haltwhistle, Northumberland, where they stayed for less than a week: then to Liverpool where they boarded an ocean-going troopship which had brought American soldiers to Europe for the invasion, and was now returning to the United States. During the crossing, the POWs were fed on porridge and nothing else. Stricken by acute hunger, Bruno bartered a ring for two bars of chocolate, and sustained himself by eating a small piece every morning and another at night. The ship docked at Boston, Massachusetts, where an American soldier searched Bruno and said, 'What's *this*?' as he hurled the treasured chocolate into a rubbish bin. Even now, seventy years later, Bruno sighs at the memory. 'I'll *never* forget that. I think I'd have killed him if I could.'

Bruno and his fellow soldiers were to spend the next two years in the United States, but they had not yet seen the last of Britain.

---

* Bruno Liebich says that, not knowing the actual name of this camp at the time, the prisoners referred to it as 'the A-B-C camp' because the subdivision into groups was according to the first letter of the men's surnames.

For Eberhard Wendler it was different. He, and many others, would spend the rest of the war in Britain. They were hustled at gunpoint from the beach on to the landing ship. Seven weeks had passed since D-Day and the shuttle service was now operating at full capacity:

> There was hardly room to sit. We were crammed in there and we sat on the rusty steel deck. We were there ages, not knowing what was going on. There were no facilities to relieve yourself, but they lowered a massive tub down with a crane and we had to take it in turns, and you sit and take your trousers off and do your job on there. There wasn't anything to wipe yourself. But what a relief. And then, when the tub was full – running over – they took it up and they made sure it slopped about all over so you got wet, and tipped it out and lowered it down again.

Eberhard found it unsettling to be separated from his comrades. 'We didn't know anybody else, only one or two you'd been captured with. We were hungry. We were all mixed up, and we were fed up and we were frightened. At Southampton we were let out into a reception camp with big cages all in the open and we were left out there for a long time. We eventually got something to eat, pre-packed food. Then we were taken on the train with guards.' Everywhere they were encircled by barbed wire. Now it was British soldiers, not American, who watched their every move. The POWs were ushered into a big hall – possibly part of an army barracks – and the Tommies brought out some stew.

'We had once been told by an officer, "Be comrades, and help each other."' But of the eight Germans at his table four were sergeants: 'These wretches who were supposed to look after us piled their plates to overflowing. I was the next to last, and I only got half a scoop and the last one got nothing. Honestly, it's niggled me all these years how they scoffed the lot!'

After the meal, they passed along still more corridors of barbed wire, and boarded another train. Predicting that very large numbers of prisoners might be captured, the Allied forces had made elaborate plans to 'process' the POWs as efficiently as possible. A special camp was set up at Kempton Park racecourse for the purpose. A minimum of four trains arrived here every day, each carrying 500 POWs. The whole reception process was supposed to take no longer than a day: official orders stated that the prisoners must be 'detrained, fed, received, searched, medically examined, their clothes disinfested, bathed, reclothed in their disinfested clothing, interrogated, accommodated for the night and entrained for base camps, all within the time stated'. It was a tall order, but the POWs would generally be on their way again within the allotted twenty-four hours.

As soon as the men had disembarked from the trains they were marched straight on to a flat area behind the grandstand which was nicknamed the 'barrack square'. Now the British would show the prisoners who was in charge. Intelligence Officer Tony Hare describes the procedure with POWs fresh from the battlefields in France:

From previous information, we had some idea which German divisions were in the area, and by learning all the numbers of the regiments and special battalions by heart, it was possible to call them out and make them fall-in in the same sequence that they had been on the front line only some hours earlier. This gave them the impression we knew a great deal about them, and any questions during the preliminary negotiations that followed were frequently given freely and in a relaxed manner, particularly as they were simultaneously told about the hot shower and meal afterwards. The aroma of this meal was usually wafting across the interrogation huts at the time. The result of this was a very strange psychological experience. For ten days we lived as if we were in Normandy, talking to prisoners who had been there some hours before, having constant detailed maps before us.

Every German knew, if only vaguely, of the Gestapo's reputation in Germany: assuming that things would be the same in Britain, the POWs doubtless found the prospect of being interrogated by the Secret Service especially chilling. They were led into 'a long hall where there were about a dozen tables in a line'.

'The interrogator was a Norwegian who spoke perfect German,' says a German paratrooper captured in Brittany. During the interview he was asked if he would go on the radio and broadcast propaganda to the German troops. 'I said, "Sir, when Hitler is dead, yes. While he's alive, no – because if you've sworn your allegiance you must keep your word. You're only released from that oath when the man you've sworn to is dead.'

'One at a time we went in and the Secret Service were there and we were interrogated,' Eberhard Wendler remembers. With the prisoner's pay-book open in front of him, along with any other documents captured from the POW, the Intelligence Officer was at a distinct advantage. 'They knew which town you came from and told me, "They're making things for the war effort there, and we'll make sure we bomb your town." And they said that Russia needed a lot of people to work there and we were warned we'd all be taken to Russia to work in the mines.'

The prisoners found it unnerving to be questioned by someone with such a perfect grasp of the German language. In fact, a significant number of the interrogators *were* Germans – Jewish refugees who had fled to Britain before the war to escape persecution under the Nazi regime. The irony was that some had initially been interned as 'enemy aliens' right here at Kempton Park.

The tables were turned. Now it was the Jews who were asking the questions.

Twenty-two-year-old paratrooper, Bernhard (Bert) Trautmann, who later became a legendary footballer, claimed, 'They knew more about us than we did ourselves.' As 'unimagined numbers' of prisoners threatened to overwhelm the system, extra interpreters were drafted in to help. A staff-sergeant by the name of Deutsch was transferred from another depot, but was quickly sent back when it turned out that – in spite of his promising name – he spoke no German at all and was, in fact, an Italian interpreter.

After being on the battlefield for days or weeks without proper washing facilities, most of the Germans were infested with lice. '[They] used to gather in the crotch of our trousers and drive us mad,' one German soldier explained. 'When we had time we would remove our trousers, turn them inside out and hold the crotch over a lighted candle. This was a horrendous job but it killed most of the little blighters.' As well as being a major irritant to the sufferer, lice could spread typhus. The major German chemical company, IG Farben, had begun during the war to manufacture a product called *Lauseto* containing DDT, but supplies were never adequate and seldom reached the front-line troops who needed them most.

As former interrogator Matthew Barry Sullivan describes, 'The cavernous areas under the stands [at Kempton Park stadium] were ideal for the big delousing parades at which every prisoner was squirted with DDT.'

'Our uniforms were all taken off and fumigated and we stood there naked.' explains Eberhard Wendler.

'A British soldier, with a syringe at least 2ft long, and full of DDT delousing powder, skilfully squirted everyone from top to bottom, fore and aft, making sure that the powder entered into every wrinkle and fold of skin,' a POW remembers.

This process was followed by the promised 'hot shower' – in reality a pathetic trickle of icy water. 'Our uniform came back again all wet and we had to put it on again.'

A somewhat different version of the procedure was sometimes adopted. The POWs were ordered to throw all of their clothes on to a huge pile prior to delousing. Afterwards, they went to a hut where, according to one man, 'Trestle tables were piled high with assorted bits of German uniforms. Each prisoner had an item of clothing thrust towards them indiscriminately, with no attempt to check the size, until every man had one of everything available … some of them were so badly shrunk that it was doubtful if they would have fitted a child.' He finished up with 'a pair of green drill trousers, grey shirt, boots two sizes too large, and an infantry jacket that hung down well below the tips of [the] fingers … permission was given to swap around, and eventually everyone was dressed in something.'

Peter Roth was in his mid-20s. He'd already seen a lot more of army life than most of the teenage conscripts who stood in line with him waiting to shower. Long before the Canadians captured him he'd acquired a reputation as a bit of a rebel. In fact, it had all started in his early teens. 'I lived in a staunchly Catholic village. All the other boys were in a Catholic youth organisation, and I didn't think it was genuine. They were all good boys – but only when the priest was near. I like everything to be straight, you see. I was one of only seven or eight who went into the Hitler Youth. We went out on night exercises and so on. It was the best time I ever had, absolutely brilliant.' He was glad when he received his call-up papers, but military life didn't turn out entirely as he had expected. 'The first thing they do when you start in the army is to make you like a machine. All you do is what you are ordered, no questions asked. They made you like a computer. I didn't like that sort of thing; I wanted to do my own things. I got into a hell of a trouble about it. The thing was to outwit the authority. If I could outwit anyone who was in charge, that was my plan.'

As he stood in a long line of weary prisoners, it was not immediately apparent to Peter how he was going to outwit the British army, who seemed very much in control at that moment. But his chance would come, of that he was sure.

A posting to France had offered more scope to do as he pleased:

> I had a very big position in the German army because I spoke fluent French. I was in charge of an army food depot in Mont de Marsan, south-western France. I loved France – I had a girlfriend whose mother owned a hotel in Biarritz. Her mother was lying on her deathbed and the last thing she ever said to me was, 'Peter, when this war is over, and I hope it's soon, if you still love each other this is all yours' – a big hotel in Biarritz. She took to me, you see.

As he pondered these things, the queue of men shuffled forwards under the gaze of the guards. Those ahead of him were undressing. It was not a very dignified procedure. Peter felt an undercurrent of anxiety – not because he was embarrassed about taking off his clothes. The fact was that for some time he had – somewhat alarmingly – been swindling the German army out of large sums of money. And now he was worried that the British would get their hands on the wads of cash he'd stashed in his clothing.

After the good life in Biarritz he'd been transferred to northern France, to a village near Abbeville. 'I was responsible for the soldiers' accommodation and I made sure I got good quarters for myself. I was always on the winning side, you see. Later, I was interpreter for the whole area.' Here he hit upon a scam with the potential to make him rich:

> We expected an invasion, and I was in charge of French people who worked for me erecting telephone poles in the fields so your gliders wouldn't be able to land. And I told my boss I would put them on piecework – they'll do more work that way. I said, 'You tell me how many poles you want there and you'll get them.' I gave each worker 10 *francs*, but I charged my boss 13 *francs*. So there was 3 *francs* for me, and I always had plenty of money. I wouldn't ever cheat an ordinary man, but I'd cheat the system if I could make some money.

Finally, Peter's turn came to strip off all his clothes and shower. 'I've never had such a quick shower in all my life,' he remembers. 'We had to run through that shower; we hadn't got ten drops of water on us. And when we got our things back, all the money and everything had gone.'

He accepted the forfeiture of the cash with stoicism, expecting to make up for it later, perhaps. But some things simply couldn't be replaced:

If they just took the money I'd have understood, but the worst thing was when one of the guards took our photographs and burned them. There were men crying like babies. Some of them, their families had been bombed out and they only had one picture of their wife and children. Things like that make you bitter. If any of the guards had come in to where we were at night we would have killed them. It leaves a lump in your throat – you don't forget it – I'm *still* bitter about it now.

Behaviour of this kind was not unknown, but it was not typical either: the POWs generally received humane, if somewhat dispassionate, treatment. 'They looked after my injured arm, treated it with iodine,' says Eberhard Wendler. 'Then we went outside in the open again. Next morning we went on again by train. In every wagon there were English soldiers with guns. They couldn't speak to us, and we couldn't speak to them.' The Germans were by no means an uncultured people, but under the Nazi regime schooling for most young men centred on learning a practical trade, with very little emphasis on languages and other 'arts' subjects. Any remaining time was mostly spent being force fed Nazi doctrine. 'Our lessons comprised the history of the lives of Hitler, Göring, Goebbels and other famous Nazis. If we knew all the details we would pass any exams,' claimed one POW. Even the few Germans who *did* know a little English were perplexed by the many regional accents of the Tommies and their Yankee allies. For their part, of course, the British were proud of their inability to learn other languages. The guards contented themselves with a handful of useful phrases – such as *'Hände hoch!'*, and *'Schnell, schnell!'* ('Hands up!'; 'Quick, quick!').

A long journey through the night via Newcastle and Edinburgh brought Eberhard Wendler and his companions to Camp 16, Gosford, East Lothian. From here, they could see the Forth Bridge in the distance. The camp was a former British army barracks which had been hastily laid out in the grounds of a mansion prior to D-Day. Afterwards it was converted for POW use, when it became evident that space would have to be found for significant numbers of German prisoners. That summer it had room for 3,000 men with fifty men crammed into each hut. Even so, some 400 had to sleep in tents until more permanent accommodation was erected late in the year.

'It was an enormous camp, and lovely to be at last somewhere, but there were SS men, navy, air force and infantry like us,' says Eberhard. A significant number of SS men, paratroopers, Luftwaffe aircrew, and submariners were strong adherents to Hitler's National Socialist doctrine, and one of the first tasks to be undertaken by the British administration would be to identify the ardent Nazis and segregate them from the rest of the prisoners. 'On a different day for each hut we were interrogated again in a large hall.' It was here that each man was assigned an individual prisoner of war number. 'I don't remember my German army number, but I still know my POW number.'

A major worry for the captives was that loved ones at home would not know whether they were listed 'missing' or had been killed, wounded or taken prisoner. The procedure was that the British authorities forwarded details of each POW to the International Red Cross in Geneva, where an index was kept, enabling any enquiries to be answered. In addition, each man could send a postcard to his family via Switzerland: it bore a simple preprinted message: 'I have fallen into English captivity. I am well. Permanent address follows.' The card bore a stamp, which read 'Transit camp. Do not write until the POW has notified you of his final address.'

Eberhard sent this card on the last day of July 1944. Only when the prisoner had been transferred to this 'final address' would there be any possibility of two-way postal correspondence.*

Every new arrival was issued with a *Seesack* (a kitbag of the kind used by sailors), a shirt, a pair of underpants, two pairs of socks, two handkerchiefs, one pair of braces, one toothbrush, one nailbrush, one comb, one bar of soap, and a sewing kit. The German Red Cross provided each prisoner with six cigarettes and a small quantity of tobacco. The POWs were handed a set of cutlery for their personal use and had to sign for it.

Food was scarce. A large cauldron of soup or stew had been prepared one evening, and the men queued up to be served. 'As we were coming near to it, and it was getting low, one of the cooks just poured a bucket of hot water in.' Eberhard's diary shows that on 13 August, 'Our group had kitchen duty, and I ate so much I was sick.'

'In Germany we ate rye bread at home and it's filling,' he recalls. 'But in England we got white bread – that was lovely, we'd never had it before. But it was like eating cotton wool, you bite into it and it's gone.' Before long they were hungry again. And there was another unwelcome side effect. 'For a fortnight you went to the toilet and you only produced water. And finally the first one in the hut shouted, "Hooray, I did something!"'

This difficulty was later remedied by introducing rye into the bread. Later, baking was carried out in camp by experienced bakers from among the German POWs. A significant number of other prisoners would eventually serve an apprenticeship as bakers while in captivity. At one location, the bakery supplied several other POW camps as well as a number of British army barracks in the area.

Separated from his family, and hundreds of miles from home, Eberhard felt terribly homesick. In the new camp he found himself mixed up with many people he didn't know, a situation he found completely daunting, and to make things worse hundreds of prisoners went away and hundreds more new ones arrived every day. Soon, however, he discovered a welcome distraction. 'One man, a schoolmaster I think, formed a choir with just a few who wanted to sing. Germans love to sing, and when we heard them singing we joined in. We sang lovely songs about home.'

Hans Reckel was at the same camp and later recalled that the prisoners had little to keep them occupied. 'There was nothing to read except a special newspaper for POWs, *Wochenpost*, which no one took seriously.' This German-language publication with a

---

* He reached his permanent camp on 19 September 1944 and sent a card and a letter within a week of arriving. The first reply reached him on 26 January 1945.

circulation of 70,000 was produced by the British government and purported to give a balanced, impartial view of the war as well as other events. Typically, it reproduced reports on the progress of the conflict from both British and German sources side by side: in this way the authorities hoped that the prisoners would recognise the German reports as blatant propaganda, which was often the case. However, the POWs were not so easily convinced. Many felt that it was the British version that was untruthful. 'The question of how far one could believe the different statements at that time aroused the first serious disputes [among the prisoners],' says Reckel. 'On 31 October one of the dissenters … was horribly beaten up.'

At this camp, followers of the Nazi doctrine were generally described as 'politicals' while, conversely, less ardent supporters of Hitler were called 'non-politicals'. An attempt was made to separate them, Eberhard remembers. 'The non-politicals were put in a hut by themselves but overnight they were attacked by the SS men and nearly killed. Some of them committed suicide.'

Both Eberhard and Hans were relieved when the time came to be transferred to another camp. 'We had to walk a long way in the dark to the station – we had a job to walk we were so weak,' says Eberhard. 'We were taken by train to Haltwhistle, and then walking again. We were worn out.' They arrived at Featherstone Park, a former United States Army base which lay in a deep valley with hills all around. The Americans had called it 'Death Valley' – now it was simply known as Camp 18. 'The sun didn't come there until nearly two o'clock. It was so depressing and miserable.'

The camp was encircled by a barbed-wire fence complete with tall watch towers. 'Now, Germans are very proud of their wedding ring,' says Eberhard. 'You never, ever, part with it; it's the most precious thing. The guards would lower a string and the Germans wanted 'fags' and sold their solid gold ring for seven cigarettes.' As a single man, Eberhard didn't have a wedding ring, but he was determined not to part with any of his valuables and promptly gave up smoking.

One of the functions of the transit camp was to separate the POWs according to their political beliefs and, in so doing, limit the threat of Nazis attacking non-Nazis. What some prisoners refer to as an 'interrogation' was – almost certainly – a screening interview to weed out the hard-line Nazis, and not a belated attempt to extract any further military intelligence. It was therefore of considerable benefit to the majority of the prisoners. Typically, however, none of this was explained to the POWs themselves, who – throughout their confinement – were kept in the dark, often quite unnecessarily, about decisions which affected them. As a consequence, even when the British took steps to make the captives' lives more agreeable, their efforts were often misinterpreted and unappreciated.

Fundamental to the screening process was the division of the prisoners into three grades: A, B and C ('white'; 'grey'; 'black'). The proportions varied significantly over time.

TABLE 1: POLITICAL GRADING

Grade	Description	Percentage	
		April 1945	December 1946
A	'White' Strongly anti-Nazi	15.3 per cent	9.0 per cent*
B	'Grey' Neither strongly anti-Nazi nor pro-Nazi	30.4 per cent	82.0 per cent
C	'Black' strongly pro-Nazi	54.3 per cent	9.0 percent

(Source: Wolff, H., pp. 48–9)

* By December 1946 many of the 'A's had been repatriated to help with the rebuilding of Germany – otherwise there would have been appreciably more of them. The general change in political 'tone' over the twenty-one-month period may be attributable, at least partly, to the re-education programme (described in Chapter 9).

Those who had been given a 'C' grade were separated from the others and sent to 'black' camps, generally in remote areas in the north of England and in Scotland, where they were detained under conditions of heightened security. Typically, these camps had high barbed-wire perimeter fences and watchtowers with searchlights manned by armed guards. The men were frequently mustered for a random roll call at any time of the day or night.

Herbert Holewa was a paratrooper and therefore presumed to be a Nazi, no matter what he told the interrogator. He was given a 'C' grade and sent to Camp 183a on the English–Scottish border. This he describes as 'a bad camp', where the British commandant was an old soldier of the worst kind and the *Lagerführer* (the German camp leader) was 'a nasty man'. Holewa and some of the others revolted and were sent to Camp 22 at New Cumnock – 'a so-called Nazi camp', as he puts it. 'That was excellent. There were paratroopers, U-boat men,* SS and pilots. There were 3,000 of us there. And the commandant, a colonel, had a German-born wife and they'd married in the 1920s. And we had a fantastic choir that sang German *Lieder* every Wednesday evening.'

Eberhard Wendler was graded 'B', along with most of the other prisoners. After two weeks (which seemed to him more like two years) at Featherstone Park he and 500 others boarded another train. They were not told where they were being sent, and they are unlikely to have recognised the name of the place even if it had been disclosed to them.

Eberhard would have been dumbfounded if he had known that he was destined to live out the rest of his life there.

* Germany's surface fleet was severely limited in scale during the war in order to concentrate on the submarine war, which was showing more tangible results: thus, not all who served in submarines had volunteered for these duties. Similarly, while many hard-core Nazis joined the Luftwaffe and the parachute units, these formations also had non-Nazis and politically indifferent men among their members.

3
The Darkest Day

As more and more Allied troops poured into Normandy it soon became clear that this was no feint but the real invasion. Germany countered the attack by sending reinforcements. Among them was Karl-Heinz Decker, who says:

I was 18 years old, and I was in the 12th SS Panzer Division under the famous *Standartenführer* [Colonel] Kurt 'Panzer' Meyer. We were the pride and joy of Hitler. I'm a farmer, really, and I took my exams in agriculture and passed. I knew I'd be called up so I volunteered and as I was the leader of the lads in the village they sent me to an NCO school. I was there for about eight months. It was very hard because you had to train and to learn the work of an NCO at the same time. From there we were taken to Belgium, where the Division was established, and from there to France. Our behaviour had to be very correct, and if anything had happened people would have been court-martialled. Things happened that shouldn't have happened but I say that it's a very small percentage that were involved. As *Waffen-SS* we were combatants, trained to go to war, and we went with songs in our hearts.

But, by mid-August 1944, two months after D-Day, it was becoming clear that their earlier expectations of victory had been unfounded:

I was in command of an 8cm mortar with another eight men. We marched off with our equipment. Every night we moved – only at night – and it was backwards instead of forwards. We tried our best but we were betrayed by the Army High Command. We had no support. No Luftwaffe, no heavy artillery – nothing. We were left there to die. I was one of the lucky ones.

We were shot at from somewhere – you never knew where you were because there was no real front. The infantry were in front so we just followed behind. Then I heard an explosion behind me, right among my eight men. So I shouted for a medic, but there were no medics and no one came. So I looked to see what could be done. One man's leg was nearly off, and the second one both legs were off. The first one said to me, 'I've got a knife in my pocket – cut my leg off, will you?'

'I can't cut it off.'

'Yes you can – take the knife and cut it off.'

I had no experience of that but I had an idea what to do. So I put a tourniquet on. His leg was only hanging on bits of clothing and maybe a few bits of skin or whatever – I cut it off and chucked it in the hedge. I knew he was safe but the other poor devil was really in a very bad state. All he wanted was water. Well, you don't give 'em water, but I moistened his lips, and the blood was oozing out. So I told the men, 'Leave your equipment there.'

We took the wounded to the field hospital on groundsheets, with four men – one on each corner – carrying them. I think – I hope – that I saved somebody's life, but the other one I don't think survived.

I was covered in blood from my feet to my waist. It was the middle of summer and there were flies. I broke down in the end. I took these blood-soaked trousers off and sat in a ditch and I just broke down.

He pauses, and stares into the distance, as if in a daydream. 'It's the flies, really, that did it,' he murmurs.

They set off in the direction of Falaise, not realising that the town had already been occupied by Canadian troops. 'We marched in the direction where the Canadian artillery could be heard. What we didn't know was that we were already surrounded. We were half-dead, hungry and tired. We knocked on the door of a farm and asked if we could sleep in the barn loft. The farmer gave us some bread and milk. But he must have told the Canadians, and they were there within the hour.' Karl-Heinz and his comrades were taken prisoner and led into a wood:

They gave us spades, and told us to dig holes 6ft by 3ft. We refused to do this; we were all so hungry we didn't care any more. We were supposed to be digging our own graves. If they were going to shoot us *they* would have to dig the graves, why should we help them with that!

However, an officer appeared and the prisoners were led from the wood to a waiting lorry. 'We all clambered on to the lorry, which had guards on each corner and then we moved off. And what followed us behind – *as far as the eye could see* – German soldiers, prisoners of war. They'd surrendered by the battalion.'

The decision to throw in the towel was sometimes prompted by Allied propaganda, as Fritz Jeltsch explains. 'They bombarded us with leaflets – oh, we had a lot – a heap fell near me and I bent over and took a handful and gave them to the chaps to use as lavatory paper. We had no lavatory paper you see. [But] what it said in the leaflets was quite true.' The pamphlets carried an attractive illustration of the prisoner of war camp at Medicine Hat, Canada, with its mess hall, theatre and sporting facilities. If Fritz and his comrades would only surrender now they could spend the rest of the war in comfort and safety like this. (As events unfolded Fritz was, in fact, on what he believes to have been the last troopship to leave for Canada). Other leaflets which he remembers pointed out the hopelessness of Germany's situation: 'You know you can't win the war. The whole world knows that Germans are very efficient workers, and so on, but you're not supermen, you're just human beings and you can't protect a front which goes thousands of kilometres.'

The German High Command countered with its own propaganda to urge its soldiers to fight on, however hopeless the situation may have seemed. Troops were told that the Americans employed hardened criminals, ex-gangsters from Chicago, with orders to kill as many Germans as possible. 'We were told, "They don't take prisoners", "they mistreat you," and so on,' Gerhard Kleindt told a reporter.

John Tinker, MP, said in a speech to the House of Commons:

> We must try to remove that belief. So long as we have to fight and kill these people, it means that a number of our men are being killed too. We should let them know that when we have conquered them it does not mean that we shall treat them as though they have no right to live, except in a state of serfdom, because that is not our intention. As I understand it, it is our intention to treat these people as decent human beings when the war is over, and give them a place to carry on their work.

Immediately after D-day, the German prisoners witnessed a variety of reactions on the part of the French population. When Hans Reckel and his unit had just been captured by Canadian troops, and were being marched to a temporary camp, 'We were stopped on the way by an old French couple who looked at our wounded soldier. "*Pauvre garçon,*" said the wife sympathetically and brought him some water.'

But as the weeks went by, and it became ever clearer that Germany was losing the war, the French were emboldened and openly displayed their hatred of the men who had occupied their country for the last four years. At Le Havre, *Leutnant* Josef Huber was paraded through the streets after being captured by members of the French Resistance:

> The first French woman came and spat in my face. We were meant to hold our hands high, but I wouldn't and held them up in front of me. One of the resistance men then clapped me on the elbows with the butt of his rifle, but I was so mad that I sloshed at him and he left me alone. By the end I was grey-white from head to toe with the slime of their spit.

Fritz Jeltsch was taken prisoner on the last day of August:

> I remember we went through Caen as prisoners, and the French were throwing stones and empty bottles and calling '*raus, raus!*' – 'out, out!' – and a British soldier with a machine pistol shot over the heads of the French to frighten them and they stopped. But the other British were grinning and didn't do anything about it. Some POWs were injured when they were hit by the stones and bottles.

The Allies captured Cherbourg in the last days of June – the first major port to be taken. While substantial numbers of POWs would continue to be embarked direct from the beaches, much larger vessels could now be used as well.

'At the end of October we were moved up to Cherbourg and on the first of November we were put in one of those landing ships with railway lines inside,' a prisoner reports. This was in all probability the Southern Railway's *Twickenham Ferry*, built before the war to transport entire trains full of businessmen and holidaymakers across the Channel. The ship had been commandeered for the war. Recently it had brought a hospital train comprising eighteen carriages to Cherbourg, and on the return journey it ferried POWs to Britain.

As further harbours were captured, landing craft were diverted to them to pick up prisoners. The LCT on which John Andrews was a crewman went to Dieppe to collect German POWs, and he observed that they:

> looked healthy but forlorn … no doubt happy to be alive and away from the battlefields. They seemed very placid as they lined up for their food and their Sergeant Major called out '*Eins, zwei, drei …*' as they moved forward for their rations. Many of them were teenagers and were quite happy to do tasks around the craft such as lowering the ramp and helping in the galley.

The LCTs were later judged to be highly unsatisfactory for transporting POWs in stormy weather. As the vessel pitched about in heavy seas, water flooded the tank deck to a depth of several inches and, to avoid being drenched, the prisoners climbed to the catwalk above. On one occasion six prisoners were washed overboard from here during 'violent weather'. There were no witnesses to the actual incident.

During the Channel crossing, the prisoners who had been on the receiving end of the French civilians' anger and contempt had plenty of time to reflect on how much worse it might be when they set foot in Britain itself. In fact, though, the atmosphere was usually far less hostile than they had imagined. 'We landed in Southampton,' says Herbert Holewa. 'It was very quiet. British people may have given the "V salute", but otherwise very, very quiet, very nice.'

'Civilians stood on the pavement, their umbrellas open, and looked on in silence as we German prisoners of war were unloaded,' recalled Siegfried Mohring. 'Not one of them threw a stone or spat, swore, or insulted us, no one shouted. Something here in England must be different from over there on the Continent.'

The columns of POWs marching through the streets were the first Germans most civilians had ever seen. The British had preconceptions, of course, about the nation which had bombed their cities and towns, killing civilians, elderly people, women and children. Almost every British family had lost a relative or knew someone who had been killed, wounded, taken prisoner or reported missing. And it was the Germans who were responsible for all this suffering, having started the war – not only *this* war, but the one before as well.

One man remembers, as 13-year-old boy, jeering and shouting as he watched German POWs being marched along the street. Another schoolboy, Bernard Higgins, skipped lessons to watch the prisoners being led past. 'We used to follow them for miles and asked

them for their badges and helmets, which sometimes they gave to us. The prisoners usually
marched in silence and I remember one time we got near to a big, heavily-built German
prisoner and he lunged towards us and shouted, and we ran away across the fields.'

Yet it was hard to reconcile the sight of these defeated soldiers in their ragged
uniforms with the stereotype of the 'ruthless Hun'. 'I felt some empathy for them,'
Higgins said in retrospect. 'They were in a desperate situation. They'd been thrown into
battle without knowing what they were going into.'

German infantryman Arno Christiansen's home was in Hamburg, though he was of
Norwegian ancestry. He remembers the overwhelming sense of relief the prisoners felt
on arrival in Britain. 'In spite of their unkempt appearance and haggard faces they felt
their spirits lift, just slightly,' he claims. As they marched through the streets they were
intrigued to find themselves in a land that was not so very different from Germany, on
the surface. Then again, it was an odd place – a mirror-image world where people drove
on the wrong side of the road. Other things were different, too. Shops actually had
goods in their windows in contrast to the picture painted by the German media. The
soldiers had been led to believe that Britain was a shattered nation, smashed by German
bombing and brought to the edge of starvation by the U-boat blockade. Yet the town
was 'alive and busy'.

Arno felt relieved to be out of the war, and, when the time for delousing came, he
'threw off' his clothes in what was to him a symbolic gesture, 'the end of a link with
home – even the tattered uniform belonged to the past'.

Richard Schlener, too, noticed a distinct change of atmosphere in Britain. 'The
English civilians didn't pelt us with stones like in Belgium. The English stood at the
side of the road, and just said, "Hitler's last army!" No stones – just "Hitler's last army!"'

In early September 1944, Willi Hildemann – a family man, 43 years of age – was posted
to the Channel coast near Boulogne, from where, he observed, the English coast was
clearly visible in the morning sun. He and his comrades were becoming aware of the
worsening prospects for the German army as the enemy closed in. Unable to write a
letter home – the postal service was by now entirely disrupted – he jotted down his
thoughts in the little notebook he had bought in Amiens for 20 *francs*:

> **Sunday, 10 September**: A glorious summer day. I feel like taking a dip. My thoughts
> are mainly back home with you, my sweetheart. It's a pity that the accommodation
> is so poor. There are twenty of us soldiers in a room no bigger than 20sq.m with no
> lighting. There's nothing to occupy us in our free time, no radio; we're cut off. But
> we'll hold out until the final victory. If only I could send you a letter!

Nine days later, when he was captured by Canadian forces, he described it as 'the darkest
day of my life'. He spent the next three weeks in a transit camp at Dieppe under harsh
conditions:

Thursday, 12 October: Unable to wash, haven't removed my clothes since I was in Küstrin.* No sleep, uniform ripped and dirty …

Yet he ends on an optimistic note by emphasising his 'hope and belief in a German victory'.

Forty-eight hours later, he disembarked at Southampton at 5 a.m. and was then transported to Kempton Park. In spite of his devout loyalty to Germany, Hildemann's praise for the processing of POWs was unstinting. 'The British organisation was remarkable. The way they dealt with 1,500 men in just three hours was masterly. It's a strange feeling to visit England in this way. I haven't seen much yet, but one thing I have established is that there is little traffic on the railways, the trains are clean, and the heartbeat of an orderly life, albeit adapted to wartime conditions, continues.' In what is doubtless a reference to the V-1 and V-2 missiles which had been falling on British territory for the last few weeks, he adds with more than a touch of disappointment, 'The impact of German weaponry is undetectable as far as I can judge from the areas I have been through.'

By September 1944 only the most fanatical of Hitler's followers still believed the propaganda: to everyone else it was clear that Germany was losing. Arthur Riegel had once been put on trial for 'defeatist' comments he is supposed to have made, and had been acquitted. Having been posted to Belgium he was now caught up in the mass withdrawal of German troops. 'The soldiers were retreating on foot in droves, disorganised and without weapons, helmets or gas masks. Above all, I completely lacked any motivation at this late hour to risk my life for the brown-shirted gang of criminals.'**

His arm hurt: this was not exactly a war wound but probably what we now know as RSI – repetitive strain injury – an occupational hazard for signallers who were constantly writing, typing and sending Morse code. Riegel was taken prisoner on 6 September and flown to a military hospital in Normandy. From his bed he wrote to his family, 'Treatment and food are good. Urgently need my big English dictionary.'

D-Day will forever be recognised as the most important milestone on the road to an Allied victory. It was also the point when captured Germans first arrived in Britain en masse. However, the well-rehearsed procedure for dealing with prisoners had evolved over several years, beginning with the capture of the first few German POWs only a few days after war was declared.

September 1939: the U-boat commander looked through the periscope: what he saw took his breath away – 'a submariner's dream' – the 22,000-ton British aircraft

---

*   His home town, on what was then the German-Polish border (now Kostrzyn in Poland). According to his diary, he was last there on 22 August, fifty-one days previously.

** The SA (*Sturmabteilung*), a nazi organisation, were often referred to as Brownshirts on account of their uniforms.

carrier *Ark Royal* carrying almost 1,500 officers and crew, and no fewer than sixty warplanes. The gigantic ship was only 800m distant. He could hardly miss.

U-39, a nearly new submarine, had left Wilhelmshaven on 19 August in anticipation of the conflict which was about to begin. By 3 September, Britain and Germany were at war. U-39, with its crew of forty-four men under the command of 30-year-old Gerhard Glattes, was stalking prey north of Ireland but no enemy ships had been seen. Eleven days later the submarine was on the point of returning to base when Glattes sighted *Ark Royal*. He ordered his crew to prepare the torpedoes: within minutes, he thought, he would have sunk one of the enemy's largest and most important ships. After a loss such as this the British might surrender straight away.

But it was not to be. The torpedoes exploded prematurely. Three destroyers escorting the carrier gave chase to U-39, which was seriously damaged by depth charges. Glattes gave the order to surface and abandon ship, and the entire crew were picked up by the destroyers. They had the dubious distinction of being the first German POWs to be captured by the British in the conflict.* However, in the various theatres of war Britain would eventually capture 3.5 million German servicemen.

Despite Hitler's rise to power in 1933 and the militant rumblings subsequently emanating from Germany, Britain had been slow in almost every respect to prepare for war. Only at a late date were any provisions made for dealing with prisoners and, in retrospect, those measures appear makeshift and inadequate. Early prisoners were taken to the Tower of London for questioning. The austere, menacing appearance of this fortress was no doubt sufficient in itself to persuade many captives to talk. Other interrogation units were established later: perhaps the most famous (or infamous, depending on one's viewpoint) was the so-called London Cage at 8 Kensington Palace Gardens, London, 'the requisitioned home of a margarine millionaire'. Officers, in particular, passed through this facility and often imparted information of inestimable value to the British intelligence services.

After interrogation, the prisoners were transferred elsewhere. At the beginning of the war Britain had only two POW camps which, with unassailable logic, the War Office designated 'Camp No 1' and 'Camp No 2'. Both were hurriedly created by converting existing buildings.

Camp No 1 was located in Cumbria at Grizedale Hall, a forty-room mansion which had previously belonged to the Forestry Commission and was now set aside for captured German officers. These reluctant guests could console themselves with the fact that the accommodation was of a very high standard. It was, in fact, so comfortable that Colonel Josiah Wedgwood, MP for Newcastle-under-Lyme (and great-great grandson of the famous potter), asked how much it was costing to keep the Germans there.

---

* *Korvettenkapitän* Glattes himself would spend seven and a half years in captivity and, at the time of his final release in April 1947, was 38 years old. His period of detention as a POW is believed to be the longest of any German during the war.

'The cost is about £50 a day, of which £45 is in respect of staff,' the Secretary of State for War replied. 'There are twenty-one prisoners at present in the camp, which is adequate to accommodate 200.'

'Would it not be cheaper to keep them at the Ritz?' Wedgwood challenged. From then on, Grizedale Hall was known as 'the U-boat hotel'. This exchange of words also gives an indication of just how few Germans were being taken prisoner, with only twenty-one officers in captivity by November 1939.

In comparison with the 'U-boat hotel', Camp No 2, Glen Mill, was positively downmarket. Situated in the deliciously named Wellyhole Street in the Lancashire town of Oldham, the former cotton mill was 'the last in a row of huge mills with tall chimneys all around. The building is several storeys high with but a single staircase and has several long spinning halls. The main windows are all permanently painted over because of the blackout. Every ten minutes an LMS train roars by on the embankment above the camp.' Glen Mill had room for as many as 2,000 men, and when its first occupants, the crew of U-39, arrived they must have felt lost in the 280,000sq.ft edifice. The outside toilet block had sufficed when it had been a cotton mill, but it was entirely impractical for guards to escort prisoners every time they needed to go to the lavatory. Werner Völkner, a later inmate, remembers:

There were a few big buckets there, the stench was terrible. Some of the guards complained to the commandant that there were rats in the camp. And the commandant – through the interpreter – said, 'If anybody kills a rat and brings it to me, he'll get five cigarettes.' Well, everybody wanted to get in the act to get the extra cigarettes but too many people being about with sticks made the rats hide away in their holes. Then some of the prisoners got hold of a spade and started digging and some of the others were waiting at the holes with sticks and as soon as a rat appeared they would hit it and use it like a trophy and present it to the camp commandant to get their five cigarettes. The camp commandant would then tell one of the guards to get rid of the rat and he just slung it on to the rubbish heap. The prisoners were not slow to find out what was happening and promptly went back to the rubbish heap, cleaned the rat up a bit and presented it as a newly caught or killed rat again and therefore another five cigarettes went the prisoner's way.

Speaking many years later, Siegfried Gabler claimed, 'I've seen Colditz on the television and, believe me, it was a holiday camp compared with Oldham. We saw nothing of the outside world. All we could see was a graveyard. Funerals were the only excitement we had.' By March 1940, more prisoners – mostly U-boat men – had arrived, but the total was still only 257.

In the spring of 1940 Germany invaded Denmark, Norway, France, Belgium and the Netherlands. After the British Expeditionary Force retreated to the Channel coast, a third of a million men were rescued from Dunkirk. Yet despite this 'miracle of deliverance' (as Churchill described it), some 45,000 British soldiers had been taken prisoner, giving the Germans a powerful bargaining tool. For the time being, Britain had to handle the POWs with care, as otherwise Germany could easily have retaliated.

With Hitler's army at the Channel coast, a German invasion of Britain seemed almost inevitable. Wild rumours began to circulate. Armies of fifth columnists and spies were thought to be already in place in Britain, poised to assist the invaders; the enemy was suspected of having secret weapons of extraordinary ingenuity and power; Nazi paratroopers would descend from the skies disguised as nuns. In the context of such terrors, the suspicion that invading forces might release their imprisoned comrades from the camps, or that the Luftwaffe could drop weapons with which POWs could overpower the guards, seemed relatively level-headed.

Indeed, these concerns were not quite as far-fetched as they might seem. As we shall see, something of this sort very nearly came to fruition much later in the war, when German prisoners hatched a plot to escape and to attack Britain from within.

All things considered, the British government decided that it would be safest to ship its prisoners overseas. They asked the Dominions of Canada, South Africa and Australia to hold all existing and future prisoners on Britain's behalf, but in the final reckoning only Canada participated in this scheme to any significant extent. The government half expected that Germany would exact reprisals against British POWs in respect of these shipments, but this did not happen. In any event, Britain could have excused its actions by arguing that the Geneva Convention requires prisoners to be 'evacuated to depots sufficiently removed from the fighting zone for them to be out of danger'. The first batch of German POWs left Britain for Quebec on 21 June 1940 on the SS *Duchess of York,* and afterwards, when there were enough POWs to fill a troopship, they were immediately sent on to Canada. As a result, for much of the war the number of German POWs in Britain did not exceed 2,000. But after D-Day the situation changed dramatically.

TABLE 2: GERMAN POWs IN BRITAIN AND CANADA (1941–43)

	BRITAIN					CANADA
1941	March	550		September	300	By comparison, 8,940 POWs had
	June	950		December	550	been sent to Canada by 'autumn
	September	1,700	**1943**	March	900	1942'.
	December	1,850		June	650	
1942	March	1,150		September	650	
	June	200		December	1,100	

(Source: Hellen, J. A., *Revisiting the past ...,* p.4; and Held, p.79 (figure for Canada))

4

The Ones That Got Away

In late summer 1940, in the Channel ports of Boulogne, Calais and Ostend, hundreds of invasion barges assembled to carry German forces across to England. The men on board would rush down the loading ramps and on to the beaches. They would storm the makeshift defences and overpower the troops spread thinly along the south-east coast. Britain would soon collapse under the onslaught of superior German forces and be forced into a humiliating defeat. That was the plan.

However, the commander-in-chief of the Luftwaffe, Hermann Göring, persuaded Hitler that he could beat Britain into submission from the air, without the need for a military invasion, and gave an initial forecast that the RAF in southern England would be vanquished within four days. As a successful invasion depended, in any case, on air superiority, Hitler granted Göring permission to carry out his plan. During the Battle of Britain, which began on 10 July, combat took place over the British mainland and the surrounding waters.

Oberleutnant Ulrich Steinhilper had been born during an air raid in September 1918, in the last few weeks of the First World War. His family home was in a tiny village in Swabia, the region of Germany around Stuttgart. As a young man Ulrich's ambition was to bcome a Luftewaffe officer. He studied hard and tried – with only partial success – to lose the strong rural accent of his birthplace. From the earliest days of the Second World War he saw action during the German invasion of Poland and, from August 1940, flew in the Battle of Britain. Sometimes he undertook as many as seven missions in a single day.

The morning of 27 October was chilly and autumnal. It was just after 9 a.m. when Ulrich took off in his familiar Messerschmitt 'Yellow 2' to escort a squadron of fighter-bombers on a raid on London. His formation was attacked by RAF aircraft, and after a bullet in his plane's radiator put paid to any hope of returning safely to base, he crash-landed near Canterbury. He had left his base in northern France only ninety minutes previously, but it might as well have been in a past life:

> Now I had to accept the fact that there was no more decision-making for me. From here, my life would be shaped by forces which I could not influence. As I mulled this over in my mind I saw people coming … To my relief, far in the lead were two men in khaki uniforms, soldiers. Things might be all right then. I was worried at first when I thought that there were only civilians. Some stories had been circulated

of our airmen being badly beaten up, if not killed, by angry people. But with some military influence I hoped that things might not become too serious … Already, high above us there in the sky, we heard the roaring of the aircraft engines. The third 'wave' was on their way. Their business was going on but this time without me. 'Yes, fellow comrades,' I thought, 'I have been knocked out for now, and I shall have to wait and see whether you can get us out of this situation.' We had already been informed about our pilots who, having been shot down in August, were alive and British POWs. The Red Cross information system for those pilots had begun to feed back lists to Germany and we had some idea of how many of our friends were now in custody.

Flying, as I did, from the Calais area I had seen the masses of barges and ships that had been assembled ready to take the Sixth Army across the Channel when *Seelöwe* [the invasion of Britain] started. I, and the majority of my colleagues, really believed that the invasion wasn't far away and any imprisonment in Britain would be short … I was only 22 years old, but I'd come a long way. What I didn't know was how far I still had to go before I would know any form of peace again.

Steinhilper was subsequently taken for interrogation at the London Cage and then transferred to Swanwick Camp near Derby. Here he became reacquainted with an old comrade, Franz von Werra (renowned as 'The One That Got Away'*). Together they made an escape attempt but this was unsuccessful.

On 10 January 1941 both men were transferred to Canada on the *Duchess of York*. On arrival they were loaded on to a train which was to take them to a distant POW camp but von Werra escaped en route. His story has been so well documented that a brief summary here will probably suffice.

He, too, flew as a fighter pilot in the Battle of Britain and gained considerable publicity in Germany when his photograph appeared on the cover of a popular magazine with his pet lion cub, Simba. Soon afterwards, he claimed to have destroyed nine British aircraft on the ground, although there was not a shred of evidence to substantiate this assertion. On 5 September 1940, von Werra was detailed to fly as escort to a formation of bombers attacking Croydon aerodrome. As they returned from the raid he was shot down near Maidstone, Kent, and taken into captivity. This time he succeeded not only in escaping from the camp but in entering a high-security airfield near Hucknall, Nottinghamshire, where Rolls-Royce aero engines were tested. Using considerable guile, and pretending to be a Dutch pilot, he actually managed to sit at the controls of a Hurricane fighter plane and was about to start the engine when his ruse was discovered.

Following his escape from a train in Canada he returned to Germany, where he received a decoration from Adolf Hitler himself. He resumed combat flying, spending

---

* His story inspired a book and later a film under that title.

some time on the Eastern Front before being transferred to Holland. On 25 October 1941, he took off on a practice flight: the aircraft suffered engine failure and he was killed. His body has never been found.

Although von Werra has gone down in history as the only German to escape from British captivity and return to Germany to fight again, he was, in fact, neither the only one to do so nor even the first. That distinction goes to a man named Walter Kurt Reich. This 25-year-old sailor was on board a U-boat, U-63, which sank in February 1940 after a British attack. Reich and twenty-five other survivors were taken prisoner and subsequently transferred to Canada in July 1940 in a small convoy of ships. These were the Polish vessels, *Batory* and *Sobieski*; the *Monarch of Bermuda*; the cruiser *Bonaventure*, and HMS *Revenge*. Between them they carried what was probably the most valuable cargo ever to be transported on the high seas: a substantial portion of Britain's gold reserves amounting to about £200 million worth of gold bullion, together with a dazzling selection of art and cultural treasures from Poland which included the Polish coronation sword, a Gutenberg Bible, and thirty-six original Chopin manuscripts. These priceless objects were being shipped to Canada to prevent them from being seized by the Germans if the feared invasion came, having already been brought to Britain when Poland was occupied.

The *Sobieski* carried, in addition to these treasures, some 1,700 'passengers', most of whom were Luftwaffe and *Kriegsmarine* prisoners of war. Some reports have intimated that they were being carried as 'protection' – to ensure that German U-boats would not attack the convoy – but this assertion has been neither proved nor disproved.

On 15 July, as the *Sobieski* entered the St Lawrence River at the end of its transatlantic voyage, Walter Reich squeezed through a porthole and swam ashore. He fought his way 'through dense woods' to the United States, travelling by night and allegedly 'living on berries' during the two-day trek. He was arrested by an American border patrol and put on trial for 'illegal entry'. This charge was, however, dismissed when a judge ruled that escaped prisoners of war were entitled to seek sanctuary in a neutral country. Before being returned to Germany, Reich achieved the status of a minor celebrity, even giving interviews to the press.

On 5 September 1940 *Leutnant* Heinz 'Hannibal' Schnabel took off at the controls of a Messerschmitt fighter plane at 8.40 a.m. as escort to a formation of bombers. On the return journey Schnabel's plane was engaged by RAF Hurricanes and Spitfires: the engine was hit and he made a forced landing at Handen Farm, Aldington, 4 miles south-west of Ashford, Kent.[*]

Schnabel was taken to the nearby farmhouse, where the owner's daughter mended his torn sleeve. As this was taking place, he calmly chatted with the farmer's wife,

---

[*] He was shot down at almost exactly the same time as Franz von Werra and the two crash sites were only 35 miles apart.

explaining the significance of the emblem on his aircraft – the *Tatzelwurm*, a mythical creature resembling a lizard. Schnabel was still recovering from a chest wound sustained during Germany's lightning advance into France a few months earlier and, shaken up by the crash, he was taken to the Royal Herbert Military Hospital in Woolwich, where wounded Luftwaffe personnel were treated.

A few days later, a Heinkel-111 bomber piloted by *Oberleutnant* Harry Wappler was on the way back to base after attacking Ellesmere Port, Cheshire, in the early hours of the morning. The bomber ran into trouble as it passed over Tredegar Park, Newport, Gwent. Though he could not have known it at the time, Wappler had the distinction of being the first enemy pilot in the Second World War to be downed by a barrage balloon. He later recalled:

It all then happened very quickly. The cockpit disintegrated and the same second I found myself out of the plane, feeling a blow to my right arm. I never flew with the safety belt done up and this must have saved me. Before falling unconscious, probably because my right arm had been broken in three places, I managed to open my parachute. I then suffered a blackout until about 10.00 hours the next morning when I awoke in the hospital. The other three members of my crew were killed.

His bomber crashed on to a house, killing two members of the Phillips family who lived there. Soon afterwards he was transferred to the same hospital at Woolwich where Heinz Schnabel had been taken. An accomplished cartoonist, Wappler drew caricatures of other Luftwaffe POWs on the ward. (They included *Leutnant* Max Himmelheber who, in 1932, had invented that ubiquitous product – chipboard).

Harry Wappler's and Heinz Schnabel's beds were only a few feet apart. Soon the pair got to know each other, and they discovered they had much in common. Both were pilots. And both had every intention of escaping as soon as they were fit and well again.

On recovering from their wounds, they were sent to Camp 15, Shap Wells Hotel, near Penrith. Here they succeeded in forging identity passes. They also fabricated what would pass for RAF uniforms, with realistic buttons made from a shiny tin can. A U-boat officer made convincing dummies to stand in for Wappler and Schnabel at the afternoon roll call, while a Luftwaffe pilot with a talent for ventriloquism impersonated their voices when their names were called.

While this charade was taking place, the pair had hidden themselves in laundry baskets, which were collected by a van with the intrepid pair inside. On the way to the laundry Harry and Heinz jumped out.

They made their way to an RAF flying school near Carlisle and began to size up the situation. Many training aircraft were parked around the airfield – 'a hundred at least'. While waiting for a suitable opportunity to enter the flying school, they even risked going into a pub, where they fell into conversation with the landlord. They pretended to be Dutchmen, and the publican treated them to drinks.

Next day they sauntered on to the airfield as casually as they could, ordered one of the ground crew to take the covers off a Miles Magister training aircraft and took off. When their fuel ran low they landed at another RAF airfield, and when they asked for the fuel tanks to be refilled, obliging ground staff complied.

Finally they cleared the British coast and set out across the North Sea. Freedom seemed to be within their grasp. But partway across the sea they realised that the fuel they had would not take them all the way across. They turned around and landed at yet another RAF station – this time the important Bomber Command station at Horsham St Faith, Norfolk. Here they were given tea and offered a bed for the night. But while they were settling into their temporary accommodation in the officers' mess, news came in that two Germans masquerading as Dutch flyers had stolen an aircraft. Both were returned to captivity, although a rumour went around the camps in Britain that the two Luftwaffe pilots had in fact made a 'home run', and this was generally believed. Squadron Leader Victor Brooks, the officer in charge of operations at Horsham St Faith, was impressed by their feat: when he learned how far they had got, he is said to have declared that 'These fellows have put up a jolly good show'.

The bombing offensive continued through the winter of 1940–41. Pilot Max Probst, a man said to have had an 'ebullient and exuberant nature', had already completed a number of bombing missions over England and had a low opinion of the ability of the British gunners to hit their targets, bragging that he 'normally flew straight through' the curtain of anti-aircraft fire. On 9 November he was detailed to participate in a raid on London, but 'He'd been invited out to a dinner on the evening of his mission and rather than bother with changing when he got back he'd decided to fly in full evening suit under his overalls'. This time, however, his luck ran out. Over Bromley, to the south-east of London, he was hit by anti-aircraft fire in spite of his boast. One wing of his Heinkel 111 bomber was ripped off by a shell and the aircraft went into a dive. Probst baled out just in time, and parachuted into the grounds of the Sundridge Park Hotel. The rest of his crew were killed, and so was a civilian, a resident in the house upon which the aircraft crashed. Probst, meanwhile, discarded his flying overalls and walked toward the hotel to give himself up:

Approaching people with his heavily accented English and claiming that he was a Luftwaffe pilot only seemed to make them laugh. They took one look at his dinner suit and dismissed him as a prankster or a drunk. Gradually he made his way towards the hotel and ended up in the foyer, which was crowded with people. A private dinner party was in progress. In the happy throng, Max went unnoticed and apparently thought that, as he was going to miss his evening out in Germany, he might as well dine in style where he was. He therefore took a table for one and sat down to enjoy a good meal and a few drinks.

Probst was eventually taken to the RAF interrogation centre at Cockfosters, where Luftwaffe crews were quizzed by specialists on subjects such as aviation hardware and tactics. Here he revealed that the Luftwaffe was planning to mount large-scale attacks on Coventry. Because this did not correspond to information already held by the British he was disbelieved: days later, however, on 14 November, his predictions were proved correct when a massive raid on the city destroyed the cathedral as well as over 4,000 homes. About 570 people were killed and over 1,000 injured. The accuracy of the Luftwaffe bombers had been enhanced by a new guidance system known as *Knickebein* ('Crooked-leg').

Probst finished up at the POW camp at Swanwick, newly opened to take the overspill from Grizedale Hall, which had finally reached full capacity. He was debriefed by a committee of German officers. Probst complained bitterly that 'He'd tried very hard to explain the *Knickebein* beams to [the British], and they'd been too thick to understand, always wanting to return to more mundane matters ...' The German camp leader considered subjecting Probst to a court martial, but they finally all concluded that 'Max was just Max' and left him alone.

At sea, still more Germans were being captured. In May 1941, the pride of the German fleet, the battleship *Bismarck*, had sunk the British battlecruiser HMS *Hood*. British aircraft and ships (including the *Ark Royal*, which had narrowly escaped being sunk by U-39 a year and a half previously) pursued *Bismarck* and sank her. Of her crew of 2,200, all were lost except for 110 men who were rescued by the Royal Navy ships *Dorsetshire* and *Maori*. Two others were picked up by a German vessel. One of the survivors, 20-year-old Johannes Zimmermann, was a member of *Bismarck*'s forward damage control team. He later described the carnage on board as the battleship came under fire.

> An officer told us to try to get to the upper deck so as to have a chance of escaping. We reached the deck near the 150mm gun on the starboard side. There were pieces of comrades, you couldn't be sure what pieces belonged to which person. The ship turned over on to its port side. Where I stood it was 6½ to 7m above the surface of the water, and I was afraid to jump. Maybe that saved my life. I took off my sea boots and combat gear and, as the ship rolled further to port, I just sat down on the deck and slid into the sea. I found myself in a cocktail of oil and seawater. The waves were 10m high. I was swimming together with a friend. He'd been a neighbour of mine; we lived only 20 yards from each other and went to the same school. Before abandoning ship we'd agreed that if one of us died the other would tell his parents what had happened. And I lost him – he died. After one-and-a-half hours in the water I saw a ship – the *Dorsetshire*. There was a small sailor boy on board who gave me a big bottle of gin. I drank it all by myself, and then all my inside came out. I'd swallowed salt water. I never touched gin again. Two men took me down near the boiler room and took my wet clothes and gave me a blanket. They put us in the

library on board and I found the book *Last of the Mohicans* and started to use it to teach myself English. I was treated well – the crew made us feel like shipmates.

Interrogation of POWs produced copious amounts of intelligence of widely varying usefulness. Prisoners divulged information on such matters as the German command structure, weapons, tactics, communications equipment and the design and performance of aircraft and naval vessels. The pilot of a Messerschmitt 109 fighter which crash-landed near Dover admitted that the latest version of this aircraft suffered from a serious design fault: two pilots had sheared the wings off their aircraft when trying to follow Spitfires in a dive. Less pivotal to the outcome of the war, perhaps, was a captured sailor's revelation that the railway line between Berlin and Hamburg was soon to be electrified.

In distant parts of the world, events followed which may have seemed quite unconnected with German prisoners of war, but which eventually would have serious consequences for them. The attack on the United States fleet at Pearl Harbor on 7 December 1941 forced America to declare war on Japan. Four days later Germany and Italy in turn declared war on the USA.

But it was not until late 1942 that the United States and Britain fought side by side against the common enemy. For two years Britain had already been waging war in North Africa against an Italian–German alliance under the overall command of Erwin Rommel. Now, in a joint campaign with the Americans, the British invaded Algeria, Morocco and Tunisia with the aim of attacking Rommel from the opposite flank and ending the conflict in that theatre of war.

Hans Teske was a member of the *Afrika Korps* – the German forces in North Africa. In peacetime, he had intended to follow in his father's footsteps by becoming a compositor for the local newspaper in his home town of Stolp, Pomerania. But his career plans were put on hold when he was called up. Although only 18 years of age, he was already a seasoned paratrooper when, in 1943, he fought in Tunisia against the British. During fierce fighting that February he saved the life of an Allied soldier who lay injured in no-man's-land between the German and British lines. The area was heavily mined, and was overlooked by a British machine-gun post. 'I had a choice of leaving him there or of having him on my conscience,' he later said. Hans brought the wounded Briton to safety and was awarded the Iron Cross, second class, for his bravery in carrying out this deed. Later he distinguished himself in battle once more, this time receiving the Iron Cross, first class. However, he was wounded during this action and was withdrawn from the front line. At a hospital in Tunis, he was one of a large group of German casualties who were waiting to be evacuated by sea. 'American aircraft bombed a brand-new Italian hospital ship on her maiden voyage. One of the patients on board was our battalion surgeon who had been wounded in the shoulder and he lost his arm in the attack, ending his career. In other words, 7,000 of us were stranded.'

On 7 May 1943, gunfire could be heard not far from the hospital. Teske said:

A doctor came to me and said, 'Can you make out what's happening over there?'
And I told him, 'It's artillery.' But how could artillery be engaged just outside Tunis?
Moments later the RAF came – we saw wave after wave of bombers and they
dropped bombs fairly close. We realised there must have been a breakthrough and
that afternoon we were told to destroy documents which could be of use to an
enemy and prepare for captivity.

After a long delay, British soldiers arrived in an armoured car: although only lightly
guarded, Hans and his comrades were now technically prisoners of war. 'Troops only
arrived much later in the day. They settled down in the forecourt of the hospital, and
on the steps they set up a cooker and boiled some tea, and offered us some. We'd never
had English tea with milk – it was something new. But it tasted all right.'

A few days later, on 13 May, the war in North Africa drew to a close. 'The end was
inevitable,' *Afrika Korps* soldier Martin Schenkel admits. 'Outnumbered five or six to
one, and with very few heavy weapons left, the Axis surrendered to the Allies. We
marched over a hill to some British tanks. The Brits gave us cigarettes and we gave
them chocolate, and they were very friendly.' Overnight, the Allies found themselves
with around 260,000 POWs on their hands. Roughly half of these were Germans and
the rest were Italians.

Housing and feeding this number of men proved difficult. The solution was to keep
the Germans in camps in the Middle East, and ship the Italians back to Britain, where
they would be used to relieve a chronic manpower shortage in the country. One of the
first tasks of these Italians was to build semi-permanent accommodation for their own
habitation. On 8 September 1943, Italy surrendered and allied itself with Britain and
America, and the status of the Italian POWs changed dramatically. Those who agreed to
remain in Britain as voluntary workers were classified as 'co-operators' and lived under
a comparatively relaxed regimen with minimal security. Many were relocated to hostels
near the farms where they were employed, and some lived at the farms themselves.

At the beginning of 1943, Britain and America had agreed that any prisoners they
captured during joint campaigns would be shared on a fifty-fifty basis. (This meant, for
example, that all POWs captured in North Africa were equally split between British
and American 'ownership' even though the majority of prisoners in this particular
campaign had, in fact, been taken by the British). However, as the war progressed and
thousands more enemy troops surrendered, Britain balked at having to look after its
share: the country was woefully lacking in accommodation, food and many other
necessities of life. America, on the other hand, had wide-open country and seemingly
limitless resources. Britain therefore asked its ally to accept – in addition to the half-
share already agreed – a further 130,000 prisoners, who would be held in America
while still technically 'British-owned'. After some hesitation, America consented to
this arrangement on the understanding that the prisoners would be used as a labour

force within the USA. Almost all the German POWs who came into American hands in this campaign (including those who were actually prisoners of the British) were immediately taken to camps within the United States.

The practice of sharing POWs on a fifty-fifty basis remained in force for the rest of the war. As we shall discover later, one of its consequences was that 'Many prisoners would experience an appreciable extension to their imprisonment', as the German official history puts it.

Britain's POW camps were run by the War Office: for the purposes of military administration the country was divided into regional Home Commands (Northern, Southern, Eastern, Western, Scottish, and so on). Each camp therefore came under the authority of the Command in which it was situated. Most of the early prisoners were U-boat men and Luftwaffe personnel. As such they were considered a danger to the public and sent to the remotest of these camps. Since there was a genuine fear of a German invasion, the authorities decreed that camps should not be sited within 50 miles of the coast, or near sensitive locations such as airfields or munitions factories. Whoever issued this instruction seems to have overlooked the fact that Britain is an island, and a fairly small one at that: the War Office, having been given the near-impossible task of implementing these provisions, replied in February 1941, 'We haven't measured distances accurately [but] the proposal not to create camps within a 50-mile limit from the coast looks like limiting sites to a very small area in the country!'

In spite of the difficulties, War Office staff gave it their best shot. Featherstone Camp was located near Haltwhistle, which has the reputation of being at the exact centre of the British Isles and therefore, one would imagine, as far as possible from any coast. But as the threat of German invasion receded, these factors diminished in importance and eventually camps were built in all areas. Their placement seems in some cases to have been based on a whim: a former member of staff from Camp 295 at Cattistock near Dorchester claims, 'When it was opened the incoming Commanding Officer was given the choice of Cattistock and a rather more convenient site at Charminster with better road communications … The Colonel chose Cattistock because the fishing was better.'

As well as the purpose-built camps, a variety of existing places were used, including former British army barracks, and establishments previously occupied by American and Canadian troops in the run-up to D-Day. As many as 1,500 separate camps may have existed at various times, but it is most unlikely that a definitive catalogue will ever be compiled. When the Geneva office of the International Red Cross asked its London delegation to supply a list of all camps in the country, it received a reply which said:

> We think it would be almost impossible to compile such a list … Not only have numbers and location of camps in Great Britain changed continually, but as you know, it has frequently happened that a camp at the same location has had a succession of different numbers, and a camp with the same number has moved to a succession of

different locations … We ourselves could certainly not compile a list of all camps which have ever existed, and we very much doubt if the War Office could either.

As far as the Germans captured in North Africa were concerned, none would set foot in the United Kingdom at this point, except for those en route to the USA, who would typically spend a few days at a British transit camp before crossing the Atlantic. Their short stay in Britain generally made no difference to the monthly statistics, as they came and went in the space of a few days. Not until the Normandy invasion in June 1944 would German POWs arrive in substantial numbers and be detained for an extended period of time.

TABLE 3: GERMAN POWs IN BRITAIN 1944–1945

1944	March	2,550	1945	March	156,100
	June	7,900		June	207,000
	September	90,000		September	208,950
	December	144,450		December	211,300

NOTE: the September 1944 figure shows a marked increase in numbers of POWs after the Normandy invasion, with further increases over the following months. From June to December 1945 numbers remained static, as very few POWs were now being brought to the country.

5

All Walks of Life

After a journey lasting half the night, the train carrying Eberhard Wendler and hundreds of his comrades pulled into a railway station shortly before midnight. 'We were taken to the camp in lorries – it was pouring with rain and we hadn't a clue where we were. We were directed to our huts.' Not until the following day did the POWs discover their new location – Camp 78, High Garrett, near Braintree, Essex. This was Eberhard's first and only permanent camp, and he would live in it for the best part of two years.

Like most of the POW camps around the country, this was designated as a GWC – German Working Camp, also known as a Base Camp. These were for 'other ranks' – men ranging from private up to sergeant major. Officers could not be compelled to work and were held in separate camps.

Since the hard-line Nazi troublemakers had been identified – as far as this was possible – and sent to special camps, elaborate security precautions such as watch towers and searchlights were considered unnecessary. A simple barbed wire fence around the perimeter and routine patrols by guards were deemed more than sufficient for these low-risk POWs, who posed no measurable threat to the British public, and were unlikely to run away. The odds were against a successful escape, as crossing the Channel would have been difficult in any case. Besides, the average prisoner was relieved to be out of the war, and an escape to Germany – even if it were possible – would only mean a return to the fighting.

Not knowing how long they would be here, the men settled in as best they could and got to know their new neighbours. Hans Behrens spoke of his own arrival in camp:

> There were army, navy, air-force, all mixed up. After a few roll calls and initiations we were divided into various huts and naturally you look around at your hut-mates and you strike up a relationship. Sometimes it's with someone from another hut, so you ask for permission to move so you're nearer each other – someone from your area or your home town.

'There were about twenty-five huts,' Eberhard Wendler remembers. 'Mine was hut 13, and I was together with two or three others who I was captured with.'

As Arno Christiansen recalls, 'The other German POWs came forward and subjected the newcomers to severe scrutiny, searching their faces, hoping to see someone they knew, or someone from their former unit, someone with news. But it didn't often work out that way; each group was just as confused as the other.' The new arrivals and the 'residents' quizzed one another:

'How long have you been here?'

'When were you captured?'

'What happened to your lot?'

Finally, to Christiansen's delight, he bumped into an old school friend, Erwin, whom he hadn't seen for years. And Werner Reinhold, while detained in a Northumberland camp, renewed his acquaintance with an English doctor on the staff whom he had first met in Germany in 1938. However, an unwelcome feature of camp life was that comrades might be moved away without warning or explanation. Some friendships which began in camp survived only until one of the POWs was transferred elsewhere. Others have lasted a lifetime.

The camps varied significantly in size; the smallest accommodated about 200 prisoners, while the largest had room for several thousand. The typical German Working Camp, of which there were probably at least 200 around the country (and possibly twice this number), had a population averaging about 750. Many of the camps were laid out to an almost identical design: this fact was highlighted when one group of Germans was en route by train from one camp to another and had worked out the hut allocation before they even arrived.

A massive brick-built water tower, which could be seen from a considerable distance, dominated the view of most of the camps. (In many cases this is the only structure that survives to the present day, High Garrett being just one example.) A common layout consisted of a central path or roadway with huts leading off on either side, and the water tower at one end of this path. A Red Cross inspection report from February 1945 states that on a previous visit the POWs had been living in tents 'surrounded by a morass of mud'. Since then, the situation had greatly improved. 'The compounds have been provided with an extensive drainage system, concrete-slab pathways have been laid out and roads are being built. The mud has disappeared.'

As time went by the POWs decided to make their surroundings as pleasant as possible. 'Every hut had a garden, and that was our pride. We tried to make a home of our camp,' Henry Metelmann explained. A camp newspaper produced by the prisoners contains this description:

Anyone who sees our base camp in its present summer finery can be justifiably delighted with the scene. Thank God there are a considerable number of comrades who have the feeling and the vision to undertake such a task. Approaching the camp from the forest road one walks or drives to the guard post. Then, to left and right, are the huts, freshly painted and surrounded by soft green grass or multi-coloured flower beds. Bordered by floral arrangements and lawns, the sparkling-clean light-coloured concrete roadway is also a testament to our industrious and worthy gardeners.

At some camps the POWs were allowed to keep rabbits as pets. A story came to light that POWs at a camp in Kent would be forced to kill the rabbits to supplement their ration. The issue was actually debated in the House of Commons. It transpired that there had been a misunderstanding on the part of the commandant and, to their relief, MPs heard that no such order had been issued. The prisoners' rations had always been up to scale and the rabbits were reprieved.

Still existing in virtually its original form, Eden Camp, Malton, Yorkshire, occupies an 8-acre site. It consisted of two main sections, one for prisoners and one for the British contingent. Of the twenty-seven near-identical huts in the prisoner compound, two-thirds were used as living accommodation for the POWs, while the rest served as recreation rooms, laundry, cookhouse, sickbay and so on (see Table 4, p.52, and Plate no. 16).

The Nissen hut, with its distinctive half-round design, was a design dating from the First World War and featured prominently among POW camps of the 1940s, though a number of other styles were also used. Typically, the huts would measure about 18ft to 20ft in width, and about 100ft in length. A structure of this size would accommodate fifty to sixty men. The POWs slept in two-tier bunk beds with straw mattresses – or palliasses as the army generally referred to them – supported on a wire grid. Prisoners were issued with two grey army blankets with a border of coloured thread, which they sometimes unpicked and used to embroider designs on their clothes and kitbags.

During the day, the men's bedding and other kit had to be arranged in a specified manner: the routine was drummed into the prisoners' heads so thoroughly that decades later they still remembered every step.

'We were shown how to make the bed,' says Erwin Hettwer. 'The mattress was to be folded in half. The kitbag placed on the head end. One blanket was to be folded in a way that it could be wrapped into the second blanket and then placed on the folded mattress.' He adds, 'Spare shoes were to be cleaned and placed, soles up, against the folded mattress. A towel was to be folded, placed on the wire mesh at the foot end and the plate and cutlery placed on it.'

'Apart from the beds, the only furniture consisted of two tables and four benches,' another captive recalls. 'Prisoners squatted on the edge of the bed, or lay on the two-tiered bunks.'

The huts themselves were filled with an all-pervading smell of burning wood and coal from the two stoves, a fog of cigarette smoke, and the aroma of damp washing. The stoves were the only source of heat and in cold weather were kept burning the whole time. The type in use was not very efficient: 'Sometimes it glows and sometimes it says *krrr*, thrusts out a few clouds of smoke and goes out. Unluckily for the wet socks and cardboard soles to which it lends a deserving edge.'

As much as 56lb of coal per man could be consumed every week, though this ration varied according to weather conditions. The lighting was often poor, with as few as two or three 60-watt bulbs to illuminate an entire hut. A Red Cross inspector remarked that the addition of some table lamps would have helped the prisoners carry out delicate tasks such as sewing.

The remaining huts served a variety of functions: a cartoon map published in *Die Pforte,* the prisoner of war magazine for Camp 247 at Ripon, Yorkshire, shows just how self-contained the camp was and illustrates the administrative and recreational purposes to which the huts were put.

TABLE 4: ALLOCATION OF CAMP BUILDINGS, CAMP 247, RIPON

Handwerker	Craftsmen (Cobbler and tailor)
Furier	Storekeeper. (A more usual name for this individual is *Quartiermeister,* but in camp this title was apt to be confused with that of the Quartermaster – a member of the British contingent. The much less common word *Furier* seems to have been adopted to distinguish between the two.)
Lagersprecher	Camp spokesman. Formerly known as *Lagerführer* (Camp leader; see p. 61–2 for explanation. His office and living quarters were often formed by partitioning off some space in one of the huts used as general living accommodation for the prisoners.)
Kalabusch	Detention cell. (The word *Kalabusch* is not found in any known German dictionary. It is almost certainly the 'Germanisation' of the American colloquial word, 'Calaboose', meaning a prison or jail, and was probably introduced by prisoners formerly held in the USA.)
Uhrmacher	Clock and watch repairs
Bäckerei	Bakery
Schreibstube	Writing room
Waschraum	Washroom (Ablutions)
Kino / Theater	Cinema / Theatre
Kapelle	Chapel
Presse	Printing press (Camp magazine)
Revier	Sickbay
Leseraum	Reading room
Küche	Kitchen
Kantine	Canteen (Always used in its military sense, meaning a shop where everyday items such as soap and writing materials could be bought. It was not a place where food was served.)
Friseur	Hairdresser

Eberhard Wendler's journal shows the extent to which prisoners relied on facilities such as these. After losing the glass from his watch, he visited the camp watchmaker to have another fitted and subsequently had the timepiece itself cleaned; during September and October 1945 he used the services of the tailor and a carpenter:

9 September 1945: I had a cap made (dark blue) for three shillings: Rolf [fellow prisoner] received my old one.

23 September 1945: I had a shelf made for two shillings.

He made several purchases from the canteen:

> **9 January 1945**: bought a mirror (1s 11d), shoe polish (8d), a ruler (3d), an eraser (4d) etc. Hair-oil (2s 2d), skin-cream (10d).
>
> **24 May 1945**: bought a brown suitcase for 9.7 *Schilling* [presumably 9s 7d]. Had a cover made for it out of my *Wehrmacht* coat.

Eberhard also paid an artist in the camp to paint a picture of his family home from a photograph, and subsequently had this framed by another prisoner. For 2s 8d a tailor made a pair of gym shorts for him. He spent 1s having a mountain landscape painted and the same to have a new collar sewn on to his shirt.

'There was nothing that couldn't be produced by the craftsmen in camp,' one POW proudly claims.

Eberhard Wendler had to visit the sickbay several times. Most camps had a resident German doctor from the ranks of the prisoners, and there was often a visiting British medic as well.

> **2 October 1944**: the English doctor gave us an injection on the upper left arm.

This simple procedure impressed Eberhard no end. In the German army, men received injections in the left breast: the doctor used a huge syringe and injected some of the liquid into each man as he filed past, using the same needle for all of them.

There was a further visit to the sickbay when Eberhard was ill with a high temperature. The diagnosis seems to have been jaundice and tonsillitis. On three occasions in early December 1944, he had a 75cm-long rubber tube inserted down his throat to extract an accumulation of bile, and had to remain with the tube in place for three hours each time.

> **13 December 1944**: three comrades from my hut, Koch, Böhme and Lange – on behalf of all the comrades in the hut – brought cake, shampoo and this exercise book to me in the sickbay.

While he was in the sickbay another prisoner made of sketch of Eberhard on the back of a patient's temperature chart (see Plate no. 12). The exercise book he had been given was to become his diary – a rare, if not unique, example of a journal which was actually written up in the camp as the events took place. Eberhard could now gather together all of the notes he had kept and put them in order. He transferred them into the notebook, and from that point on kept an almost daily record. While it is a factual account of the events which took place, the thoughts, reactions and emotions evoked by those events remain, for the most part, unwritten.

The prisoners themselves were a mixed bunch, with diverse interests and outlooks. 'They came from all walks of life, and from all parts of Germany,' Arno Christiansen says. 'There were garage mechanics, a butcher, schoolmasters, bank clerks, office boys, a publican, a couple of plumbers, a tailor, several factory workers, hotel porters, a taxi driver, a dental assistant, and a few professional soldiers. Then of course, the inevitable few "Mummy's boys" … the sort that back home in Germany would be wearing pure silk pyjamas and having their nails regularly manicured.'

In age, they ranged from the very young to the very old. Perhaps the youngest of all was 'a 14-year-old Nazi soldier in full uniform', captured not long after D-Day. This lad revealed an astonishing ignorance of the true situation when he 'demanded to be sent to the German-occupied part of Britain [and] would not believe that there was no German-occupied part of Britain'.

At the other end of the scale was 'an old man who had been given an armband and a rifle in France and told he was in the German Army. The following day he was captured. On the night he turned up, the RTO [Rail Transport Officer] rang the camp from Devizes railway station and asked for a truck to be sent for a prisoner'.

'A *truck*? Is the prisoner wounded? In that case he will need an ambulance.'

'No, he is not wounded. He is just too old to march to the camp.'

The prisoner, when questioned, answered in impeccable English: 'I am a bit old for this sort of thing actually … I was too young to fight in 1870 in the Franco-Prussian war. I was too old for the 1914–18 war. Yet I am taken as a prisoner of war in 1944. Isn't that remarkable?'

A visitor walking among the huts would naturally expect to hear German spoken in all its many regional dialects. But a multitude of other languages were spoken, too. A bewildering mixture of nationalities could coexist within any of the camps, as the German forces had recruited from a wide range of territories: these included areas considered to be German territory, such as the Sudetenland, which the Fatherland had 'liberated'. In addition, some citizens of the German-occupied countries elsewhere in Europe, including Holland, Norway and Denmark, chose (or were chosen) to enlist in the conqueror's armed forces. An inspection of Camp 179 in February 1945 revealed that almost half of the inmates were not actually German, the break-down being as follows:

German	165	Yugoslavs	13
Dutch	110	Norwegian	1
Czechoslovaks	2	Luxembourg	1

Toft Hall Camp, where 1,516 prisoners were detained, must surely hold some kind of unofficial record: its inmates belonged to no fewer than thirty-eight nationalities, with some men claiming to have been 'pressed into German service against their will'.

Prisoners held by Britain were not segregated according to the branch of the service to which they had belonged: any one camp might potentially hold army, navy and air-force prisoners. (This was in contrast to the system in Germany, where Allied soldiers, sailors and airmen were kept in separate camps run by the German army, navy and air force, respectively.)

When new prisoners arrived in camp, the Quartermaster's office was invariably one of their first stops. 'In general the prisoners had arrived in this country direct from the area of conflict and their eventual capture,' explains a former member of a camp staff. 'Their possessions were very meagre indeed.' On average, only 37 per cent of the POWs still had their full uniform. The Quartermaster and his staff had the job of recording the POW's belongings and issuing him with whatever new kit was needed to fill the gaps.

Eberhard Wendler's diary says:

21 January 1945: I got a smashing new pair of trousers because my old pair was ripped. Had to stand outside waiting in the cold for two hours to get them. But they let me keep the old pair.

Wendler explained:

We arrived in the uniforms we had on when we were taken prisoner, and used them till they wore out. Naturally, they were already old, and then [later] we worked in them all the time. Once a month on a Sunday we went outside the camp to the British compound where there was a hut where you could change things. You stood outside in the cold *for hours*. If your trousers were worn out, you'd tear them a bit more to make sure, but you'd get there and the Sergeant might suspect you'd ripped them. So then you wouldn't get a replacement. None of it was new – the clothes came from British soldiers who'd been demobbed or something. When it came to the jacket, that was the English army 'blouse' – as it was called – dyed maroon. In the back was a big diamond-shaped patch in a contrasting colour. It was sewn on and underneath the patch was a hole in the jacket.

This last measure was taken to eliminate the possibility of POWs using these as escape clothes by removing the patches and passing themselves off as either British soldiers or civilians. With all three branches of the armed forces in one camp, it was hard to tell just by looking at his uniform which service an individual prisoner belonged to.

'One parachutist in particular owned, for some inconceivable reason, two uniforms: a German and a brown-coloured English one, and offered us his original parachutist's trousers for sale,' Hans Reckel declared. 'The price was around thirty cigarettes. A dark blue woollen scarf could be purchased for twelve cigarettes. Non-smokers were undoubtedly the exploiters of every useful situation.'

The new arrivals at High Garrett soon spotted near the gate a statue of Romulus and Remus, crafted by the previous inmates of the camp.* 'The rubbish dump behind the barracks was still smoking,' Hans Reckel remembered. 'Our predecessors could only have moved off a very short time before. From the graffiti on several walls, one gathered that they had been Italians.' In some camps, signs on doors still bore Italian words such as *Medico* and *Gabinetto Dentistico* [doctor; dental surgery].

When Italians had been moved on to the farms where they worked space became available in the camps, and from mid-1944 this spare capacity was taken up by the German prisoners who were beginning to arrive in significant numbers. However, the two groups were kept well apart. 'Germans and Italians are not to work together,' the *Daily Express* reported. 'The Italians will work in one area, the Germans in another, so placed that they are not likely to meet.'

'We felt the Italians stabbed us in the back when they switched sides, and our army had to go in and defend their country for them,' one German says. For their part, the Italians felt that they were victims of the Germans, who had dragged them into a war they did not want.

The Germans had been encouraged by their High Command to think only in terms of victory. 'Being taken prisoner was for the other side, not us,' one German claimed. The average soldier therefore had no idea what to expect as a POW and had probably given the possibility little thought. But he was mistaken if he thought that arrival at a permanent camp would be followed by a lazy, if uneventful, life. The camps were run by the military: POWs were subject to a regimen that was every bit as strict as in the *Wehrmacht*.

In overall charge of each camp was a British commandant – usually a Lieutenant-Colonel, but occasionally a Major. Many had seen action in the First World War, and held decorations such as the Military Cross or the Distinguished Service Order. 'He always looked smart,' Eberhard Wendler says of 'his' commandant. 'He was very old, very tall and *very* strict.' Despite their stern manner, some commanding officers looked on the prisoners with the sort of affection one might expect from a kindly headmaster. A woman once phoned the nearby prisoner of war camp to complain about the behaviour of the POWs on work parties. She explained that when they arrived at their place of work they were in the habit of urinating in plain view of anyone present. The commandant listened to her grievance. Clearly this had something to do with the watery porridge served every morning for breakfast. He replied, 'I am very sorry Madam; I cannot do anything about it. It is an old German custom!'

---

* Similar statues of Romulus and Remus were created at various places around the country. An extant example may be seen at Stoberry Park, Wells, Somerset. The sculptor was an Italian stonemason, Gaetano Celestra, who is said to have copied the image from a 50 lire banknote. This statue is now a Grade 2 listed monument. At Lamb Holm in the Orkney Islands and at Henllan Bridge POW camp, Camarthenshire, Italian POWs created highly ornate Catholic chapels, both of which survive today.

At Norton Camp in Nottinghamshire the commanding officer, Major Boughton, was referred to as *Father* Boughton by the prisoners. 'He was a lovely person,' Arthur Riegel declares. 'He was always there for the POWs who were entrusted to him – whenever a prisoner was sick and had to go into hospital Father Boughton would collect him afterwards in his own car. At Christmas he appeared in the camp at midnight and greeted every single one of us with a handshake, wished us a happy Christmas and an early return to our homes.'

While the personality of the commandant – more than any other factor, perhaps – set the 'tone' of the camp, the interpreter was vital to its smooth running. The ever-present language problem meant that he was usually the only staff member who could speak with the prisoners face to face in their own language. He spent longer in direct contact with the POWs, and almost certainly had a better sense of their mood, their problems and their frustrations. The interpreter was usually a sergeant or junior officer in the British army, and liaised between the prisoners and the British administration. Many of the interpreters were German Jews. Herbert Sulzbach had volunteered in the First World War for service in the German army and fought from 1914 to 1918, winning two Iron Crosses in the process. When the Nazis came to power he fled to England and joined the British army. During the early part of the Second World War he worked on defences against air or sea landings by the Germans. As the threat of invasion diminished he offered his services as an interpreter and worked initially at Comrie Camp, later at Featherstone Park, Haltwhistle, where he likened the relationship between the commandant and himself to that of 'Lord Mayor and Town Clerk'. He records in his memoirs how one POW, startled to hear a man in British uniform speaking perfect German, said, 'Sergeant – if you weren't in that uniform I'd have said you were a German.' Sulzbach retorted, 'I was till Hitler threw me out.' Despite having lost his home and his nationality, Sulzbach realised that not all POWs were to blame for the war just because they had joined the Nazi party. 'Every postman, every railway worker, every policeman had to join the Party, if he didn't want to sacrifice his family or himself,' he declared.

Heinz Greilsamer was 13 in 1939, when he and his sister, Hannah, fled Nazi Germany on a *Kindertransport** to England, leaving their mother, father and grandmother behind. He changed his name to Harry Grenville, attended a grammar school in Camelford, Cornwall, and became, in his own words, 'pretty thoroughly assimilated'.

News of his family was scarce. He says:

We were pretty sure that they wouldn't survive. My grandmother and parents were deported to a concentration camp at Theresienstadt. We knew they were there because the International Red Cross allowed a twenty-five-word message once a month in each direction. We also knew there were transports from Theresienstadt to

---

* A scheme under which Jewish children came to Britain to escape Nazi persecution before the outbreak of war.

the extermination camps in Poland. In twenty-five words you can't say a lot, but the last message I had through the Red Cross was 'We are going east'. That's all they said and it was perfectly obvious what that meant.

Harry was recruited into the army and took an intensive course to become an interpreter. In 1945, he received a commission and in about September of that year he was appointed to a POW camp in Devon. In spite of the near-certainty that his parents had been killed by the Nazis, he experienced no problems with the German prisoners:

> I was very young at the time, and I didn't find it particularly difficult to deal with them as individuals. In the POW camps we knew the designation of their units: they were for the most part army, air force, and a few navy prisoners, and not many *Waffen-SS*. I didn't deal with any officers – they were all other-ranks. The only officers that I came across were the medical officers – one per camp.

It was generally arranged that for every 500 prisoners there would be one interpreter. Harperley Camp, County Durham was responsible for 2,000 POWs and had a department manned by two British interpreters and two German clerks. After the end of the war the interpreter's office was give the additional job of checking POWs against a thick directory of suspected war criminals. Incredibly, much of this work was done by German prisoners. The interpreter's services were occasionally requested even when there was no real need for them, as paratrooper Herbert Holewa recalls: 'Our camp leader spoke perfect English, but always went through the interpreter. I asked him why and he told me, "If I converse with him I haven't got time to think of a good answer but if he speaks to me, and the interpreter translates, I know already what to say."'

The prisoners were watched over by a contingent of guards – mainly British soldiers but occasionally Polish troops in British army uniform. The Poles were usually assigned to patrol the camp perimeter, while the British soldiers looked after the running of the camp within the wire. The attitude of the Poles towards the Germans was frequently hostile. Sophie Jackson cites examples in her book, *Churchill's Unexpected Guests*, of prisoners being shot by Polish guards. And as the German army had also recruited large numbers of Poles, conflict occasionally arose between the two sides. One German prisoner witnessed an extraordinary event. 'One of our paratroopers came from Poland and his brother had joined the British army and was standing guard in the same camp. He was on one of the towers, shouting down in Polish and his brother shouted back in German. It was quite a ding-dong!'

With only one guard to about 135 prisoners, the British staff can hardly be said to have maintained an intimidating presence: in fact, there were five times as many administrative staff as there were guards. In the early part of the war the guards had tended to be men who, for reasons of age or infirmity, couldn't serve as combat troops. They were later replaced in many cases by soldiers who had seen action and were being given a relatively 'cushy' posting prior to being demobbed. Unexpectedly, those who had been in combat were often more sympathetic towards the POWs than the non-combatants had been.

Ulrich Steinhilper, the Luftwaffe pilot captured in 1940, tells how he was guarded by:

> an elderly soldier, complete with rifle and fixed bayonet … He was about 50 years of age and, in the conversation which followed, he mentioned he was now serving his twenty-sixth year in the army … From time to time he had been promoted then, for various reasons, he'd been 'busted' [demoted]. At that time he'd just been reduced to the ranks again because he'd been drunk on duty a few weeks before. His stories about his service and the different countries in which he'd served were a true delight to listen to and certainly helped to pass the time for both of us.

Peter Roth spent some time at Glen Mill camp, where there were two buildings, with a road in between. 'One of our lads saw someone he knew and went across. We weren't supposed to go there, and a British guard kicked him in the arse. But he'd kicked the wrong man. This one was trained in karate!' The guard was left sprawling on the ground. 'You never know who you come against, do you?' Peter comments wryly. 'Some guards were quite brutal and others were just the opposite. They did their duty and treated you as a human being but others went to extremes: you get it anywhere. Some of the guards took personal revenge. Something happens in the war – somebody gets killed – this was a chance to get even with us. And when they got even with us we had to get even with them again.'

The memoirs of prisoner Otto Funk show that, as well as British soldiers, men from all around the Empire served as guards: they included South Africans, Canadians, Indians, Australians and New Zealanders. 'My personal recollection is that all of them were very *korrekt* and adhered to the conditions of the Geneva Convention.'

6

Nazis Rule the Roost

While prisoners were aware of the Geneva Convention's existence, very few knew much about it. Most soldiers believed it to be international law. In fact, it had no legal force and served only as a set of guidelines which the signatories had undertaken to follow. (Britain, the United States and Germany were among those who had signed: Russia and Japan had not.) Its scope did not include those on the battlefield, only those who had been taken prisoner. (The fine distinction between the two would be a reason for disharmony later.) Broadly speaking, the Convention dictated that prisoners of war were to be treated no worse than the capturing power's own troops: and this extended to accommodation, food, medical treatment, freedom to engage in religious worship and the ability to communicate by mail with one's relatives and loved ones. Indeed, almost every aspect of a POW's life was included. But the Convention had a number of shortcomings. Having been drafted in 1929, it failed to predict the ways in which modern warfare would develop, and its lack of precision in certain areas would give rise to various problems, as we shall discover.

Each side in the war relied on the other to look after its own prisoners with respect, dignity and fairness. The British, it could be argued, have always had a reputation for 'fair play', sportsmanship and 'correctness' – to the extent that the English words *fair* and *fairness* have been imported, unchanged, into the German language. Thus the Germans had very high expectations in this regard: and when the British failed to live up to these standards the disappointment was all the greater.

A neutral country acted as 'Protecting Power', safeguarding the interests of each side in the war by inspecting camps and monitoring conditions. At the beginning of the war Switzerland undertook this responsibility on behalf of Germany, while the United States represented Britain. When the USA entered the war in December 1941, thereby renouncing its neutrality, Switzerland became the Protecting Power to both sides – an arrangement which no doubt speeded up the administrative process considerably.

In fact, the POWs had relatively little contact with their captors: discipline within the prisoners' compound was for the most part left to the Germans themselves. The British only intervened on rare occasions when it was suspected that the POWs were planning an escape or contravening some regulation.

Eberhard Wendler says:

We didn't like having roll call in all weathers, but other than that they left us alone. An officer came through the hut checking everything but we didn't mind that at all.

It was nothing like as strict as the German army. Even in the *Arbeitsdienst* we got to know the realities of life. In the mornings we had to stand outside without a coat in a massive square – rain or snow or whatever. We weren't allowed to wear socks – I don't know why. We had *Fußlappen* – little squares of cloth as big as a handkerchief, folded over our feet inside the boot. And they inspected us to make sure we hadn't got socks on. On Saturday we had a shower – all of us stood in a row and the officer came round with a hosepipe and sprayed us all over with cold water.

Occasionally the guards would rummage through the huts looking for British money which – in the earlier years – POWs were not allowed to have. Eberhard records one such event in his journal.

> **24 April 1945**: My birthday. At midnight 3 comrades (Koch, Böhme and Kuse) woke me and congratulated me. There was a beautiful little table [and set out on it were] many flowers and the painting of my family home. [Later, we] were individually searched. We were brought on to the playing field. When we went back into the hut, everything had been turned over.

Recalling the incident, he adds that before being readmitted to their hut they were kept waiting on the playing field for a very long time. Every hut 'had a good thrashing'.

The British and German staffs held a daily meeting attended by the British commandant, the adjutant, a senior British interpreter, and the German camp leader who was in charge of the day-to-day administration of the prisoners' compound:

> The purpose of the meeting was to liaise and discuss, in an amicable manner, matters relating to the efficient running of the camp, and resolve any current problems … The prisoners' compound was a completely self-contained unit, where all the facilities provided were run by the resident prisoners of war.

At least one camp had a loudspeaker system enabling the camp leader (*Lagerführer*) to communicate easily with the prisoners. While the arrangements generally ran to everyone's satisfaction, the choice of *Lagerführer* was controversial in some instances. 'Everyone was surprised to see how the camp leader – a warrant officer of the "concrete navy" (coastal artillery) … got fatter and fatter as the months went by, in complete contrast with the increasing thinness of the ordinary camp inmates.'

In the House of Lords in May 1944, Lord Strabolgi claimed:

> The camp commandants are mostly retired officers, men with very distinguished careers but of a certain age, who, to put it quite plainly, do not want trouble. They look after the health and other interests of the men, but if they can arrange for the prisoners in the camps to run themselves they allow that to happen … In practice it

means that the ardent Nazis rule the roost. They keep order and take very good care to suppress, and in some cases oppress, their fellow-countrymen who have seen the error of their ways ... great care should be taken to separate these dyed-in-the-wool Nazis, these strong party men who are probably incorrigible, from the others. We think they should be put in separate camps so that the others may have some chance, by discussion, reading, listening to the wireless and other experiences, of seeing the evils of the régime which they have hitherto served.

In the House of Commons, John Dugdale, MP for West Bromwich, made the point even more directly. 'The *Lager*führer is chosen not because he is the most democratic, the least unpleasant German. He is chosen because he is the most Nazi and the best disciplinarian ... I submit that is not the best way of running our prisoner of war camps or inducing Germans to cease upholding the Nazi régime.'

George Wolff, a German Jew, had come to Britain as a young man, and served in the RAF. As an interpreter at a British POW camp shortly after the war, he experienced these problems at first hand. He states:

These POWs had been screened in Scotland by the army and sent down as non-Nazi personnel – 'safe' people. But I found on arrival that there was a core of very hard Nazis who'd somehow managed to slip through the net ... On the first day I was in my office and a *Feldwebel* – a senior NCO – walked in, sat on the edge of my desk and told me what the orders were for the day. I just looked at him and said, 'Well, *my* orders for the day are this: you get yourself off my desk, get outside the office, knock at the door, and when I say "Come in" you come in and stand to attention and then I'll give *you* the orders for the day.' And I realised immediately that he was one of these very arrogant types who thought he was running the camp. A lot of the ordinary German soldiers in camp were very unhappy about being more or less bullied by this small group of about ten or twelve people.

Wolff notified his commanding officer, saying, 'I want them packed off back to Scotland' – and they were.

The camps operated to a strict timetable. 'Very early in the morning a bugle sounded. There were a couple of washrooms for us to use then another bugle call and out for roll call. Rain, sunshine, snow, we were always counted,' says Eberhard Wendler. The prisoners stood in groups of fifty – five abreast and ten deep – and the British soldiers checked that everyone was present.

Do you know, some of them couldn't count, and *we* had to tell them! That's the truth. The longer we had to stand there the more frozen we were. And then the commandant arrived and everyone stood to attention. And if anyone was missing – in the toilet, or still in bed or anything – straight away it was twenty-eight days' solitary confinement for that man. Then we marched off and went for breakfast. This was often porridge – something we'd never had before. Thick porridge, no sugar, no milk. Sometimes with salt, sometimes without. But it filled us up.

Immediately after breakfast the men were taken out of the camp to work on local farms.

The concept of using captured Germans as a workforce was nothing new. A precedent had been set during the First World War when about 65,000 men had been put to work in both agriculture and industry. Early in the Second World War, in February 1940, the question had been asked 'whether German prisoners from scuttled ships may be usefully employed on dredgers, trawlers and lightships instead of keeping them in idleness for the rest of the war'. The reply was that it would be undesirable for a variety of reasons to adopt this practice. Nevertheless, the idea kept simmering in the background, and a couple of years later Commander Oliver Stillingfleet Locker-Lampson raised the subject once more.

The son of an eminent poet, Locker-Lampson had served with distinction in the First World War, prior to becoming a politician. In June 1943, in an exchange with the Secretary of State for War, he was told that the possibility of German prisoners being used as a labour force had been flatly ruled out. The Commander was not the sort of man to be easily deterred, though. He represented a popular sentiment in Britain that the Germans must in some way make reparations for the damage and suffering they were inflicting on the nation.

'Does not my honourable and learned friend agree that German vandals who have tried to destroy this country should be employed to help us to restore it?' he insisted.

'For security reasons it is preferred not to use Germans in this war,' was the reply. 'We prefer to use Italian prisoners of war, of whom there is a plentiful supply.'

'Are we to be afraid of the Germans in our own country?' harrumphed Locker-Lampson. And in the following weeks and months he persisted with this line of questioning. During a debate on the reconstruction of war-damaged buildings in London, Locker-Lampson shouted, 'Why not employ German prisoners of war?' And when the Commons discussed the proposed new PAYE (Pay As You Earn) system of collecting income tax from employees it was claimed that between 7,000 and 10,000 additional clerks would be needed. 'Where are those men to come from?' pleaded one MP. A reply from the back benches reverberated around the chamber: 'use the German prisoners!' This time, to everyone's surprise, it was not Commander Locker-Lampson who spoke, but Andrew McLaren, MP for Stoke-on-Trent. Evidently, the idea was catching on.

Before 1939, Britain had imported half the food it needed: wartime conditions – in particular Germany's submarine blockade, which seriously limited the amount of material which could be brought in from overseas – meant that British farms now needed to double production. And all of this came at a time when men who normally would have worked in agriculture and in related occupations were away fighting for their country. The risk that Britain might starve prompted the government to take over responsibility for all agricultural production for the duration. Each area of the country set up its own War Agricultural Executive Committee (abbreviated to WAEC but popularly known as 'The War Ag'). This body oversaw farming in its county and stipulated how the land should be managed. Needless to say, farmers who had tended the same fields all their lives were often unreceptive to the 'help' given by the War Ag's officers; however, a blend of tact, persuasion and occasional coercion usually brought about the desired result. As a last resort, farmers who simply would not co-operate could have their land confiscated by the state.

To augment the pool of labour, the Women's Land Army (WLA) – an institution created in the war of 1914–18 – was reintroduced. Its members have always been affectionately known as 'Land Girls'.

In 1942, the country's chances of survival had seemed poor. The Minister of Agriculture asserted that the harvest that year 'might well be a critical factor *not only in the history of this country but in the history of the world* [author's emphasis] … Every ounce of foodstuff that we can produce at home will release *pro tanto* our shipping – shipping so sorely needed for so many other purposes vital to our final victory.'

When Italian prisoners of war had first been used as labour it was found that many came from farming backgrounds and had skills that the British farmers could exploit. But their innate abilities were outweighed by a distinct unwillingness to apply themselves to the job in hand. Mary Barnes was a schoolgirl when they came to her father's farm. 'That summer was hot and dry and the harvest should have been an easy one, except for the Italians [who were] very reluctant to work. It was too hot, too cold, or too dry. One man had excellent English but memory lapses when asked to work full time.' Egg production by the hens appeared to plummet and then the hens disappeared. Farmers and landowners also noticed that pheasants and other game were being poached by the Italian prisoners.

Nevertheless, supervisor Ted Page found them to be a 'human, happy band, up to many pranks and a sense of fun, making the most of a bad situation. We worked and played together as a group,' he wrote in his diary. Ted had left school around 1936 and – after a brief period when he was employed by a shopkeeper – he found a position with the Ministry of Agriculture. As a conscientious objector, his religious and moral convictions prevented him from taking any kind of combat role in the war, and he was assigned to agricultural work – initially as a farm labourer. He later became the foreman at a Sussex camp for Italian POWs, with whom he established a warm rapport. 'I learned for the first time the importance of breaking the language barrier … I am proud to have been accepted as their brother.'

In the run-up to D-Day in early 1944, a number of Italians were transferred to work outside of agriculture. Some were employed on transport duties and preparing camps for American troops, and in this role their contribution was described as being 'of inestimable value'. Others, especially those who had learned a trade in peacetime, were promoted to more specialised jobs consistent with their pre-war occupations. Significant numbers were used as gas fitters to repair pipework in bomb-damaged houses. The result, however, was a further shortfall in manpower for vital agricultural work, and the case for allowing Germans to work was greatly reinforced.

A small-scale experiment was held in strict secrecy in early 1944, in which '969 specially selected German POWs for labour purposes' were brought to Britain – presumably captives from the North African campaign. 'They are earmarked for agricultural work under military supervision from Camps No. 97 [Birdingbury, Warwickshire] and 103 [Moota Hill, Cumberland].' Following the success of this initial trial, a much more extensive scheme was rolled out, and was in full swing by autumn. By November, farmers concerned about 'the idleness of Italian prisoners of war working on farms', were asking their local War Agricultural Executive Committee to replace them with Germans 'who work much better and are under proper discipline'.

The Germans were still officially viewed with some apprehension, however. The media had spent most of the war portraying them as ruthless monsters who wouldn't hesitate to kill innocent civilians, including women and children, given half a chance. The very idea of letting them out to work on the land seemed far too great a risk. Unlike the Italians, who enjoyed considerable freedom, the Germans would need to be strictly supervised by armed guards. When an East Anglian MP asked why more Germans couldn't be made available in Norfolk, 'because if they are kept under proper supervision the saving in manpower more than outweighs the loss of manpower we are getting from the Italians', he was told by the Minister of Agriculture, 'It is a question of camps. For security reasons the German prisoners are limited to certain camps, and there are no more of them in that area.'

While the prevailing view was that unleashing 'dangerous Nazis' on an unsuspecting public might be a risk too far, one committee warned that, on the contrary, they might become *too friendly* with the civilian population. 'If selected German prisoners were to be allowed the same degree of freedom as Italians and proved themselves docile hard-working people, there might be a public reaction favourable to the German people in general.'

It was finally decided that screening and segregating the prisoners would effectively minimise the risk. Hard-core Nazis would be held in special high-security camps, and would not be allowed out to work. The rest of the prisoners would reside in working camps under supervision both in camp and when out working. Having satisfied themselves over these points, the authorities now had to pacify the trade unions. A compromise was reached with the National Farmers' Union: firstly, prisoners would not be used where British workers were available; secondly, the farmer must pay the minimum union rate of £4 per week for each prisoner (later increased to £4 10s). This avoided any accusation that POW labour was 'undercutting' union members. It is important to add, however, that only 5s per week (one-eighteenth of the total) was paid to the POWs themselves and, as we shall discover, this would prove to be a major source of friction.

Added to all this, the prisoners themselves wondered whether they should be working for the British at all while Germany and Britain were still at war. 'Opinions as to whether "We ought to help the Tommies to win the war" were very varied, and long and violent discussions took place,' Hans Reckel maintains. The issue wasn't merely a matter for their own consciences: it could be a question of life or death. Not long after Reckel wrote his observations, a prisoner named Rettig had contributed a piece to the POW newspaper, *Wochenpost*. This was perceived by some fellow prisoners as an act of treason against Germany. (Rettig was also suspected – wrongly, as it turned out – of having tipped off the British about an escape plot.) To punish him for these supposed crimes, the other POWs beat him up and he subsequently died from his injuries. Two men were tried by the British and hanged for his murder.

Screening ensured that prisoners who were prepared to work were not attacked or intimidated, and these measures made it possible for Britain to use most of its German POWs as a consenting (if somewhat reluctant) workforce.* Trusted POWs such as Eberhard Wendler and his comrades at High Garrett were sent out as farm labourers as early as September 1944. Immediately after roll call and breakfast the men were taken to the farms where they would work, often at some distance from the camp. According to Arno Christiansen, the transport consisted of several 'utterly decrepit clapped-out lorries. To say that they had seen "better days" would be a gross exaggeration … They would have served a better purpose if they had been melted down for scrap.'

'They weren't army lorries, but privately owned ones,' Eberhard Wendler remembers:

> One belonged to a greengrocer, another to a farmer and so on. They drove right into the camp. Then we were counted out, normally twenty-five in each squad. The commandant stood near the gate of the camp every morning and as we went past we had to salute: and anybody with hair not cut short, he shouted 'haircut'! In the lorries we sat on orange boxes and there was no cover. We were taken quite a long way to places like Felstead and Thaxted [each approximately 12 miles by road from the camp]. A German sergeant came with us and on the way to the fields we picked up an English ganger who dished out the work and showed us what to do. And the German sergeant made sure we did it correctly. There was a guard, a British soldier with a rifle, who just sat there and watched us work. A lot of the guards let us know they didn't like Germans. Some soldiers would leave and others replaced them. You never got to know any of the guards.

---

* Later, when the war was over, the threat posed by Nazi hardliners diminished considerably. By that stage, only a small minority of the prisoners felt they were betraying Germany by working for the British.

Hans Reckel, also at High Garrett, had to dig root vegetables. 'After a long journey through Braintree and Witham, we stopped on the edge of a large potato field. A foreman was already waiting for us, everyone received the usual wire basket and then the great potato-picking began. We were completely out of training and the work was mostly not easy, but we were basically happy to prove our strength away from all barbed wire, even if accompanied by armed guards.' On 18 October, Reckel noted in his diary that he 'lifted turnips all day. Had an absolutely stupid guard; grumbled because I laughed at his instructions; thinks I do not want to understand because I answer his threats with a shrug of the shoulders.'

Fraternisation between the Germans and British civilians was strictly prohibited, and every effort was made to keep them apart, even in the workplace.

'We didn't go to the farmhouse,' Eberhard explains, 'we were taken *straight* to the fields. We'd never seen such big fields, because we had in Germany only little farms. We never saw any other British people, not even the ones who lived on the farm. We didn't see any British workers, and we weren't allowed to talk to anybody and they didn't bother with us – that's how it was.'

Peter Roth explains:

When we first went to a farm we just did a normal day's work. If the farmer gave us cigarettes we'd work extra but for those who didn't give us anything we did as little as possible. Or we'd do more damage than good. Some people wouldn't even give you a glass of water. We used to say, 'Me no understand', but we *did* understand. And they'd say, 'bloody Nazis!' and they'd talk among themselves and then we had to get even with them. There were always ways and means to get even with people. We once had to plant some lettuces and out of every four plants we cut the root off three before planting them. After a few hours the farmer picked them up and went 'tut-tut', and he jumped in his car and went to the chemist's to get some stuff to put on them! [He wipes a tear of laughter from his eye.] When they said 'bloody Nazi', we gave them bloody Nazi. We wanted to be treated as a person, not as an animal, you see.

Many of the Germans were unaccustomed to agricultural work. 'I'd served an apprenticeship as a precision instrument maker,' explains Eberhard Wendler. 'I was one of the smallest, the youngest, and I was thin and hadn't much strength. It was getting on for winter and we had to go sugar beet pulling. In truth, I'd never seen a sugar beet before – they were a cross between a mangold-worzel and a parsnip. Then I found out they'd been invented by a German chemist[*] and I wasn't half annoyed!'

Almost unknown in Britain until the 1920s, this crop became indispensable during the war years after imports of cane sugar had ceased because of the U-boat blockade.

---

[*] Andreas Marggraf, 1709–1782.

The roots were turned into sugar, and the leafy tops were used as animal feed. Nothing was wasted.

But while the government viewed sugar beet as Britain's salvation, the prisoners saw it differently. Miming the action of beet-pulling, Eberhard says:

> Sugar beet was the worst. You pull them out and knock them together to get the dirt off, and then you lay them down. There were twenty-five of us in a line across the field, each with his own row, and these great big chaps of ours, some of them farmers, they got to the end of the field and waited. And then a few like me came along, we'd hardly got there and they'd start again. So *we* never had any rest. You were always disadvantaged if you were small and short. And when the whole field was done we used a tool to cut off the leaves at the top and we put the beet in heaps. The backache! You've got to bend right down – I've never had backache like it in all my life. And it was so cold you could cry. And we were always soaked right through and covered in mud. I *hated* sugar beet!

The men were permitted a short break for lunch:

> Our sergeant had a big tin with the food, and he cut the loaf into so many pieces and gave out a little bit of margarine and a bit of corned beef to each of us. Every day it was the same food. We always had tea, never coffee, in a 1-gallon petrol can. It was black tea with no sugar and no milk. If we were lucky and we were able to make a fire out there in the sticks, we could have the tea hot.

The wily prisoners eventually overcame the lack of sugar in their tea. Reg Miles, a guard at a Sussex POW camp, recalls the Germans asking the farmer's permission to take some of the sugar beet back to camp. Somewhat puzzled, the farmer agreed. He knew that beet was inedible in its raw state and had to be sent away to a factory where it underwent some mysterious process to extract the sugar. But the prisoners found a way to duplicate this operation within the camp, a procedure that took three days and produced a thick, dark, treacly substance. This was evidently going on in other parts of the country, too. Mike Arron, a Cheshire teenager, was employed to photograph POWs at the local camp for official record purposes. As a frequent visitor, he made friends with the prisoners, who invited him to tea. He says he never worked out how they had such sweet tea when sugar was so strictly rationed.

Foreman Ted Page noticed a distinct contrast between the Germans and their Italian predecessors. The Germans seemed 'abject, cowed, spiritless but not surly or … stand-offish. [They] worked hard but soullessly. They would answer in one single word, "Yes", or "No", but wouldn't sustain any conversation – one almost gave up trying.' He observed on one occasion a gang of fifty German POWs 'hoeing for dear life' in a large sugar beet field. They never spoke, even to one another, nor did they ever seem to stand up and stretch. 'One felt a great sense of depression. These men were cowed like animals who had been whipped, and one could sense the terrible things which [they] had been through … I never want to see men like that again.' As time passed, though, he detected a change: 'One began to find individuals underneath … those tattered clothes … [who] had come through such an ordeal.' Ted spoke a little German but was disappointed to be 'rebuffed' when he tried to make conversation with the POWs. Wherever possible, the German gang-leader was chosen for his ability to speak some English, and it was these individuals whom Ted first got to know: later, when he had perfected his German, he would converse with all of the men in their own language.

7

The Final Battle

On completing the work that needed to be done at one farm, the prisoners might go to another and yet another until finally, at day's end, the lorries arrived to take them back to camp. 'We sometimes had an Irishman as guard, and he was always drunk,' says Eberhard Wendler. 'When we got to the fields we made a fire so he could keep warm; and sometimes I carried his rifle for him on the way home till we got to the camp.'

After his first day as an agricultural labourer Arno Christiansen felt tired: but it was 'the healthy kind of tired feeling, not the stiff boredom tired … depending on the farms, the farmers and the guards, on balance most of the working parties seemed to have had a good day.'

Back in camp the prisoners had a quick wash before the evening meal was served. (Baths or showers were a once-weekly luxury.) Two or three huts were used as dining rooms, with long tables and bench seats. The meals were served to the POWs in shifts, and the men from each hut would go in their turn. Eberhard Wendler recalls:

> Three men would go to the cookhouse and bring the food to the dining hut. If it was a cooked meal there was a big bucket with everything sloshed in together, and they'd dish it out and each table got so much. Otherwise you'd just get a little slice of bread, a little margarine and a little bit of corned beef – that's all. It wasn't much, but I'm not complaining. One man – he was a big chap – he was always hungry. And another one who was a mate of mine and old enough to be the first one's father was serving the food. And the young one accused him of giving himself more food than he'd got. And he took it to heart. He dished out the food and left his own there, he wouldn't eat it. And I thought, 'Oh dear, what's going to happen now?' And the old boy beat the youngster black and blue – he had black eyes.
>
> Another man took a slice of bread back to his hut to eat later and somebody pinched it and ate it. And the one who pinched it was beaten up. On your mind all the time was something to eat – we weren't starving, but we were hungry.

German prisoners manned the kitchen and, depending on their skills and imagination, the quality and variety of the meals could be greatly enhanced. A report by the International Red Cross detailed a typical day's menu at Camp No. 54, Hampton Lovett, Worcestershire, in July 1945:

Breakfast: Coffee, ¼ loaf, jam.
Lunch: Porridge, cooked liver, mixed salad.
Dinner: Potatoes, Corned Beef Goulash (about 23 grams per man), carrots, bread.
(*Allowances shown are per person.*)

During the evenings, the men had to amuse themselves in conversation or card games. A prisoner writes:

There was not a single moment of real peace to be obtained because one was continuously surrounded by games of cards, stories, discussions, lessons and other noises. After roll call in the morning, no one was allowed to set foot in the huts until 11.45 [a.m.], and during this period, the crowds of POWs loafed around the huts and inside the narrow circle of barbed wire fence. Singly or in groups, the POWs crowded past each other in a permanent circuit round the huts – nothing but men, always the same faces, the same voices, the same conversation, the same environment

And Werner Völkner says:

… Day after day went by, the same routines. It was absolutely soul destroying … Everybody knew about everybody else, they knew about their families, they knew about their sweethearts, they knew about their youth, where they spent their time at school. There was nothing any more that we didn't know about one another.

Conversation consisted of 'concentrated imbecility, fiction and fact, experiences with the fair sex and various curses. So some twenty men talk men's talk through the noise of the radio … Over the double bunks hang damp socks (those which have not found a place on the stove), wet washing and, put there by prisoners who cannot come to terms with captivity, a [picture of a] naked woman.'

Notwithstanding the drawbacks of life in captivity, Kurt Bock looks back quite fondly on those times: for him the companionship was important. 'Talking to friends, talking round and round. Have we ever again had time for these discussions? I certainly have not and I regret it. Everybody had his own life story and there was also the present and even more important the problems to come: what would happen to us and when? … But I do not think this time was lost; I even think of it as a nice time … I cannot help thinking of it in this way.'

From their camps in Britain, the POWs caught occasional glimpses of history in the making as war continued on the Continent. 'Huge squadrons of twin-engine aircraft towing gliders flew over the camp,' Eberhard Wendler wrote. This was the opening phase of Operation Market Garden – an ambitious Allied expedition intended to bring the conflict to the enemy's doorstep and shorten the war. It was hoped that by capturing the bridge at Arnhem and pressing on through Holland the Allies would be able to proceed quickly into Germany itself. The operation – later the subject of the film *A Bridge Too Far* – failed to fulfil its objectives; however, this could in no way diminish the impact that this show of military power must have made on the prisoners.

That winter, a shock resurgence by the Germans in the Ardennes left the Allies reeling and filled some of the more optimistic Germans with fresh hope. Willi Hildemann took cheer from this news, and wrote in his journal, 'The situation in the scenes of battle is communicated to us via the English and German military reports. May this be the final battle, which will lead us to victory.' But his wish was not granted. German troops had delayed the Allied advance, but only temporarily. A few weeks later the Allies were at Germany's frontiers.

As 1944 ended the prisoners faced what was, for most of them, their first Christmas in captivity. On a page of his diary, richly-decorated in colour to mark the occasion, Eberhard Wendler records how he, as an impressionable 18-year-old, perceived the event:

CHRISTMAS 1944 – BEHIND BARBED WIRE

On 24 December 1944 we celebrated German Christmas, the festival of joy, behind barbed wire. Everyone looked forward to the festival and the preparations were in full swing. We had the most beautiful Christmas tree in the camp and we had decorated our hut with pictures and fir-twigs. When the Holy Eve arrived the preparations were complete. Outside on the camp square the Christmas tree lights were lit, the choir sang carols and the camp leader spoke some appropriate words. Then we all went into the huts, each to celebrate the Christmas feast.

Assembled under the glow of the Christmas tree we sang the most beautiful songs about Christmas and about home. One of the comrades spoke about home and about our fate, and brought us so near to home that all of us had tears in our eyes, and thus many went out silently into the holy night. At every bedside the candles burned and every one of us dreamed of home, and in our thoughts we were at home in the midst of our loved ones.

Eberhard reflects:

I don't know where they got a Christmas tree from, but they must have chopped something off a tree outside. It's unbelievable what you can do with a few twigs, a bit of string, and a few odds and ends. And that's where I learned how to make stars out of paper – another prisoner showed me how to make them and I still do it. I've never sold them, I always give them away. I must have made hundreds, if not thousands over the years. The camp commandant announced a competition for the best-decorated hut with a prize of cigarettes for the winners. Actually he seldom came into the huts. But he must have known that Christmas meant a lot to us. On Christmas morning somebody came through saying, 'The commandant is coming round!' So we were all excited. At first he went past our hut! So one of our lot ran after him and said, 'What about us?'

Eberhard's diary entry for that day concludes:

> Ours was second best out of twenty-five huts. The commandant was very pleased
> with the cleanliness and order in the hut, with its Christmas decorations.
>   We'd shown him a real German Christmas.

Even at this late hour some people in Germany still believed that Hitler's
Vergeltungswaffen – 'revenge weapons' – could defeat Britain, and a prolonged attack
using these weapons was launched. An unintended consequence of this assault was that
Germans imprisoned in the south-east of England had been on the receiving end of
these missiles for several months. Hans Reckel says:

> On 23 September I saw a V-1 for the first time; its explosion shook the whole hut. V-1
> rockets thenceforth became almost daily visitors. We heard the motorbike-like rattle
> of their engines and waited for the explosions with mixed feelings. One evening we
> even saw two German aeroplanes caught in English searchlights. So we could never
> think that we were living well protected on a peaceful island.

Early in January 1945, Eberhard Wendler recorded in his diary: 'At 21.00 hours two
V-2s exploded near our camp with a terrifying din.' In the House of Commons one
MP asked the Secretary of State for War, 'whether, in providing camps for German
prisoners of war, he will segregate, as far as possible, those who have had anything
to do with the robot bombing and put the camps for these in situations where these
bombs are most likely to operate.' The Minister replied, 'Even if the suggestion were
practicable, it would be considered as a reprisal contrary to the Geneva Convention
and contrary to the interests of our own prisoners.'

When Germany's temporary change of fortune in the Ardennes fizzled out, morale
reached a low point in the camps. In February 1945, a number of prisoners escaped from
Glen Mill Camp. An immediate roll call was held to establish how many POWs were
missing, but the remaining prisoners were defiant and obstructive. After several hours, the
POWs grew ever more restless and abusive towards the British camp staff: at one point
they began to move forward and one of the British guards, intending to fire over their
heads as a warning, hit a young German prisoner, Paul Hartmann, fatally wounding him.

While this was a tragic and most regrettable incident, such events were rare. In general,
relatively few of the German prisoners lost their lives while in British captivity.[*]

While POWs in British camps experienced the war 'through-the-keyhole', so to
speak, those still in action on the Continent saw everything at first hand.

Hans Behrens was a signaller in a tank regiment. He had already seen action in the
Ardennes, and in February 1945 his unit had been moved to Germany's border with
Holland. He recalls:

---

[*] By January 1947, the number of fatalities from all causes was 1,254.

We experienced great losses. It was very cold. Food was getting extremely difficult and so was fuel. I remember not having washed properly for three weeks; we must have stunk, I would imagine. My tank commander had gone off to headquarters for new information and I was left alone with Hans, the other wireless operator and machine gunner, in our little half-track. I was just sitting doing the paperwork for the decoding of a message and suddenly all hell was let loose. There were sparks inside the vehicle and I felt pain in my legs. I heard voices I couldn't understand. Then the door was ripped open and there was standing an American with his sub-machine gun. I had a terrible fright. I do remember pulling the plug out of the wireless set and ripping the top sheet of paper off my communication pad which I put in my mouth and swallowed as an obedient soldier.

The American gestured to him, 'Come on, let's go, let's go!':

And I virtually fell out because my legs wouldn't support me any more. And then an American sergeant in his battle gear came over and spoke in reasonable German. All he was interested in was to get to Brunswick to see his grandmother.

Hans was taken away to the American lines and saw at close quarters the huge formation of armour that he would have been pitted against next morning. 'Thank God we didn't attack them,' he says, 'or I wouldn't be sitting here now.'

Eduard Friedrich Winkler had joined the Luftwaffe, but colour blindness had prevented him from becoming aircrew. Instead, he became an armourer in the Luftwaffe Field Division, servicing the guns on aircraft. He was sent to Arnhem shortly after the Allied assault on the city, and on two occasions narrowly escaped being killed by 'revenge-weapons' which had gone off course. 'We were out on an exercise and a low-flying V-1 hit a tree and came towards us, and belly-landed without exploding. Later, in Arnhem, we were billeted in a block of flats and a V-1 hit the building and we lost fourteen men. I was asleep in bed – there was a very bright light and the wall on one side had disappeared.' Finally he was sent to Riess on the eastern bank of the Rhine to defend Germany's border. 'The area was under heavy fire from the Americans and we lost two ferries to the artillery fire. We were only there to stem the advance.' Eduard and the others in his unit had their machine pistols taken away for use by other troops: in their place they were astonished to be issued with French rifles from the Franco-Prussian war of 1870. These were, to say the least, at the opposite end of the spectrum from the sophisticated V-1 and V-2 missiles.

'We had no transport whatsoever,' Winkler adds. 'Only wheelbarrows and bicycles without tyres and whatever we could find to transport our stuff. We knew it was finished. On 2 March 1945 we went to Winnekendonk and when we saw the British coming it was out of this world for us. For each of us there were about twenty people there. We knew it was hopeless. I raised my hands and the first English words I heard were, "Shall I kill the f****** bastard?"' Eduard already understood the word 'kill'. The Tommy didn't carry out his threat and Eduard spent the next few years as a prisoner in Britain, where he would have ample opportunity to learn what the rest of the soldier's utterance had meant.

Morale among the German soldiers reached a low ebb: Dieter Hahn had long suspected that they were now on the losing side. He says:

When Hitler declared war on America we knew we couldn't possibly win. After D-Day, although I was only a youngster, I felt deep down we could *never* win. Just before I was taken prisoner in Mainz I was still walking about with my rifle, and I was so fed up with the damned thing I took the bolt out and threw it down a drain, and broke my rifle over a wall and said, 'To hell with you, Adolf, and your war!'

By mid-March 1945, the Americans had crossed the Rhine and the defending forces were in complete disarray. 'The conditions in Mainz were indescribable,' Dieter told a researcher. 'Hundreds, if not thousands of soldiers were milling about, no one knew who was who or what was what. No one was in command.' Dieter and his comrades took shelter in a wine cellar. 'There were little barrels all around the wall and we were just sitting there. There were a few drops of wine in the barrels and – on an empty stomach – I was a bit tipsy. We could hear the American tanks, their tracks rattling in the street. The Americans appeared at the top of the stone steps and just shook their heads because we were only lads. I was 17.'

Another 17-year-old, Theo Dengel, had been posted to Mainz to help defend the city against an American attack. The town lay only 85km from Kaiserslautern, where he'd grown up, and where – even as a schoolboy – he'd somewhat grudgingly done his bit for the Fatherland:

When we got into the sixth form at high school in about September 1943, the whole class was called up to be *Luftwaffenhelfer* – air force auxiliaries. We were moved into a camp 6 miles outside Kaiserslautern at a railway engineering depot. The idea was that at night we were under military command and we were trained to use anti-aircraft guns and searchlights. And in the mornings, between 8.00 [a.m.] and midday, our teachers came out to give us lessons – that was the theory. In fact, most nights we were awake on the guns and in the day we went to sleep in class. At 17 I was called up, first in the *Arbeitsdienst*. This was compulsory. Instead of guns you had spades and you marched around – it was absolute nonsense. The only purpose was to put drill in you. It was supposed to be for a year but we were sent home after about three months. It was November 1944 and we were called up in the army. I won't go into that; it was just awful.

In early March their captain had gathered them together:

We were required to countersign a new order from army headquarters, informing us that should a soldier allow himself to be captured by the American forces, his family would be subject to reprisals. If one of the soldier's parents was in government service, local or national, this person would be dismissed regardless of his or her position. [Theo's father worked for the tax authorities.] The captain also stated that it was our duty to defend the left bank of the Rhine, and that we were not permitted to retreat to the right bank of the river. We were all absolutely terrified, but were forced to sign the document. In effect this order meant that each one of us had to face almost certain death; we were given no alternative.

As the enemy approached, Theo and another young soldier were ordered to guard an empty house. The other soldier disappeared without warning and Theo ventured outside in an attempt to make contact with any remaining German troops in the area. As he approached a tunnel under a railway embankment he came under fire and began to run:

> Whilst I was dashing down the hillside, I noticed several soldiers on the ground who had been caught in the fire and then I was hit. I was flung to the ground by the impact and felt a stabbing pain in both legs, blood was running over my rifle from a small wound on my right hand. I appeared to have been hit by shrapnel. I lay there, too terrified to move; eventually more German soldiers ran down the hill into the tunnel without being shot at. It was worth taking a chance and I ran as fast as I could that last hundred yards into the tunnel to be met by several other soldiers who had also got through.

He made his way to a field hospital and while he was there the Americans entered. He was taken prisoner and, like so many others, experienced uncertainty about the future, worried about the plans he'd had to put on hold, and feared the unknown dangers he would have to face. 'An episode of my life was over, and I was being sucked into an unknown and unpredictable future. Would I see my parents again, and when? The threat of retribution on my parents by the Nazi regime, as a result of my capture, worried me for a long time.'

Theo was treated for his wounds and taken, eventually, to a field hospital in Normandy. 'It was spotlessly clean and food was adequate – far, far superior to anything I had ever received in the German army. The standard of nursing was excellent. I could not but admire the care with which the American staff looked after the wounded German prisoners of war.'

Henry Metelmann was born near Hamburg on Christmas Day, 1922. In common with most other young Germans, he was taught to revere Adolf Hitler. 'I remember the day, 30 January 1933, when Hitler was appointed to lead Germany into a glorious future. My father, probably to let me witness history in the making, took me to a celebration in the large square in our town, the name of which was changed on that day from Kaiser Platz to Adolf Hitler Platz.'

Later, he wrote:

> Even though Father hated everything connected with the Nazis, I liked it in the Hitler Youth. I thought the uniform was smashing, the dark brown, the black, the

swastika, and all the shiny leather. Where before we seldom had a decent football to play with, the Hitler Youth now provided us with decent sports equipment, and previously out-of-bounds gymnasiums, swimming pools and even stadiums were now open to us. Never in my life had I been on a real holiday – Father was much too poor for such an extravagance. Now under Hitler, for very little money I could go to lovely camps in the mountains, by the rivers or near the sea.

In 1941, as an 18-year-old recruit, he joined a tank division and served on the Russian Front. In the closing stages of the war he was transferred to Schifferstadt – a town close to the Rhine a few kilometres from Ludwigshafen. By now, though, his enthusiasm for the war and his devotion to Hitler had diminished considerably:

> We were an odd collection of disillusioned survivors thrown together from once proud fighting divisions. Our unit did not even have a name, only a meaningless number, and our equipment was ridiculous considering that we were to do battle with General Patton's powerful tank army, which was now moving in from France.

Surrounded by American troops and hopelessly outnumbered, Metelmann and his companions decided, after much soul-searching, to give themselves up. 'From leaflets I knew what the word "surrender" means, and how it is pronounced. I walked about … rehearsing "Surrender, surrender!" and my friends thought that it sounded good.' Henry improvised a white flag by fixing a white cloth to a broomstick. They ventured out of the house in which they had been hiding and came upon two American soldiers. He says:

> They [the Americans] carried no weapons, had their hands in their pockets and whistled, and when I waved at them with my broomstick and shouted: "Surrender, surrender!" they must have misunderstood and probably thought that we wanted them to surrender to us. In any case they turned on their heels and ran as fast as their legs could carry them out of sight into some doorway … Whatever these two brave soldiers reported to their base, I will never know, but it must have been something hair-raising. For it did not take much longer than five minutes and we were as good as surrounded from all sides. There were several jeeps, an armoured car and not much less than a platoon of infantry with machine guns positioned at each end of the street.

With Cherbourg now in Allied hands, a new procedure was adopted for American-held POWs starting around September 1944. Instead of being taken first to Britain they were gathered at large camps in France situated in Cherbourg, Rennes, Le Mans and other locations. They were then taken to the United States on large troop-carrying ships – usually without any intermediate stop in Britain. Theo Dengel found himself:

[at] a huge transit camp outside Cherbourg with about 100,000 POWs in it – an
enormous place. The only way the Yanks could cope was to divide the camp into
what they called "cages" – each had about 10,000 POWs. There was constant traffic,
people coming and going. The people were divided up, not by their date of arrival or
where they came from, but by their surname. So I went into a cage where we were
'C' to 'H' or something like that. It all went by your initial letter – 'D', in my case.
We heard that men in some of the other cages went to coalmines in France, but after
about three weeks they told us, "You will be going to the States." They said, "You're
going tomorrow … you're going next week …" And then it actually happened. They
marched us into Cherbourg docks, and loaded us on to Liberty ships. [!]

'I suppose I was a bit excited,' Dieter Hahn exclaims. 'Normally I would never have
got to America.'

As well as the mass-produced Liberty ships, some of the world's most famous
passenger liners were used to transport the POWs, including the *Queen Elizabeth*,
Queen Mary and the *Ile de France*, which had been pressed into wartime service as
troopships. But when German prisoners crowded on to the *Queen Mary* they couldn't
believe they were on the famous vessel despite the name painted on the ship's side.
They were sure that this must be a propaganda trick on the part of the Allies, because
Hitler had previously declared the liner to have been sunk by German U-boats.

After a short sea crossing to the Solent, Theo Dengel caught his first glimpse of
Britain. Ahead was the mainland, while a large island which he correctly identified as
the Isle of Wight lay astern. It was a glorious summer day and Theo 'spent the whole
day lying on deck, sunbathing'. Next morning the convoy had 'grown so large that
I could not count all the ships,' and they moved off into the Atlantic. The prisoners
didn't set foot on British soil at any time: in fact, their ship did not even enter the port.
These facts play an important part in the POWs' later perception of events.

The convoy set out across the Atlantic Ocean. 'I was seasick the whole three weeks,'
Theo says. 'When you went up on deck you saw ship after ship after ship – a *huge*
convoy going towards the west, and on the outside you could see the warships. The
worst of this was, there was a U-boat alarm and you could hear bangs from the attacks
on the ships and the destroyers dropped depth charges. It was a particularly unpleasant
feeling to be down in the bottom of the ship with no means of getting out, and there
were Germans likely to torpedo you.'

'We slept on the steel deck in the hold,' Dieter Hahn recalls. 'The cover of the
hold was open to let in fresh air, and when the convoy was attacked we saw flashes of
explosions and star-shells and Americans going mad and rushing about. Every time we
saw a big explosion we shouted "Hooray! Give 'em hell, lads!" Little did we know that
we might be the next victims.'

'I realised that for the first time in my life I was at sea,' says Hans Behrens. 'I was very
seasick; it was terrible. I was hoping one of the U-boats *would* get us because I was so
ill I wanted to die.'

'We landed first of all in the port of New York,' says Hans Teske, 'and we were disembarked a few hundred yards from the Statue of Liberty. And there we were in little ferries which took us away from the Liberty ships and we saw "the symbol of the free" – and there were more guards than there were of us.'

Although the German prisoners' experiences in America may seem beyond the remit of this book, their relevance to the story will become apparent later. As in Britain, a network of camps had been established across the United States. These housed as many as 370,000 German POWs including the 130,000 who, under the Anglo-American agreement already mentioned, were technically prisoners of the British. Living conditions within the USA were relatively unaffected by the war, and the Americans kept their POWs in a degree of comfort which Britain could not have provided and which would also have been unimaginable in the German forces they served in prior to capture. Hans Kuhn described the accommodation in America as 'a fabulous luxury prisoner of war camp where we had excellent food, unheard-of steaks, and marvellous facilities'. Gunter Mauff raved about the Chesterfield cigarettes, Coca-Cola, ice cream and real coffee they were given. 'It was an unforgettable experience,' he told a German television reporter long afterwards.

'In our entire military existence no one had ever served us food like this,' said Reinhold Pabel, describing his stay at Camp Grant, Illinois.

'When I was captured I weighed 128lb,' another prisoner stated. 'After two years … I had gotten so fat you could no longer see my eyes.'

When they were not eating, drinking or smoking, prisoners could pass the time watching movies, pursuing hobbies such as woodwork and attending educational classes in a wide variety of subjects. But their stay in an American POW camp, comfortable as it may have been, did not only consist of recreation. Like their counterparts in Britain, the prisoners had to work. Bruno Liebich was one of thousands sent to the southern states to pick cotton for 80 cents a day (the same pay as an ordinary soldier in the American army). 'It's the worst thing you can imagine. In the open sky, no trees, no shade, very hot. And cotton weighs almost nothing – and we were supposed to pick forty pounds of it a day. Forty pounds! To make up the weight we put sand in it, we'd pee in it. But they found out we were doing this swindle and transferred us elsewhere.' Sometimes they worked alongside African-Americans, who had been doing this work for generations. Karl-Heinz Decker was shocked by the discrimination shown towards the black farmworkers and appalled by the conditions in which they existed.

'They used to say to us, "You're the slaves now, but when you go home *we'll* be the slaves again."'

8

An Eternal Yesterday

In contrast with the United States, Britain was suffering severe shortages of food, fuel, clothing and most other commodities. The German prisoners were, of necessity, kept in Spartan conditions because the authorities needed to balance the requirements of the Geneva Convention against the reactions of the British public if they treated the Germans too kindly. 'The other day a neighbour of mine had not a bucketful of coal in her cellar,' a civilian complained, 'but there was plenty at the nearby prison camp.'

Apart from the restrictions on physical comforts, the lack of news from home weighed heavily on the prisoners' minds. Terrible rumours circulated about the destruction of German cities and towns. The majority of the men had received no word from their loved ones since advancing to the battlefront: in the meantime anything could have happened, and it was human nature to fear the worst. They had sent the one card to inform their loved ones that they had been captured. Until this card was received, families had no idea whether the soldier was alive or dead, and even then they were given no address to reply to.

This changed, however, when they reached a permanent camp. Upon his arrival at High Garrett, Eberhard Wendler had written in his diary, 'At this base camp we got our first permanent address.'

The significance of this, he explains, is that: 'It was the first time we were really allowed to send a letter home. [Until then] my Mum didn't know where I was, she hadn't a clue.'

Mail took several weeks to reach Germany via Switzerland: no communication left Britain without first being checked by the censor in case it contained information of use to the enemy. Then, on arrival, it was checked again by German military intelligence. (There is some evidence that officers were instructed in how to send encoded information back to Germany in letters, and that snippets of useful intelligence were successfully transmitted in this way.) After the secret service had finished with the letter it was passed to the German censor. Any comments suggesting that Germany was losing the war, any hint of 'defeatism', or other undesirable material would be rendered illegible, or the letter would simply be 'lost'.

After writing home to his mother, Eberhard Wendler waited for eleven weeks before a letter and a parcel arrived in the post in reply. Among the contents of the package he discovered a mouth organ. At first it seemed a strange gift, because Eberhard's mother knew very well that he had never learned to play the instrument. It fact, though, it proved to be an inspired choice. He says:

Some of the others *could* play, and so I just handed it around – and *they* could play, those others. At ten o'clock when the lights went out at night they kept playing. All in the pitch dark they played. They played right through the night and you could hear them sobbing. All our songs were about home. Not marching songs or anything, but so many songs about *Heimat* – home! That word, *Heimat*, is holy – you can't translate it – it's sacred to us.

We *lived* for a letter. Then I got a letter from my Dad who'd been taken prisoner and was in a POW camp in France. As far as I can remember, we could send a card once a week and a letter once a month. So I had to share my allocation of letters, writing to my Dad one week and to my Mum the next. They could send parcels, but we couldn't – we had nothing to send. They sent what they could – a handkerchief or a pair of socks they'd knitted themselves. A little cake they'd baked. It was all very, very welcome, but they had nothing themselves!

Hans Reckel received his first letter from home at the end of January 1945:

Three names appeared on the noticeboard. We could collect the letters from the office. So that I should not have to answer curious or sympathetic questions, I read it out in public immediately: my family house was undamaged and my next of kin were in good health; but one of my cousins had been killed in Russia; another was in an American POW camp. My joy was not complete, but a feeling of great relief soon swamped everything else. I was generally congratulated and a few days later I had to report to the less fortunate in the *Lagerspiegel* (the camp news bulletin) on the condition of the letters, the length of time they had taken and their contents.

For others, the news was often far worse. Some endured the purgatory of receiving no reply at all, and wondering, fearing, what might have happened. German civilians in their thousands were being killed, injured or made homeless by the Allied bombing campaign. Hamburg, for instance, had been the target of a week-long aerial attack by British and American bombers in 1943. The city was almost destroyed. In that week alone, 42,000 of its inhabitants were killed and 37,000 injured. A further million fled from the ruins.

In 1945, the city of Dresden was attacked: schoolgirl Karin Busch and her mother took shelter in the cellar of their house. A bomb landed in the cellar, but did not explode: but in trying to escape Karin and her mother were separated:

The city was in ruins, ruins – just rubble and chimneys standing up. In the distance I could see a person walking and cried 'Mother, Mother!' and the chimney stacks fell down by the echo of your voice – like an avalanche. It's so eerie. I was trying to look for her, and I clambered back into that hole and saw these two little shapes. When you put wood into a furnace it burns and it gets red-hot and it still keeps its shape, somehow, with an inner glow, but when you touch it, it disintegrates. There was a pile of ashes in the shape of a person. I didn't know who it was, but then I recognised the earrings.

The bombers which flew these missions were frequently based in East Anglia near Britain's North Sea coast. The airfield at Wethersfield was only 6 miles from High Garrett where Eberhard Wendler was a prisoner. 'Every day we saw hundreds of these planes going off to our homeland to smash everything to pieces. A lot of prisoners received letters to say their parents had been killed, children killed, wife killed, house and everything smashed to pieces. And we saw them flying off every single day.' Eberhard found it impossible to ignore the threat made at his initial interrogation: 'They're making things for the war effort there, and we'll make sure we bomb your town.' As he saw and heard the massed formations of aircraft he couldn't help thinking of his mother, his younger brother and his friends at home, and wondering whether they would survive.

Although Eberhard maintains that he and most of his fellow prisoners felt no hatred toward the British, he has always felt that this intensive, indiscriminate bombing caused resentment.

By December 1944, it was clear to most people that the war was nearly over and that it was not going to end well for Germany. Some of the prisoners in Britain, however, long out of touch with the real turn of events, still clung to the conviction that Hitler would be victorious. The introduction of the V-weapons, combined with the German resurgence in the Ardennes, brought the prisoners hope that Germany could still win, and they were ready to do their bit to help. Accordingly, POWs at Le Marchant Camp, Devizes, began to hatch a stunningly audacious scheme. The camp in which they were detained was just a small part of a significant military complex in Wiltshire, bordering Salisbury Plain. At the time, 7,500 prisoners of war were held there.

The plan involved overpowering the camp guards and opening the main gate – a difficult and dangerous undertaking, but not impossible if carried out by twenty experienced SS men. The camp inmates would be released, and would arm themselves with weapons from the adjoining barracks. The next stage in the plot was to seize Sherman tanks from a nearby depot and Mosquito aircraft from an airfield in the vicinity. Finally, reinforced by the long-awaited paratroops they were expecting to arrive from Germany, they would march on London, releasing still further prisoners from the many camps they would pass on the way. In this way they would secure a triumphant victory for the Fatherland even at this late hour.

Together, the 150,000 German prisoners held in Britain at that time represented eight or nine infantry divisions, probably outnumbering the Allied troops in the country by a substantial margin, as most active units were currently overseas. The plotters saw themselves, quite literally, as Hitler's Last Army.

Nine hardened soldiers escaped from the camp and reconnoitred nearby military and air bases, of which there were several. They then returned to camp pretending to have given up their quest for freedom, and passed the necessary intelligence to their comrades. However, two American soldiers with a command of the German language overheard the ringleaders plotting and the conspiracy was thwarted.

The failure of the proposed breakout at Devizes did not deter others from planning escapes even at this late stage in the war. In March 1945, a civilian in Bridgend, Glamorgan, was woken by a noise in the street. On looking out of the bedroom window he saw a number of men pushing a car. His suspicions were alerted and he called the police. A constable turned up in response to the call and discovered that the doctor's car had been stolen. (It wouldn't have been the first time: previously, a group of servicemen from the RAF base at St Athan, about 13 miles distant, had 'borrowed' the vehicle to get back to base after a night out.)

On the late BBC news that night the top story had been the mass break-out of prisoners from the POW camp at Island Farm just outside the town. Only later did the police put two and two together and realise that the theft of the car was part of the most audacious escape by German prisoners during the entire war.

Island Farm Camp had previously housed American troops who had assembled there in preparation for the Normandy invasion. General Eisenhower himself had visited the camp and inspired the men with one of his pep talks. The Americans lived in great luxury and were said to be furious when they learned that enemy prisoners were to move into the comfortable accommodation after they had gone.

In fact, the quarters were deemed too plush for ordinary soldiers and the camp was finally used for officers only. Following suspicions that the Germans might attempt to break out, security at the camp had been heightened, and during the night a guard heard a sound and saw movement outside the perimeter fence. He opened fire and a prisoner was wounded: two others approached out of the darkness with their hands up. But later it was revealed that this was only a feint to draw the British guards' attention away from the real escape. No doubt this group had not expected to be fired upon.

On the other side of the camp, under cover of a noisy concert, men had already begun to slip away. Since 10 p.m. they had been crawling along the 20m-long tunnel they had painstakingly dug over a period of many weeks.

A group had already reached the town and had unlocked the doctor's car. Unable to start the engine, they had begun to push it. By chance, a group of guards on their way back to the camp after an evening at the pub arrived at that moment. The POWs told them they were Norwegian servicemen and asked for their help. The guards obliged by pushing the car until the engine started: this was the commotion heard by the civilian who had called the police.

By now, the first escapers were already 8 miles away in Llanharan. A roll call was held at the camp where, to the commandant's horror, it was found that seventy men were missing. A huge manhunt began, involving troops, police and civilians. Since the beginning of the war, church bells had not been rung in Britain: they were only to be used as a warning to the population that an enemy invasion had begun. But the escape of so many German POWs was seen as an emergency of such magnitude that the bells now rang out across the valleys. A local man, identified only as 'Ivor', was approached by one of the search teams who asked him to help them find the fugitives. 'I don't care two hoots if the whole German army's out,' he retorted, 'I'm out for a walk.

If I find them I'll let you know.' He did, in fact, see some escaped POWs and they were later caught.

Elaine Jones, the daughter of a shopkeeper, was 18 years old at the time. She remembers hearing on the BBC radio news that three of the escapers were still at large a full week after the escape. She recalls:

> Before the bulletin finished there was a knock at the door and my mother thought someone had come for something from the shop. Next minute the three Germans walked into the room with a farmer who had met them on the mountain road. They were obviously very cold, tired men, they'd been living rough and they'd eaten what they could forage in the fields. When the police arrived they thanked my mother for her kindness and they shook hands with us before being handcuffed and marched out.

One by one, the other escapers were recaptured, some in groups of two or three, others alone. One man wearing jackboots and a Luftwaffe greatcoat calmly knocked at the door of a house and asked for food. The small group who had stolen the doctor's car abandoned it after travelling about 70 miles and were caught near Castle Bromwich. (On learning that the car belonged to a doctor, one of them offered to recompense the medic for the petrol used.) All of the 1,600 prisoners at Island Farm were promptly moved to another camp in Worksop, Nottinghamshire. From then on, Island Farm housed only a handful of the most senior German officers, including Gert von Rundstedt, Erich von Manstein and Johann von Ravenstein.

As British and American ground forces advanced into Germany from the West, Russian troops now approached from the East to within a few kilometres of Berlin. Adolf Hitler and his closest associates took shelter in a bunker beneath the Reich Chancellery on Wilhelmstraße. On 20 April 1945, his 56th birthday, Hitler emerged to bestow the Iron Cross on several lads of the Hitler Youth. It was the last time he was ever seen in public.

In Britain, at Camp 29, the men decided to celebrate the Führer's birthday, as Arno Christiansen describes:

> Hut 16 acquired, by what means no one ever found out, a white sheet and some pillow cases from the hospital hut. From other quarters a supply of red ink had been organised. The inmates set to work, and in a short time their self-inflicted task was complete. They had manufactured a German swastika flag, about 6ft by 3ft, and accurate in every detail. As dawn broke on 20 April, this flag was flying high from the top of the water tower in the very centre of Camp 29 ... A great roar went up. The entire camp burst into ribald laughter ... just for a few moments it really did enjoy itself ... One of the Tommies was ordered to remove the offending object, and as he clambered up the tower, and tore down the rag, he was greeted by a prolonged round of applause from the prisoners assembled below.

Ten days later, as Soviet forces came within shooting distance of the bunker, Hitler committed suicide. Some POWs in Britain simply dismissed this news as 'British propaganda'. When newspaper headlines announced the dictator's death, they accused the British of printing special editions of these publications in an attempt to deceive them. These were the few who still refused to accept the inevitable: 'islands of men living an eternal Yesterday. To them Today is strange and incomprehensible ... Their Yesterday is Hitler's empire'.

Interpreter Herbert Sulzbach wrote in his memoirs, 'Until the end of April many clung to the prospect that they awaited liberation from their captivity, that paratroopers would soon land to occupy England from the air and set the POWs free.' The majority of the captives, however, accepted what had happened with an overpowering sense of relief. In Nazi Germany every soldier had, soon after enlisting, sworn a solemn oath:

> I swear by God this sacred oath, that I will give unconditional allegiance to Adolf
> Hitler, Führer of the German nation and people, and that, as a courageous soldier, I
> will lay down my life at any time for this oath.

Hitler's death released them from this vow; most of them felt that they could now renounce the Führer without being perceived as traitors. 'Ninety per cent of the people didn't like Hitler,' says Peter Roth 'but we weren't fighting for Hitler. I was fighting for *Germany*. I was in the Hitler Youth in the beginning, but I hated Hitler in the end because I didn't like the things they did to the Jews.'

Luftwaffe pilot Gunther Rall – the third most successful fighter ace in history – had flown in the Battle of Britain and throughout the war. He had actually met Adolf Hitler on several occasions, having received medals from the Führer. After surrendering, Rall was asked by an American intelligence officer if he would fight against the Japanese – but he refused.* (Karl-Heinz Decker states that the French Foreign Legion actively recruited men from the *Waffen-SS* from within POW camps in Britain. Some sources go so far as to claim that they formed a separate division which fought in Indochina. While it is likely that some former SS men did serve in the Foreign Legion, the assertion that they formed a separate division is open to some doubt.)

However, Rall no longer felt that he was betraying Germany by divulging the information the Allies wanted from him. He was taken next to Latimer Park for further questioning. He says:

> We were treated very well. The camp was run by the British forces but the interrogators
> were American. The questions were about tactics, about very special aviation
> problems and about the Messerschmitt Me-262 [the pioneering jet fighter developed

---

* The British War Office also considered recruiting German POWs into its armed forces to assist in the war against the Japanese, though the plan was beset by too many political and other problems to be taken seriously.

by Germany]. Three of us were in one small cell and we knew exactly where the microphones were built in. But it was of no interest because the war was over – it was senseless to have secrets and we talked freely and openly about these things.*

Later he was questioned further at Tangmere aerodrome in the south of England, of which he says:

After five minutes a very smart Wing Commander came – Wing Commander Stanford-Tuck. He treated us very gentleman-like and took us to the officers' mess and we stayed for three weeks for interrogation about tactics – everything about aviation. I answered absolutely freely. Strangely enough, we had great sympathy for the West. And there was a slight thinking when the war was coming closer to Germany that we could turn around and unite with the West against the Russians. Irrational thinking – but that's how it was.

The German forces in Italy realised that for them, too, the war was almost over. The MP for Taunton, Lt-Col Wickham, said in a speech:

I cannot help recalling the experience which a distinguished [British] officer in Italy related to me. He was travelling in a jeep with a German officer as a prisoner. As they passed through a village they received a great welcome from the villagers who threw flowers into the car, and he said to the German officer, 'I suppose they did the same for you.' He replied, 'Yes, sir, and what is more, they did it in this village, yesterday!'

On 2 May 1945, Lt-Col John Profumo** was present at the surrender of the German forces at their regional headquarters in the mountains of northern Italy. Profumo naturally had some misgivings about entering an enemy fortress, in case the offer to surrender had been a trick. Then he heard a familiar voice and saw a man who'd been with him at Oxford University. 'Profumo? Why, we haven't met in ages … yes, it's true, we're giving in.'

In Trieste, German soldier Heinz Elfner realised that the time had come to give himself up to the Allies. This turned out to be more difficult than he'd thought. He explains:

---

* Covert listening to captured Germans had earlier generated huge quantities of transcripts which include, in some cases, damning evidence of war crimes committed by those under investigation and by others. This project is described in considerable detail in the book, *Soldaten* (Neitzel and Welzer: see bibliography).

** Profumo became Minister of Defence in Harold Macmillan's Conservative government. The scandal which bears his name precipitated the defeat of the Party in 1964.

The British HQ was an imposing place so I walked in, climbed a flight of stairs and knocked on a door. An English officer greeted me but told me to go and get a job at the Town Hall! This was not what I had imagined. I went to the Military Police. This time I got some sandwiches and directions to a nearby hotel manned by New Zealanders. It was 5 p.m. on Saturday and they all wanted to go off duty. Couldn't I come back on Monday? I told them I had nowhere to go and at last I was taken in as a POW.

Guenter Wulff's regiment was stationed on the border between Hungary and Austria. As the Russians advanced from the east, he and his unit retreated into Austria in a half-track vehicle. 'At one point we were in Vienna city centre. Hitler sent out an order, "Nobody retreats – fight to the death!" But we could see how things were working out and said "Let *him* fight" … we'd fight, but not to the death. We'd fight to save our lives.' They encountered a Russian tank in the street. 'The tank came after us and fired. We made a sharp turn into a side street – a half-track can make a tight turn.' They hid in the ruins of a building. The tank returned, the turret opened, and a head popped up and looked all around. Guenter and his comrades held their breath. Each man had only a rifle and a pistol to defend himself and they knew their chances of survival were poor. Then, to their relief, the Russians drove off. They decided to get out of Vienna while they still could, but a dreadful sight awaited them as they crossed to the other side of the river:

There were all these German soldiers and officers hanging on the lamp-posts and telegraph poles. They'd collaborated with the enemy and the Germans had shot them. The Germans sent out special squads, and if you couldn't identify yourself properly they shot you there and then as a deserter. That's what they did in Austria. Pretty much on every lamp-post somebody was hanging. They hung them up and left them.

In early May, just as the war was coming to an end, Guenter and his men had pulled back to a village not far from the Austrian city of Linz. Behind them, the Russian army was pursuing them from the east. In front, they spotted American troops, who were close, but not quite close enough for an exchange of fire. They were trapped:

The Americans radioed our company and said, 'The war is over. If you want to be *our* prisoners you've got to come into Linz by 3 p.m. If you come after 3 p.m. we've got to hand you over to the Russians' – because we were in between the two. Our German officers said, 'We're going into the hills, you can come with us if you like, otherwise you can go over to the Yanks.' We said, 'You can go if you want, we're not coming.' All the officers went off on their own and we stayed with our guns and drove towards the Americans. So the Russians advanced towards Linz. And we made sure we got there by 3 p.m. [he says with a laugh].

The Americans seem to have been unprepared for the overwhelming influx of prisoners. The Germans were still driving their vehicles and were fully armed when the Americans directed them all into a field. 'We had supplies for six months, ammunition and all. We drove in with the Americans and – silly buggers like they were – all they wanted was pistols and watches. The boys handed over what they had. They gave one Yankee soldier a pistol and there must have been still a bullet in there, and he shot himself in the stomach and he made a somersault like a rabbit.'

Werner Völkner, a corporal in the SS, was wounded in Russia and had been transferred to Munich to recover. When the situation in Berlin became critical his unit was initially sent there to reinforce the defending German forces. But when the city was overrun by the Russians, and the situation became hopeless, they were diverted to the German lines in the north or even 'as far as Denmark if it was ever possible'. On the way they encountered a village where:

> from most of the upstairs windows of the bedrooms there were white sheets and tablecloths hanging … on broomsticks or anything else that could be used as a flagpole. The inhabitants of the village had obviously given up any thought of action against any intruding enemy … suddenly I had a terrible thought. The Russians could never have advanced and outflanked us that far; it was impossible. The roads were full of refugees mixed up with army vehicles and troops trying to go to the front line and the front line was almost non-existent.

As the end of April approached, Germany was crushed between two advancing armies – the British and Americans from the west and the Russians from the east. The two forces met at the River Elbe. Jubilant headlines appeared in the British press as it became clear that Germany's fate was finally sealed.

RED ARMY CROSSES THE ELBE

AN ENTIRE NATION ENVELOPED – EFFECT OF GIGANTIC PINCER MOVE

HALF A MILLION GERMANS CAPTURED IN 24 HOURS

On 7 May, at Reims in north-eastern France, in a modest brick building that had once been a school, *Generaloberst* Alfred Jodl signed the document accepting Germany's unconditional surrender. Moments afterwards, his voice choked with emotion, he made a short speech:

> With this signature the German people and the German armed forces are delivered up for better or worse to the victors. Both have achieved more and suffered more in this war than perhaps any nation on earth until now. In this hour I can only express the plea that the victors treat them leniently.

By the end of that day, 11 million Germans – virtually the whole of the Reich's armed forces – were in Allied captivity. General Johann Theodor von Ravenstein* had commanded the 21st Panzer Division in the *Afrika Korps*. Taken prisoner in 1941, he was the first German general to be captured by the Allies, and was sent initially to Canada. He was there on 8 May when he learned that Germany had surrendered, and he gathered his fellow POWs together:

> My young comrades, I know that it is a sad thing to a soldier to have said to him, 'You have lost'. But let me tell you this: it is better for Germany, better for us, that we have lost, because if we had won we should have lost ourselves.

Arno Christiansen describes the day when the news was broken to the POWs in his camp. After roll call one day, the British commandant addressed the prisoners through an interpreter, saying 'Germany has been defeated and has surrendered.'

'The camp stood absolutely still and in silence. They were momentarily stunned by the baldness of the announcement, and they did not know how to take it, or what reaction was expected of them. Then quite suddenly a voice at the back said, "Bloody good job! Now perhaps we can all go home!"'

But of course it wouldn't be that easy.

As late as mid-May some members of Germany's armed forces were still managing to avoid capture. Werner Völkner was one of them. 'Some of the chaps had previously gone to the River Elbe in the hope of finding a boat or swimming across, but they found there were Russians on the other side, and so they changed their minds and came back.' Having served on the Eastern Front and participated in the great tank battles of Kursk and Kharkov, Werner and his companions were familiar with the brutal behaviour of Russian troops. If he was to be captured, he would make sure it was by the Americans:

> As a battle group – or *part* of a battle group – we hid in farmhouses near wooded areas behind the American lines as such. I was in a big communications truck when the door was ripped open and there was somebody in a very strange uniform that I hadn't seen before with a Thompson sub-machine gun. They shouted, 'Gun, gun! Pistol, pistol!' I had a P38 and a machine-pistol we'd just been issued with – a Schneider, I think. I handed over the P38 and was rather hesitant, and to my surprise they handed me a pack of 200 American Lucky Strike cigarettes. And I thought, 'Things are looking up.' I went outside. Another American took the Schneider and

---

* Von Ravenstein completed his time as a POW at Island Farm, Bridgend, in the UK. He was repatriated in either 1947 or 1948.

gave me another 200 cigarettes. That was the first meeting with the American forces. There were rumours that the Americans would hand us over to the Russians, but this threat didn't materialise. Instead, we were told we were going to France to the coal mines. Until then, I had no contact with my parents, except for a postcard we were given to write on. It was pre-printed with the wording, *Ein Mitglied der geschlagenen Wehrmacht sucht seinen nächsten Angehörigen* – a member of the defeated German army seeks his next-of-kin. There was only space for about five lines of writing. So I bundled up some of my remaining cigarettes with a note which said 'I'm going to France', and threw the note out of the train as we crossed a bridge over a road. Somebody found it and wrote to my parents. But then the Americans said, 'No, we're going to Belgium instead.' And there we lived through the winter in tents.

The 1.4 million men taken prisoner after Germany's capitulation (as opposed to those captured during the war) were described by the British not as prisoners of war, but as 'Surrendered Enemy Personnel' (SEP). (The Americans used the designation DEFs – Disarmed Enemy Forces.) By creating this distinction, the Allies avoided their obligations under the Geneva Convention which, strictly speaking, dealt only with those combatants who had been captured during the fighting, and not those detained *after* the surrender. Food and water in the camps in Germany were in short supply and shelter was entirely lacking in some instances. To care for these men adequately would have been hard enough; meeting the high standards dictated by the Geneva Convention would have been impossible. The British Secretary of State for War said, 'Though we have not recognised their right to be treated as prisoners of war, we have, whenever practicable, given them similar treatment.'

Reports vary as to the death toll in these camps, but the figure may have been as high as 10,000.[*] Under pressure from the Red Cross, some improvements were eventually made, but in the end the only solution was to let the captives go as soon as possible. Among those set free by the British was Helmut Schmidt, who would later serve as West German Chancellor from 1974 to 1982. The Americans released teenager Joseph Ratzinger – later to become Pope Benedict XVI. By November 1945 all of the SEPs and DEFs had been freed, with the exception of known war criminals. This was in stark contrast to the prisoners of war *per se* in Britain and the United States, who – for the time being – would be held without so much as a hint of when they might be set free.

---

[*] Canadian scholar James Bacque has claimed much higher figures of between 790,000 and 1,000,000. Günther Bischof and Stephen Ambrose, among others, have challenged Bacque's conclusions, suggesting a considerably smaller number. See Bacque, *Crimes and Mercies*, and Bischof & Ambrose, *Eisenhower and the German POWs* (listed in the bibliography).

9

The POWs Are Guarding the Camp

At POW Camp No. 78, Eberhard Wendler makes only the briefest of references to the German surrender: 'On 7 May 1945 the war was over, and on 8 May and 9 May we didn't have to work. As of 6 May we couldn't send any more letters.'

The exchange of mail – which had become fairly regular in recent months – abruptly ceased again, because Switzerland's role as a go-between had finished with the ending of hostilities. The turmoil in Germany meant that contact was often not re-established for months. Families there had left their homes when they were bombed out. Millions fled from the East to evade an advancing Soviet army. Within the Russian sector, entire cities were renamed: Chemnitz, for example, became Karl-Marx-Stadt. Letters addressed to the former place names were simply dumped.

Squares and streets named after Adolf Hitler and other Nazi leaders had been promptly relabelled by the conquering allies in both east and west. However, POWs had no idea of the new names of the places where their families lived, thus adding to the confusion and delay.

People who participated in the war – on both sides – had long recognised that whatever plans they had for the future would need to be put on hold until peacetime. Those on the winning side could at least look forward now to a gradual return to normality, a chance to pick up where they had left off. But for the defeated there was only doubt. Was it tempting fate to look ahead? Or would their destiny be decided by others?

'When the total surrender came we wondered what our future would be like,' says Werner Völkner, 'and we wondered what had happened to all the others. We were still alive after all the bloodshed, but what was it all about? What had it all been for? In a way I, felt secure at that time – I knew that at least I was still alive. But what was the future going to hold for me?'

'What I really wanted to do – if things had gone a different way – was to become a forester,' Werner reflects. 'When I was a boy I used to spend a lot of time in the countryside with one of my aunts who lived in a forested area. I saw the wildlife there out in the open … it was a dream, so to speak. There was a farm next door where they had a boy of the same age, and I learned how to put harnesses on the horses, and they even let me drive the horse and wagon, which was an adventure in itself. But when the war was over they said they wanted to "stamp out militarism", and we were told that the *Waffen-SS* would have to be imprisoned for twenty years.'

'To realise it was all over and we'd lost the war and it had all come to nothing – for us, of course, it was very depressing,' Bruno Liebich admits. He had been a prisoner in America for almost a year by now. 'But we had to accept that. And the next thought was, "When are we going home?" And the Americans said, "Don't worry, it'll happen – one day."'

Henry Metelmann, having been captured a short time before, had made the three-week Atlantic crossing on a troopship only to arrive in New York on the day after the surrender:

> Having no idea what was happening anywhere, we were a bit surprised when an *Ami* shouted to us while we were still in the holds that the sirens were howling all over New York because Hitler was dead and the war was over. We received the news with a strange and confused feeling. I did not quite know whether I should feel sad or shout 'hurrah'. We did not even feel like discussing it amongst ourselves, as the deadweight of the Nazi past was lying heavily on us. All us younger ones like myself could not really imagine a Germany without Hitler, and none of us had ever dared say anything adverse about our Führer while he was alive. We could not be all that sure that he was really dead now, anyway.

In Britain, meanwhile, civilians thronged the streets and linked arms with strangers – dancing, cheering, weeping tears of relief and joy. Winston Churchill addressed them on the radio, telling them that victory was theirs: Germany had been defeated and was now awaiting Britain's judgement and mercy.

By contrast, at Camp 165 near Wick, Caithness, it was a sombre scene as Willy Hildemann and his comrades huddled around the radio set. Immediately afterwards, he wrote in his diary:

> It's 3 p.m. and a grave piece of news has reached us. The British Prime Minister has spoken to the world on the wireless and announced the unconditional surrender of Germany. I am incapable of expressing in words how every German feels – including me. So end almost six years of self-sacrifice on the part of the German people. Something we simply couldn't have believed has turned into reality.

Horst Rossberg was at work on a local farm when the news came through.

> On 8 May, a very sunny day, the owner came in her car to where we were working and told us that Germany had surrendered and it was all over. We threw our arms round each other and shouted with joy. She could not understand our happiness and said, 'You have lost the war; how can you be so pleased?' We told her that we were happy that at last the war was finished, no more bombs would fall and our families would no more need to fear for their lives.

Off Portland, Dorset, *Oberleutnant* Uwe Kock ordered his submarine, U–249, to the surface to surrender, the first to do so following the capitulation. The U-boat was escorted into harbour by two British sloops. One by one the rest of the underwater fleet surrendered. On 14 May, one of Germany's latest and most sophisticated submarines, U–2326, surfaced at Dundee. The crew had been unaware of the German capitulation, they maintained, their wireless having been out of order. The U-boat 'was escorted up river by a motor launch and a naval fishing smack', the *Derby Evening Telegraph* reported. 'A Royal Navy Chief Petty Officer went aboard, lowered the German naval flag and hoisted the White Ensign. As the flag was being taken down a German officer stood at the salute on the conning tower. The crew, numbering fifteen, two of whom were wearing Iron Crosses, were brought ashore and searched in the presence of about 1,000 spectators.'

At the 'Nazi camp' (as Herbert Holewa described it) in New Cumnock, the *Lagerführer* told the POWs, 'The war is over; Germany is now completely decimated and apparently there isn't one stone left on another.' He proposed to write to the War Office requesting that the prisoners should be allowed out to work if they wished, and the POWs supported the plan. The authorities consented and in August 1945 the men were taken to German POW Working Camp No. 256, near the racecourse at Market Rasen, Lincolnshire. 'On the third day we saw a forest fire opposite the camp,' says Holewa. 'We jumped the three barbed wire rolls and before the fire service arrived we already had the fire under control. They marched us all back, counted us again and again and we were still all there. And they took away the three rolls of barbed wire, and left just one wire. And the major said, "If anyone wants to go out, just go through the gate." That was the thank-you.'

For POWs in British camps, Germany's surrender did not signal an end to their captivity: it merely marked the beginning of a new phase. 'When the war was over we thanked God that it was finished and we were happy to be alive. But you wondered, "What's going to happen now?"' Eberhard Wendler declares. Until this time they had been treated reasonably well, but now he and his comrades felt deeply insecure. British POWs who had been in German hands were being set free: if Britain now chose to mistreat its German prisoners it could do so without fear of retaliation. 'We lost and they could do what they liked with us. And we thought they'd take it out on us.'

Other safeguards which the prisoners could have relied on during the war were removed. The Protecting Powers had no further role to play now that the war was over, and withdrew. The International Red Cross – which took over where the Swiss government had left off – theoretically had access to all British camps. It was authorised to inspect accommodation and facilities, and to interview prisoners: but in practice it was virtually powerless, having only four representatives to cover the entire country.

'In all the time I spent as a POW, I had never seen anybody from the Red Cross,' claims Erwin Hettwer. Instead of actively scrutinising the conditions in which POWs lived, the four inspectors had to confine their visits to 'cases where requests are made by the British authorities, the camp leaders, or the prisoners through the medium of their camp leaders.'

Significantly, the Geneva Convention had failed to provide for a situation quite like this. The Convention dictated that arrangements for the repatriation of prisoners should be agreed 'when belligerents conclude an armistice convention'. It goes on to say, 'in any case, the repatriation of prisoners shall be effected as soon as possible after the conclusion of peace'. But there had been no 'armistice convention'. Instead, Germany had surrendered unconditionally, and the Reich had ceased to exist. Even if Britain had wanted to negotiate, there was no one left to negotiate with.

Germany's defeat caused some POWs in British camps to question the beliefs they had once cherished. Willi Hildemann wrote:

> I ask myself again and again how it's possible that the Anglo-Saxon democrats can be conquerors twice, while Germany was defeated under two separate forms of all-powerful state. And I wonder whether history repeating itself within a generation represents 'God's judgement'? Many people – myself included – feel that intolerance and envy have got the better of the Germans, especially in the years since 1933 [the year Hitler was appointed Chancellor].

In the days leading up to Germany's surrender, Allied troops had come upon concentration camps for the first time. In shock and anger they forced 'thousands of German prisoners' recently captured in Germany 'to see the conditions, the filth, disease and death'. On 24 April, the mayors of six small towns around Belsen were also taken to view the scene. At the beginning of May 1,000 citizens of Weimar, escorted by American Military Police, had been marched 6 miles to the Buchenwald camp and 'were there made to view the conditions under which thousands of prisoners were confined, starved and put to death'.

'What else can and should be done?' asked Lord Denham. 'I think it is absolutely vital that every German prisoner of war, wherever he may be, should be made to see the films which I understand are being taken at these ghastly camps, so that when he does go back to Germany he may know something, which otherwise he would not believe, of what has been going on there.' Lord Denham's suggestion was taken up and by early June all German POWs in Britain and America were required to watch the film. While some of this material was also shown in public cinemas, the version exhibited to the POWs included footage deemed too grisly for a general audience to view. The prisoners' responses varied widely.

Bruno Liebich was in the USA when the images were screened. 'In our case we started laughing. "Don't be stupid, we haven't done this. We couldn't do *this.*" The Americans said, "*You've* done it" … as if *I'd* done it. But in some camps it was much worse, they had riots about it. It happened in every camp in America.'

Immediately after watching the film, a POW in Canada declared, 'It was a really crude, cheap bit of propaganda. Lampshades made of human skin! There was a lot of shouting and yelling [from the prisoners].' Dieter Hahn, imprisoned in an American camp, was similarly incredulous. 'We laughed because we could not and *would* not accept that anything as horrific as that was carried out in the name of Germany. We thought it was nothing more than a gigantic American propaganda stunt.'

Karl-Heinz Decker says, 'We knew people got arrested and Jews had a little yellow star on their clothes. I knew all that. But – about those camps – we didn't know. We were told when they were arrested they were sent to camps where they had to work because Germany couldn't afford to keep them.'

But some prisoners grasped the enormity of what they were watching straight away. 'It was as if a ton of bricks had hit me,' says Werner Völkner without further elaboration.

Herbert Holewa saw the film while at Camp 22, Cumnock. 'We were forced to watch it. Many prisoners vomited – they said "That's an impossibility."'

'Many didn't want to believe it and yet it was the plain truth,' says Arthur Riegel. 'We were often overcome with despair, knowing that there would be no one in the world who would stand up for our battered, dishonoured people.'

'I couldn't believe it,' Bert Trautmann avows. 'How can your own people do that to other human beings? It was terrible.'

Horst Rossberg says, 'We simply could not come to terms with the fact that those capable of such acts had formed our government. For young people like us, the world in which we had lived as children, and in whose schools we had been educated, crumbled.'

Theo Dengel writes:

We were all absolutely horrified, ashamed and disgusted that such brutalities and murders could have been organised by the Nazi regime. As a youngster I must have been very naive, as I had no idea such extermination camps existed. Whilst at junior school, it never occurred to me to ask what had happened to Jewish classmates and their parents after they suddenly disappeared … I had quite frequently heard the comment: "Mind your tongue or you will finish up in Dachau!" But the sight of the inhuman and degrading practices shown in the films from the Belsen and Auschwitz concentration camps were absolutely horrifying. For many days, after seeing these films, we were all very subdued and distressed; most of us were quite unable to come to terms with the horrific sights we had been shown.

Eberhard Wendler's diary mentions the film only fleetingly:

6 June 1945:   In the evening the concentration camp film was shown. It was compulsory to watch it. I bought one bottle of hair-oil for 1s 5d and a toothbrush for 1s 10d.'

But almost seventy years later he revealed how the revelations changed the course of
his life:

> I was so stunned. I never heard of anything like it. And I thought, 'That lot, they did
> this and wanted me to lay down my life.' I fought for them and risked my life and lost
> my home … I was ashamed to be German. I thought, 'I don't want anything to do
> with them, I don't want to go home.' And I made up my mind, there must have been
> more who knew about it; it couldn't have been just a few.

Bruno Liebich, on the other hand, suspects that most people *were* unaware of the
atrocities: 'It's a blot – not on me personally, but on the country – that just can't go
away. But we were all puzzled. There's not a single person that I've met, soldier or
otherwise, that has actually taken part in it. Probably only 0.02 per cent of the entire
German population took part in this.'

Author Matthew Barry Sullivan notes that in twelve camps, 'a manifesto was drawn
up expressing disgust at the Nazi regime, though at six they rejected responsibility
on behalf of the people.' Some camps held collections for the concentration camp
survivors; elsewhere a religious service was held immediately after the screening of the
film. In some places Nazi emblems were removed and thrown away.

After the concentration camp film had been shown, the prisoners noticed a
worsening in the treatment meted out by the British, and concluded that their captors
were avenging the Nazi atrocities. Hans Reckel states that on 11 May, 'All POWs had
to stand at attention on the parade ground for four hours, because one or two English
officers had not been saluted by a few prisoners.'

'Our meagre rations were cut even further,' Erwin Hettwer says. 'It was assumed that
it was done because Germany no longer had Allied prisoners and could not retaliate.'
At some camps the men were made to start work earlier. In fact, the reduction in
rations and longer hours of work on the farms were not so much retaliation as a
reflection of the new wave of austerity affecting the country. Reduced rations for the
population in general were announced in mid-May. Some civilians still complained
that while their own rations had been reduced, POWs still had plenty to eat. But the
House of Commons heard that:

> Non-working German prisoners of war have never received more of the nationally
> rationed items of food than civilians in this country. But in view of the worldwide
> shortage of food it has been decided that the normal scale for these prisoners held
> by His Majesty's Government must be further reduced, and instructions have been
> issued for a new scale providing approximately 2,000 calories of all items, that is
> irrespective of whether they are rationed for civilians in this country or not. Two
> thousand calories is, of course, substantially less than the average civilian consumption
> in this country. Suitable additions of non-rationed foods, mainly bread and potatoes,
> will be made to cover the minimum extra needs of working prisoners, but otherwise
> they will receive the same scale as non-working prisoners.

TABLE 5: RATIONS, POWs AND CIVILIANS

WEEKLY RATIONS IN OUNCES (c. 1945-46)

	CIVILIANS	PRISONERS	
		Non-working	Working supplement (i.e. in addition to non-working rations)
Meat (bone-in)	1s 2d value (equivalent to 1lb 3oz approx.)	14	
Margarine	4	4	
Cooking Fat	1	1	
Bacon and ham	4	3	
Bread	NR	70	+56
Flour	NR	4	+5
Semolina, Macaroni, Barley	NR	–	
Oatmeal	NR	7	+6
Offal or sausage	NR	10	
Cheese	NR	2	
Cake	NR	–	
Preserves	4	3	
Dried Fruit	Points	4	
Tea	2	2	
Coffee (if available)		6	
Sugar	11	6	
Skimmed milk powder	–	7	
Potatoes (old)	NR	70	+70
Potatoes (new) if available		49	+49
Vegetables fresh	NR	56	
Vegetables dried	Points	11	
Salt	NR	Appx 2½	

(Source: Hansard, 9 July 1946 (HC))

NR = not rationed. Some foods available to civilians were not rationed, but nevertheless may not always have been available.

'Points': civilians were each allowed up to 24 points' worth of ration stamps monthly for canned, dried, frozen and certain other goods. With this points allocation it was possible to buy, for example, 30oz of tinned pineapple or peaches.

Bread: civilian bread rationing was introduced from July 1946 – essentially because grain was being sent to Germany to feed the population there.

Milk and eggs were available to POWs but usually only in powdered form.

It is emphasised that rationing regulations varied all the time and thus direct comparison between civilian and prisoner of war rations is seldom, if ever, possible.

German POWs did receive larger quantities of *some* foods than their civilian counterparts (see Table 5). The scarcity of food was caused in part by a general shortage of produce: moreover, after the war Britain had begun to send foodstuffs to Germany to prevent a famine there. Perhaps the prisoners would have found their meagre diet more tolerable if they had known of these outside influences, but – true to form – the British government considered that they didn't 'need to know'.

The Geneva Convention required nations to feed its POWs to the same standards as its own troops. Britain appears to have made reasonable efforts to follow this rule by endeavouring to give prisoners equivalent rations to those its own men received. However, questions were asked as to whether the food was equivalent in quality and nutritional value as well as quantity. Mr Reginald Paget, the MP for Northampton, said in October 1946:

> The sort of menus which I have come across, and I hope they may be improved, is a breakfast consisting of bread and tea, sometimes with some jam on the bread, but no butter. Then they go out to work, and they take two very thick sandwiches consisting almost entirely of bread and a little very thin meat or fish in it, but no butter or margarine. Later, in the evening, when they get back, they get a meal of stew. That may all add up to a great deal of calories, but one is struck by the tremendous shortage of fats, and I think that there are a good many of us who would feel that the hope of a good meal in the evening would not really assist one through a day's work in which one had had inadequate food for breakfast or lunch.

The government could do little to improve the POWs' diet. However, the load on prisoners lightened a little when security at German working camps was stepped down a notch or two in mid-1945. 'The British guards have been sent away. The labour groups went to work without guards,' writes Eberhard Wendler. With no intended irony he adds: 'Now the camp is being guarded by the prisoners.'*

Although showing the concentration camp film to the prisoners had not always evoked the desired response, the British evidently felt that it had been a step in the right direction. Perhaps, with a guiding hand, the Germans – or some of them at least – could be shown the error of their ways: maybe in time they could be converted into peace-loving democrats. In America, President Roosevelt had already hinted at a possible future for Germany once the Nazis were defeated:

> We bring no charge against the German race as such ... but there is going to be a stern punishment for all those in Germany directly responsible for this agony of mankind.

---

* A small contingent of British guards remained in an administrative capacity and to carry out occasional security checks.

The German people are not going to be enslaved ... But it will be necessary for them to earn their way back into the fellowship of peace-loving and law-abiding nations.

A sense that the German people could be 'de-Nazified' and 're-educated' took hold. In a speech in December 1944, Lord Lang opined, 'There must be every effort to re-educate the Germans ... to recreate the moral basis of that country.' It would be a tremendous task. The German people had been under a military dictatorship for twelve years: many of the younger soldiers who had fought in the war could scarcely remember any other system of government. From now on, re-education would require a colossal effort on the part of those entrusted with its implementation.

As important to the Allies as the reorientation of German minds was the challenge of reconstructing Germany itself. Following the country's unconditional surrender, it came entirely under Allied military control, and was divided into four main zones of occupation – British, American, Russian and French.*

The Times reported on 20 April:

No plan for military government in Germany, however foreseeing, can have reckoned with the reality of the fearful retribution that has fallen on the cities of the Rhineland ... There are simply no words with which to describe the devastation of Cologne, which sprawls in awesome testimony to the destructive power of the perfected bomber.

With the aim of destroying Germany's ability to continue the war, Britain and America had resorted to carpet bombing. Two million tons of bombs had been dropped, wreaking havoc in towns and cities: some sixty towns were to all intents and purposes destroyed; half a million citizens lost their lives. The country's infrastructure was shattered; communications were, by the end of hostilities, almost non-existent.

Out of a population of 70 million people, 30 million were searching for someone. A missing persons' bureau in Hamburg received 50,000 enquiries in a day. A vicious circle arose where no transport was available to carry coal; trains could not move unless track and bridges were repaired; repairs could not proceed without steel; and steel could not be made without coal.

'Every time you saw a group of people you would call out names,' Karin Busch declared. 'At the cinema, after the newsreel, there were reels and reels of names on the screen – this person is seeking that person and so on.' The problem of homelessness, already acute, was made worse in the final days of the conflict when uncountable refugees fleeing the Soviet army poured into the West.

Nora Doerfel was 15 years old when the war ended. She says:

* Military rule in the British, American and French zones lasted until September 1949 when the Federal Republic of Germany ('West Germany') came into being.

We were almost starving; anyone who didn't have anything to get black market goods was really quite lost. People would pay anything to get coffee or tea – or cigarettes, of course. We had to beg the baker for a bit of extra bread over and above the rations. At the time the bread was yellow, made from maize. And I used to go to the local dairy and queue for *Molke* – whey – thin, milky stuff, and we made soup with that. At the butcher's there were crowds, masses of people pushing, wanting to buy meat. Sometimes you got this awful stuff – I *couldn't* eat it now – where they'd boiled the sausages in a big container and the liquid still had grease and fat in it and a bit of taste, and people bought that to make soup.

From such chaos the Allies hoped to create a new society. In the months and years ahead, the British and Americans would take advantage of this opportunity to de-Nazify Germany. A number of ambitious, near-Utopian schemes were suggested. According to one, Germany would be demilitarised and never again allowed to have any armed forces; in another, the country's industries would be completely dismantled and Germany would become a totally agricultural economy.

Not everyone believed that these plans would work. During the advance on Germany, General George S. Patton was asked for his views on de-Nazifying German prisoners. 'Trying to do that would be like trying to fertilize a forty acre field with a fart,' he snapped. (Following the surrender, he was appointed Military Governor of the southern German province of Bavaria, but after publicly ridiculing American re-education plans he was sacked.)

However, the official view was that these measures *could* work, and must be made to work. The collapse of the Nazi dictatorship would leave a vacuum and the Western Allies saw it as their responsibility to fill that void with a new template for the future conduct of the German nation. What's more, the hundreds of thousands of prisoners on either side of the Atlantic would form an integral part of the plan, acting as guinea pigs for the re-education of Germany itself. Re-education might even make it possible for the Allies to transform the POWs into ambassadors who would one day return to Germany and help to instil democracy in the rest of the people.

The man given the daunting responsibility of putting the scheme into practice in Britain was Henry Faulk, a former schoolmaster from Dundee. He had spent a year in Germany as part of his studies and was in Berlin when Adolf Hitler came to power. Faulk even underwent part of an *Arbeitsdienst* course just to find out more about the Nazi movement. His command of the German language was second to none, and he was the author of a 1938 textbook for adults learning German. When war broke out he volunteered for military service, where his language skills singled him out for work in intelligence. A motorcycle accident which resulted in a protracted stay in hospital prevented him from taking part in the D-Day invasion: instead, still hobbling with the aid of crutches, he was assigned to the interrogation of prisoners. At one camp in the Midlands he persuaded the POWs to co-operate with the British and join work parties: every single one went along with this suggestion, whereas in other camps in the area none had agreed to help. To quote Matthew Barry Sullivan, 'This sympathetic and formidable Scottish schoolmaster was given the chance of his life.'

Re-education would be implemented by an assortment of methods, the most important being talks by visiting speakers. Interpreter Harry Grenville recalls:

> The War Office sent all kinds of lecturers to the camps to talk to the prisoners in an effort to persuade them that there were other points of view. This was done by a Foreign Office department run by an off-the-scale attractive young woman called Miss Stern whom I met once or twice in London. She sent MPs, trade unionists, business people and even a Swiss secondary school teacher who explained the Swiss system of government. Many of the speakers were fluent enough in German, some I interpreted for, and some carried on just in English in the hope that they would be understood.

Reports on the lectures were sent to headquarters in London so that their effectiveness could be gauged. Following a talk at Normanhurst Camp in Sussex entitled *The Idea of Justice and Nuremberg*, Interpreter Officer Leroux wrote:

> Mr. K— was very competent and well informed and held their attention well, but tended to give the impression that *all* Germans were responsible for the concentration camp horrors. German POWs in particular are very sensitive on this point and when one considers their extreme youth in many cases, and absence outside Germany at the time, one can understand their sensitivity on these matters. I am quite convinced myself that none (or at least extremely few) had any idea what was happening.

Other speakers engaged with their audience more effectively. The German Study Leader at the same camp wrote of a Swiss speaker, 'The impression was so profound … the listeners thanked the speaker by shaking his hand at the end, something that has never happened before.'

Historian Renate Held observes that the lectures initially made a welcome change from the drudgery of camp life and 'While the content of the lectures was probably of only secondary importance, the fact that the talks were always held in well-heated tents was – especially in winter time – a motivation for many prisoners to attend.'

Other strands to the re-education scheme included film shows and discussion groups. The POW newspaper, *Wochenpost,* was another way to put across the British point of view, although prisoners, suspicious about the motives behind it, nicknamed it 'Wochenpest'. Camp newspapers produced by the POWs themselves were more readily accepted by the men. The British authorities encouraged these publications on the basis that they would help the Germans to understand the principles of free speech and democracy. Accordingly, they supplied paper, ink and equipment.

Libraries were provided, in which the prisoners were surprised to see copies of Adolf Hitler's *Mein Kampf* on the shelf alongside *Hansard* (the daily record of proceedings in Parliament). POWs were allowed to attend local council meetings in the towns near their camps, and some were even taken to the House of Commons to sit in the Visitors' Gallery and listen to the debates.

With an emphasis on demilitarisation, the use of ranks was abolished in the camps. As Harry Grenville explains, 'The senior German, the camp leader, was not *Hauptfeldwebel* Schultz but *Herr* Schultz and so on right down the line. Despite my best efforts I could not reverse the process: all the clerks in my interpreter's office insisted on addressing me as *Herr Leutnant* and when in due course I acquired a second pip on my shoulder, as *Herr Oberleutnant*.' Eventually, the term 'camp leader' (*Lagerführer*) was replaced by 'camp spokesman' *(Lagersprecher)*. The interrogators were renamed 'welfare officers' and 'training advisers'.

In practice, though, re-education was difficult to implement. The programme was administered by the Foreign Office, while the day-to-day running of the camps was the responsibility of the War Office. There was a standing conflict between the two authorities: it was said – albeit in a slightly different context – that 'The Foreign Office owned the prisoners' minds while the War Office owned their bodies'.

Camp commandants often felt that re-education was a waste of time, and resented the extra work involved in implementing the scheme. 'I was received very cordially,' notes a representative of the Foreign Office who was undertaking a survey of re-education in the camps. 'The officers at the camp are not interested in the slightest in re-education but helped me as much as possible.'

Elsewhere, though, officers were downright obstructive. 'The Commanding Officer's principal concern was to run a strict regimen to ensure obedience,' one interpreter wrote. 'Anything to do with politics or re-education was of no interest to him. His role model, I suspect, was Colonel Blimp. This is how he defined his role: "I don't mind if a man is a Nazi, as long as he works and behaves."'

A leaflet was sent to commandants begging their co-operation and explaining the goals of re-education. Finally, Whitehall was forced to send representatives to confront camp commandants face-to face and try to persuade them that the effort was a worthwhile one and that 'the commandants themselves could benefit from the re-education programme as it would have a positive effect on the mood within the camp and would reduce anti-British resentment'.

Those who promoted re-education felt that, for all its faults, it achieved many of its aims. Former interpreter officer Harry Grenville says, 'I think this had a big degree of success, really. In *my* experience it was *very* successful. The men we graded 'A' could be relied on to play a part in the emerging German administration on the other side.'

If the overall results were 'patchy and qualified' from a political viewpoint – as writer and politician Adam Fergusson claimed in a piece for *The Times* in 1973 – it was perhaps because a relatively small proportion of the prisoners seem to have come into contact with the programme in practice. When Karl-Heinz Decker was asked about re-education he seemed puzzled: 'I don't think we were invited to attend. We wouldn't have gone anyway. They had de-Nazification in Germany, though, and [there] they went absolutely berserk.' In Britain, he says, he was never interviewed about his political beliefs. 'That was in Germany. I have no knowledge of it happening in America or Britain.'

When asked whether there was any attempt to give the prisoners political instruction, Heinz Czieselsky firmly denied any knowledge of it. Dieter Hahn says, 'In the camp there was somebody who tried to brainwash us with democracy. I don't think he got very far. They tried to teach us the advantages of a democracy, but I couldn't see it. In a way, I suppose I still had sympathy for the German way of doing things.'

Eduard Winkler recalled:

> There must have been something, especially in the first camp. But by then we weren't totally convinced that the war was lost. We thought it was enemy propaganda. We knew there were concentration camps – one of my neighbours was an organiser for the Communist Party. He went to a concentration camp and came back rather subdued. But indoctrination? I don't remember any.'

Inspired by a 1944 speech by Winston Churchill, in which he called for democracy to be re-established and nurtured in Germany, a special training institution was set up at Wilton Park, Buckinghamshire – a former POW camp – shortly after the war. The first to attend were prisoners of war selected from those already being held in Britain. Later they were joined by other students: 'The education scheme for prisoners of war in this country has been so successful and popular that Germans have asked to be allowed to come from Germany to join in the courses and are actually here. We intend to bring others to join with the prisoners of war in these courses.' Those travelling from Germany to take part included future Chancellor Helmut Schmidt.

As one man put it, 'I was a Nazi; I came to Wilton Park and it changed my life.'

'I was suspicious at first,' another prisoner of war said:

> It was the first time I had been asked to make up my own mind and was not really ready for it but in retrospect it influenced me greatly. [The tuition] was all in German taught by German Jews, and those English who could speak fluently. Some of the staff were self-opinionated and tried to convince us (for example) that modern art was far superior to representational Nazi art. I am still unconvinced! However, I did try really hard to fit in and was nervous about failing in front of my classmates. We had influential visitors like Lord Pakenham [later Lord Longford], Veronica Wedgwood [historian], and Victor Gollancz [publisher] ... It was a good place and whilst it did not turn me from a Nazi to a democrat overnight, I honestly think it started a process which allowed me to move forward.

10

Sold Like Slaves

By the end of 1945 the prisoners held in the United States of America had been in captivity for at least a year and in some cases considerably longer. In the main, they had enjoyed a comfortable stay in their 'fabulous luxury prisoner of war camps'. But now that the war had ended they simply wanted to go home and were anxious to know whether recent developments would enable a prompt return to Germany.

President Franklin D. Roosevelt had died in April 1945, just before victory in Europe was secured. His successor, Harry S. Truman, suddenly carried an enormous burden – not least because he had only been vice-president for some twelve weeks. Truman had to make the fateful decision to use the atomic bomb against Japan – a decision made all the harder because Roosevelt had scarcely spoken to his vice-president during those three months, and, until becoming president, Truman had no inkling that America had even been working on such a weapon. Its use led to the surrender of Japan in August of that year, finally bringing the Second World War to a close.

Truman perceived his own role to be that of a peacetime leader. The buzzword at that time was 'reconversion', signifying the changeover from a state of war to a peacetime footing. Truman therefore pressed for rapid demobilisation of the military to enable men and their families to return to a normal life.

A sharp fall in industrial output following high levels of economic activity during the conflict put the United States at risk of severe economic recession. The demobilisation of so many servicemen, whose presence threatened to flood the labour market, only exacerbated the situation. Truman was well aware that the war had helped to lift America out of the Great Depression and he wasn't going to allow the coming of peace to trigger a slide back into stagnation. Jobs for the millions of returning servicemen had to be guaranteed. At the end of 1945 the United States was holding 313,000 Germans in its POW camps across the country. Most of these captives had been working in agriculture, and they had proved to be a vital source of labour. But now those jobs were needed for returning GIs and the POWs had to go. When officials of the POW Utilization Program pleaded for the prisoners to be retained for a little longer to meet a temporary labour shortage, Truman was intransigent. Every single POW, he insisted, must be sent home by the end of June 1946.

Repatriation from North America began in early 1946 after the liner *Mauretania* had crossed to Halifax, Nova Scotia, bringing with it 400 British war brides (plus 364 babies). It left again for Britain with 2,753 German prisoners of war on board.

Dieter Hahn, a prisoner in Colorado, was one of the first to leave the United States. 'In mid-January we were told, "Pack up lads, you're going back to Germany." On the way to Los Angeles we passed an aeroplane park – there were literally hundreds, if not *thousands* of American warplanes of all descriptions and sizes. And I thought to myself, "How the devil did we expect to win the war against *this?*"'

'They gave us new kit,' says Theo Dengel, 'absolutely everything was brand-new, new clothes, new shoes; everything was super!' The prisoners were allowed to take 65lb of luggage with them. Theo and his companions crammed their kitbags full of presents to take back to Germany for family and friends, as well as items which could be sold on the black market. He says:

> We loaded up with cigarettes – the allowance was 1,000 cigarettes and about twelve packets of tobacco. We could also take so many bars of soap. We had to pay for this with the money we'd earned, and it had been exhausting work. And we were told, 'You're going to Hamburg, you'll be discharged, and you'll all be home by Whitsun.'

'We came back via New York,' Karl-Heinz Decker remembers. 'It was spring in America. The trees and flowers were starting to grow.'

'The authorities in New York gave us some sheets of questions to complete and then they said "You're on your way to Germany." The ship's crew was excellent. We had plenty of food, more than we needed, and we could move around freely,' Hans Teske recalled.

'The war was over, we were going home,' another prisoner remarked, 'where else would we be going?'

'On board the ship we were spoken to as if we were passengers returning from a cruise,' a POW explained. 'But then a rumour went around that we were going to England. This rumour became increasingly strong, and an English officer was forced to deny it. I'll never forget what he said – he told us that anyone who spread this rumour would be punished.'

'After about seven days we saw an island in the distance – we were struck by how green it was – and we were told it was Ireland,' says Hans Teske. 'And this island was to the left-hand side of the ship.'

'Next morning we got called up unusually early at about 4 a.m.' Theo Dengel remembers:

> We were in a harbour – it was foggy, very gloomy – and there were glints of bayonets reflected in the electric lights and we thought, "What the hell is going on?" Then we saw these chaps all had flat helmets on – they were Tommies. "Where *are* we?" It could only be Liverpool. Then we turned around and on the decks above us were at least four heavy machine guns mounted – and all the American guards had their sub-machine guns at the ready. They expected a revolution. You can imagine how depressed everybody felt, it was really dreadful.

'In Liverpool the harbour installations were still very badly damaged,' Hans Behrens reflects. 'Masts of ships were sticking out of the water and it looked pretty bad. And I said to one of my fellow prisoners, "I hope we won't have to stop here and clear this mess up," because it looked hard work – much harder than picking oranges and grapes in the California sun.'

'We were just told we were going back to Germany and we weren't suspicious about anything,' claims Bruno Liebich. When the ship berthed at Liverpool, 'We were stunned – surprised – really angry. "What are we doing here?" Nobody tells you anything – they don't *have* to tell you.' He grins. 'We used some very strong unprintable language!'

'When we arrived at Liverpool, we naturally assumed that it would only be a port of call on our journey,' Henry Metelmann adds, 'but we were suddenly ordered to take all our belongings and line up on deck. Meanwhile, a number of British personnel came on board, there was friendly hand-shaking with their American counterparts, and we were marched down the gangway.'

'We were told the boat had broken down,' says Hans Teske:

In fact, every boat with German prisoners from America broke down in Liverpool. It was just an excuse to pacify us. We disembarked, we were met by British guards, and told to board the train. We were used to American trains, but here was a little Puffing Billy with an enormous funnel and little carriages with individual doors – like an antique. In each compartment were seven prisoners and an armed guard. We asked him as a joke, 'Have you any bullets?' and he said 'no' and opened his rifle to show us. Coming from America in peacetime with all the neon lights flashing, we saw rows of houses like Coronation Street with little gaslights and were taken aback: we said, 'Surely England's a bit more modernised than that?'

'They told us we were just passing through, and there were some formalities to complete, and we were *still* on our way back to Germany,' says Heinz Czieselsky with a hollow laugh.

Following Italy's surrender and change of allegiance, Britain could scarcely justify keeping any longer the 157,000 Italian POWs it had in captivity, and all of them were repatriated between December 1945 and late September or early October 1946. But the removal of these Italians left a gaping hole in Britain's manpower again. So now the POWs who had been kept in America on Britain's behalf would be used, especially as they were now surplus to requirements within the USA. The only drawbacks were that, firstly, the men had not been politically screened to the same standards as were used in Britain, and, secondly, that they 'would have been spoiled by the higher ration scale in America'.

Once the transfer of prisoners had begun, about 20,000 were brought to Britain monthly. The ships arrived almost daily. The following represent just a sample of vessels berthing in Britain in early 1946.

TABLE 6: SHIPS BRINGING POWs FROM NORTH AMERICA TO BRITAIN EARLY 1946

DATE	SHIP	TYPE	TONNAGE	DEST.	SOURCE & No. of PRISONERS	
1946					USA	CANADA
February						
1	General Howze	US Navy transport	17,000 (full)	L	3,050	
3	Fairisle	Not known		L	1,650	
10	Elizabeth. C. Stanton	US Navy transport	15,000 (full)	L	1,800	
11	Brazil	WSA	18,300 (GRT)	L	2,000	
14	Mormacsea	Cargo Ship	5,000 (GRT)	L	900	
16	Santa Isabel	US Troopship	7,250 (GRT)	L	1,600	
17	Marine Raven	US Troopship	12,000 (GRT)	L	2,300	
18	Ernie Pyle	US Troopship	12,000 (GRT)	L	3,000	
19	Mauretania	Cunard Liner	35,700 (GRT)	L		3,000
28	Ile de France	French Liner	43,000 (GT)	S		4,000
March						
7	Aquitania	Cunard Liner	45,600 (GRT)	S		3,300
11	Scythia	Cunard Liner	19,700 (GT)	L		2,600
12	Mauretania	Cunard Liner	35,700 (GT)	L		3,000
21	Ile de France	French Liner	43,000 (GT)	S		4,000
				TOTALS	16,300	19,900

(Source: TNA FO 939/460)

L= Liverpool; S = Southampton
WSA = War Shipping Administration (US)
Actual arrival dates may vary from the projected dates shown.

As Table 6 suggests, British ships were used to bring POWs from Canada, where many of the prisoners had, in fact, been told they were to be brought to Britain. American vessels were used for the prisoners held in the United States, as the use of British ships would doubtless have raised suspicions about their actual destination.

In all, 127,000 German prisoners arrived in Britain from the North American continent during the first half of 1946, corresponding to Britain's share of the POWs who had been accommodated in America by the Government of the United States. 'It is our intention to replace [the Italians] with additional German prisoners from North America and, to some extent, from Europe,' Britain's Minister for Agriculture and Fisheries told the House of Commons. 'Wherever possible when one body of prisoners leaves others will be made available to the farmer.'

By the end of June all the American camps were empty with the exception of just 141 individuals. America could now claim to be the first Allied nation to 'repatriate' its prisoners of war. Even if they had been aware of the true circumstances, few US citizens would have been very much troubled to learn that many of these POWs had in reality been sent to Europe for a further period of captivity. Of those held in Canadian camps, the last 4,000 or so reached British shores in the late autumn of 1946.

Henry Metelmann was taken to Altrincham, Cheshire. 'The war had been over for well over a year but when we were marched through the camp gates outside that town we woke up to the fact that the Americans had sold us like slaves to the British.' Since the majority of these men had been captured by American troops, taken to the United States by American ships, held in American camps and 'repatriated' on vessels flying the American flag they had every reason to consider themselves American prisoners.

What they didn't realise was that they had been prisoners of the British all along, and the majority went to their graves without ever being told why they had been handled in this way.[*]

'When we arrived in Britain we said, "We are not your prisoners of war", because you didn't capture us,' says Henry Metelmann. '"We are forced labour."'

'We were greeted by an English major or colonel, who was really impressive,' Martin Schenkel writes. 'He said … "You are here to help rebuild the country, in retaliation for destroying much of it." At least that guy was fair; he told us straight out what was going on.'[**]

The antiquated train carrying Hans Teske and his fellow soldiers chugged its way across the English countryside in 'a pea-souper fog' before finally arriving in Sudbury, Derbyshire. He recalls:

We were marched out, thinking perhaps we had to spend the night there, and we were met by a German-speaking officer, who said, 'Gentlemen, you are now *British* prisoners of war. Don't try to escape; you are guarded by Poles and they are only too eager to shoot you.' We were given some straw to make up a straw bag to sleep on till next morning. Then we had to register as British prisoners and we were given a British POW number. The compound was surrounded by reels and reels of barbed wire piled up high, with four guard posts manned by Poles. And the officer said,

[*] The Americans took no account of the individual circumstances of each man – where or by whom he had been captured, for example. Instead, this was a straightforward bookkeeping exercise: the USA 'owed' Britain 127,000 men and once that number had been shipped to Britain the debt was considered settled.

[**] This anecdote supports the present author's conviction that the Germans would have been much less resentful of their treatment if only they had been told what was happening.

'If you thought you were going to Germany you were mistaken. You're staying here as prisoners of war.' After America, we thought we were being treated like cattle – not like humans. We were degraded, and it seemed to us that they did their best to prolong this treatment.

Theo Dengel also came to Sudbury, and says:

We had these great big heavy Bergen bags which nobody normally carried – there were no carrying handles. The Yanks don't carry anything; they just dump it on a lorry and pick it up again at the end of the journey. We'd packed spare shoes and books; the bags were really heavy and we had to carry them a mile and a half to the camp. When we got there we saw 10ft-high barbed wire fences, watchtowers, and armed Polish guards who turned out to be particularly anti-German.

We were marched into a Nissen hut and that's where the searches started. And it's where the pilfering of cigarettes and tobacco started. Chaps had their watches stolen. It was April 1946, a year after the end of the war. That sort of thing you expect *during* a war – both sides. If you had a POW you had power over him, you took his watch and any money he had on him. But a year *after* the war it's a different story altogether. We came from America and we were 'wealthy', so to speak, and they started taking it. But we were at the end of the queue and we watched this and decided to be bloody awkward. I yelled at the guard when he started to take the cigarettes. I told him, 'I want your name and number and I'll report you at the next camp.' And that got rid of him. They took all our brand-new American clothes away – everything. What they did with them, I don't know. And they gave us dyed and patched British army uniforms and rough, second-hand underwear: it was demoralising, to put it mildly. The food was absolutely atrocious. The German camp leadership was totally corrupt – it was appalling and it's always stuck with me. We wanted to complain about being sent there – about the treatment, about the awful food and about the pilferage, the stealing. But they flatly refused to let us see a British officer.

Some prisoners stayed in Britain for only a few days before being moved again. 'They didn't know what to do with us,' claims Karl-Heinz Decker. 'We were taken to a camp in Belgium under British command.'

'The prisoners repatriated from the USA generally complain that they were not told correctly what was to happen to them,' says a report by the International Red Cross. 'In the United States they had been assured that they would be returned to Europe and set free … One can easily imagine these prisoners' disappointment, and their state of mind when they discovered that they were being brought to labour camps in Britain, having hoped to return home following several years of imprisonment.'

But one man found a crumb of comfort in the situation. Otto Funk says he felt that the journey to England had, if nothing else, brought him one step nearer to Germany, his home and his family. At least now he was on the same continent as they were. And others eventually came to realise that they could well have been worse off if they had been among those sent to France, many of whom subsequently died or were severely injured while working in coal mines or clearing unexploded bombs. Nevertheless, for some prisoners, life in a British camp was a sobering experience. 'It was a lot stricter than in America, with army discipline again, orders here, orders there,' says Heinz Czieselsky. 'In America, although we were in a camp, we had more freedom. We could do whatever we liked there, but here we couldn't.'

Hans Behrens had a somewhat different experience. He says:

I remember the train pulling in at Haywards Heath. It was a draughty station in an elevated position. I took a dislike from that very moment to this place – I *couldn't* live in Haywards Heath. We had American army uniforms dyed black with POW written on them in white. People looked at us as though we were either monsters or cattle or whatever.'

However, Hans and the other prisoners were taken by lorry to a small camp at Southease, between Lewes and Newhaven, and there his mood lightened:

The camps were totally different between here and America. America was the sunshine country but it was much stricter there. Although the British weather didn't make up for it, the freedom was unbelievable. We had one sergeant and his colleague between about 200 prisoners – that was all. We were taken by lorries up on to the South Downs where the War Agricultural Executive Committee had to clear away the rubbish to get it ready for ploughing and seeding for corn and so forth. Others were taken to various farms around to help with the farm work. Some farmers in the area weren't very nice – they treated you like you were a lot of rubbish – and other people were extremely nice.

Theo Dengel's group finished up in a camp which was not very far from Southease. 'From Sudbury we travelled by road in army lorries to Billingshurst – a fairly long journey, it took at least six hours. Same thing again – barbed wire fences, watchtowers, an unfriendly looking place.' A young lieutenant searched Theo's luggage. 'He said, "I need all your notebooks, any literature you've got, anything in writing. I promise you'll get it back." Actually, about three months later I did get it back – everything apart from one little book, where I'd written everything down about what happened at Sudbury.'

After seeing many of his comrades lose their possessions previously, Theo had been determined to get even. Before leaving Sudbury he had deliberately doctored some of the packets of cigarettes. 'Everyone had 1,000 cigarettes – five cartons, each with ten packets of twenty. So we very carefully opened a packet of cigarettes, took out the cigarettes and stuffed it with grass, and I did that to about three of the packets in one carton. I hid the cigarettes I'd removed in a pair of shoes.'

Sure enough, on arrival at Billingshurst he had some cigarettes stolen from his luggage – not by an ordinary soldier but by the British officer. 'I was furious that an officer should do that and, at the same time, laughing, "I caught you, you bugger!" You got a carton of cigarettes that's all grass.'

Theo found the dishonesty at Billingshurst shocking. 'The chaps who'd received stolen cigarettes had formed a clique with certain camp guards. It shook me; I could never get over that. Why should the Germans resent somebody teaching a British guard a lesson? The level of corruption at Billingshurst was appalling.' But there was a glimmer of hope. While in the United States, Theo had made friends with a prisoner from Saarbrücken – not far from Theo's own home. This POW had coached Theo in French, maths, physics and other subjects he had missed when the war had put the brakes on his education. Theo continues:

> We worked intensively in the States, on the ship to England, at Sudbury and then at Billingshurst. But because he spoke fluent English he was moved to another camp where they needed a clerk. Then, a week later, I got a letter from him to say he was working in the Labour Office at a camp near Chichester. And I wrote back, 'Please, please get me out of this God-forsaken place.' We corresponded regularly, and on August Bank Holiday [1946] first thing in the morning one of the camp staff told me to pack my things. On the way I asked the driver and he replied, 'I'm taking you to North Mundham. Your friend asked for you to be moved there. It's a civilised place – you'll love it.' I said, 'I don't believe a word of it!' And laughed and he said, 'Well, you'll see.'

When the newcomers from across the Atlantic met POWs who had already been there for some time, both groups were likely to experience culture shock. Gunther Wolkenhauer found that 'The other POWs were envious of the stuff we brought with us. I had a quilt. And I had an American officer's jacket – dyed. [Smiling broadly, he switches from German to English] *I was a handsome young boy!*'

'The ones who came from America even had *pyjamas*,' says Eberhard Wendler in amazement. He soon bought a pair of socks for 4 shillings from one of the 'Americans', and a blue shirt from a 'Canadian'.

Arthur Riegel was delighted when an old friend, Hanns, turned up among one of the shipments from Canada. Such encounters didn't entirely dispel the dark mood, however. A former *Afrika Korps* soldier wrote in his diary: 'Generally the people in camp are very bitter at having to spend another four to six years behind barbed wire in England.'

'They told us that in England it rains and rains and rains – and it was true!' says Heinz Czieselsky. 'We came over in May, but coming from the Mississippi, there was a difference in the weather. In Britain it was foggy, misty and very cold. We were still hoping that we'd only stay for a few days or weeks and then go to Germany, but that didn't happen.' He sighs. 'I spent another two years as a prisoner of war in England. We couldn't complain; there was no one to complain to.'

But Henry Metelmann and his fellow POWs at Altrincham *did* lodge a protest with the camp authorities, and Henry was chosen by the others to be their spokesman. 'It was the first time in my life that I had taken part in a democratic procedure. The British quickly asked us to send a three-man delegation to meet them, and discuss the problem.' Henry told the Colonel who headed the British committee, 'The Americans obviously have released us from captivity. But they have done so in the wrong place, this is England and not Germany! … You can't just take us prisoners like that. It's peace time now. No one must do that!'

The Colonel asked Henry on what legal precedent he based his accusation.

'The Geneva Convention!' Henry replied after a long silence.

'What section and what article of the Convention are you referring to?' one of the British team enquired with a self-satisfied smile. Henry had no answer. 'If I were you, *Obergefreiter*, with your history, I would not mention the Geneva Convention ever again!'

'I was conquered,' Metelmann admits, 'and when I looked at my mates, I saw only empty faces.'

Matthew Barry Sullivan asserts that the influx of prisoners from across the Atlantic had an adverse effect on morale within the British camps generally. A high proportion of the Germans who had been detained in the United States were *Afrika Korps* veterans who perceived their own capture as a personal setback, but not as the first step in a series of defeats for Germany. In particular, they hadn't experienced anything of the desperate last days of the fighting in France, Belgium, Holland and Germany, and the worsening morale of the German forces there. So while those who had been captured later in the war were usually resigned to their fate, the veterans tended to remain defiant. In addition to those from the USA, Sullivan claims, 'Some camps in Canada … were more Nazi generally than Germany itself.'

On screening the prisoners, the United States authorities had sent all of those with an 'A' grade straight back to Germany. Those who were left – many of whom ended up in Britain – were by definition somewhat pro-Nazi, and this again changed the overall profile of prisoners in British camps for the worse.

The government tried to keep the Repatriation Deceit under wraps, and succeeded for some time. However, a few suspicions were raised and on 27 March 1946, when the shipments of POWs were well under way, Richard Stokes, the MP for Ipswich, addressed the House of Commons on the subject of 'the treatment, and particularly the continual detention, of prisoners of war.'

Richard Rapier Stokes was born in 1897. He served in the First World War, receiving the Military Cross and bar, and the French *Croix de Guerre*. 'Yet for all the gallantry of his record he returned from the front with a deep horror and hatred of war.' His uncle, Sir Frederick Stokes, had been the inventor of the Stokes mortar – a significant piece of First World War weaponry. Sir Frederick earned a fortune when a grateful British government awarded him a 'royalty' of £1 for every mortar shell fired. Under this extraordinary arrangement, if all 1,600 Stokes mortars in service with the British

Empire forces had fired continuously for just one minute, the Stokes family coffers would have been better off to the tune of £40,000.

Richard Stokes – the nephew – considered that the British government had no moral right to keep the German prisoners in detention now the war had ended, and he took up their cause. As Matthew Barry Sullivan writes, the POWs viewed him as '*our* MP'. The general population was beginning to see things his way, too, but in Parliament his was still a lone voice in the wilderness.

In answer to the Foreign Secretary's assertion that the Geneva Convention no longer applied and that the Protective Power had been withdrawn, Stokes replied, 'It becomes all the more important that we should pay some regard to our obligations. It is even more important now, because, apparently, we are not decreasing the number of people we have in detention, but are increasing them. We are importing slaves from America.' This wasn't the first time he had described Britain's use of the German prisoners as 'slave labour'. In November 1945 his passion had got the better of him during a parliamentary debate:

> May I ask my right honourable friend whether these men, when employed, are paid a full and proper wage, or whether they are being used as slaves, and whether he can tell us when they will be sent home?

Another politician tried to interrupt and Stokes snapped back, 'I know some honourable members do not care a damn about slaves.'

The Speaker of the House of Commons intervened. 'That was a most improper remark.'

'I beg your pardon, Mr Speaker, but I was provoked,' Stokes replied.

On 30 July 1946, Stokes exposed the Repatriation Deceit in the House. 'Is the right honourable Gentleman aware that a large number of these people came first from America, on their exportation from which they were promised repatriation to Germany? Does he not think … that this traffic in slave labour should stop?'

Politicians are known to tremble at the word 'slave'. The British were among the foremost practitioners of the slave trade in distant times. Yet they were also one of the first nations to outlaw it. And at that very moment, Britain and her allies were conducting the war crimes trials in Nuremberg at which Hitler's architect and Minister of Armaments, Albert Speer,[*] stood accused of using slave labour. Although living conditions in British POW camps were in reality far better than those in a Nazi labour camp, for Stokes this was a matter of principle.

The press overwhelmingly supported Stokes's view. An editorial in the *Manchester Guardian* claimed that the Labour government, which had come to power a few weeks

---

[*] Speer was found guilty of using slave labour from German-occupied territories and was imprisoned for twenty years.

after VE Day, was organising the employment of prisoners of war on a large scale and 'actually importing them for the purpose fifteen months after the war is over. If we must have foreign labour to make up our shortfall … let it be free labour … forced labour is intolerable under a Labour government.' It was not until much later, on 24 March 1947, that the full extent and nature of the deception were made public by Tom Driberg MP:

> It may be that the American officers who got them on to the boats on that pretext [that they were going straight to Germany] had no authority to give that undertaking. It may be they only said that in order to get them to go quietly, but nonetheless it is an undertaking that was given, and while that is in their minds we cannot possibly preach to them that democracy is a particularly fair or desirable system of government. Surely my right honourable friend can understand their state of mind when they feel that they have been tricked in that way by people professing to be good democrats.

'Under National Socialism I was told to believe all that I was told,' a prisoner declared. 'I was promised lots of things but the promises were never kept. But in America I was promised that I was on my way back to Germany. That promise was also broken. How do you now expect me to believe anything at all?' In the light of such a remark, it becomes clear that the Repatriation Deceit significantly undermined the efforts being channelled into re-education.

11

Shilling a Day

Thousands of German prisoners captured in the closing stages of the war, and just afterwards, had been removed to British camps in Belgium. Here they were guarded, in the main, by Belgian soldiers in British uniform. As elsewhere, a lack of proper accommodation and shortages of food prevented the authorities in charge of these camps from meeting the strict terms of the Geneva Convention. The men slept in tents, even in winter, and food was in short supply.

'We had things we could sell for a slice of bread but the poor fellows who didn't were in a bad way,' says Karl-Heinz Decker. 'Believe me, if that wasn't a hunger camp then I don't know what is. The war was over – why do all of this? There was no hot water, only cold. There was still some snow on the ground. And some poor buggers had lost arms and legs … it was horrendous.'

Werner Völkner remembers:

There were twelve men in each of the round tents – no blankets we just slept in our uniforms. During the day we weren't allowed back in the tent. It was always cold. The Sergeant had to fetch the daily food ration, and so that everybody had their fair share they made a pair of scales from bits of wood and string. The bread was cut first, then a piece was put on one side of the scale and another piece on the other side. Somebody – a different person each day – had to turn round and say who that piece of bread was for. So we had a piece of bread, a teaspoonful of jam, a teaspoonful of margarine, two teaspoons full of cheese out of a tin and a teaspoonful of sugar. The tea was black tea – everybody had some sort of container to catch it. We weren't allowed to have cutlery so most of them carved a spoon or knife out of wood from the food crates.

At some of these Belgian camps, it was reported, signals such as bugle calls were drowned out by the constant howling of the wind. To alert the prisoners to mealtimes and the like, the British resorted to firing a burst of machine-gun fire over their heads. Disturbing stories about these camps appeared in the press. A front-page article in the *Daily Express* said that prisoners had accused the guards of dispensing beatings and kickings.

Frederick Bellenger (Financial Secretary to the War Office) was said to be 'filled with horror' at these revelations. Richard Stokes asked the Secretary of State for

War (Jack Lawson) whether he was aware that: 'as recently as the beginning of April, 100 men are said to have arrived at Stamford from a Belgian camp, and it is admitted by both medical officers of health that they were entirely unfitted for work through starvation.' As a result of the adverse publicity and public furore, the camps in Belgium were closed down by the end of July 1946 and all the men transferred to Britain.[*]

Werner Völkner and his compatriots were gloomy as the troopship entered Tilbury docks. But then they looked down on to the quayside. He remembers:

> The first person we saw on English soil was a bobby. All the other lads shouted, 'Look at this one with his helmet!' Suddenly it was different – they were almost elated. The journey was finished, they could laugh again. We were unloaded, man after man down the gangway. There were soldiers there and ATS women with great big steaming tubs, and someone said, 'Get your drinking vessels ready.'

The steaming tubs were full of tea, made with milk, the British way.

'Some joker had said, "The Jerries like tea and lemon", so someone added lemon as well, and of course the milk curdled. But it didn't matter, it was hot and sweet.'

By the time Robert Frettlöhr arrived at Tilbury, the catering arrangements appear to have been considerably streamlined. He says:

> You come off the boat and there's a hangar door, open just wide enough to get through, and there were big tables to the left and the right. Someone said, "You're going to get tea and sandwiches, and you'll run through there at the double." In one hand you had a jug and in the other was a sandwich. The sergeant was pouring constantly and you were running past him trying to catch some tea. You ran through because a train was waiting at the other end. That was the introduction to England.

Incredibly, later in 1946, some prisoners of war who had already been released by other Allied powers were sucked back into the POW system under a scheme known as Operation Fox. After surrendering to advancing troops near Linz, Guenther Wulff had become a prisoner of the Americans in Austria, and was released in early 1946. Wulff says:

> We were called in groups and they said, 'Where do you want to go? West Germany? East Germany? British Zone? French Zone? Or stay in the American Zone?' Well, I had an uncle in the British Zone at Osnabrück who worked in a bank and I thought I'd go and see if he could put me up, because my home was in the East –

---

[*] It was later ascertained that at least 190 men had died in British-run camps in Belgium: of these roughly half had fallen victim to dysentery or tuberculosis.

I'd seen enough of the Russians so I thought I'd better dive under in West Germany somewhere. The Americans sent about 2,000 of us by train to Munsterlager.* We'd already been discharged and had our papers and our dollars in our pockets but when we got to Munsterlager they locked us up again! They questioned us and asked us where we were going – we told them we were going home and they said, 'Oh no, you're not going home, you're going to England to work. We've had a bad summer and the farmers need help to bring the harvest in. We need volunteers to work as civilians.' We'd always wanted to go to England and we'd had no reply of any sort from our relations, and a batch of us put our hands up. They told us, 'You'll be working as civilians in the harvest.' We left by ship from Antwerp – rough sea, seasick – and we landed in Tilbury. Then by train all the way down to Plymouth, where we stayed for a week. And from Plymouth back to Kent to Goodnestone, near Dover, and when we got there it was a prisoner of war camp. We said, 'We thought we were working as civilians!' [He laughs] From there – still prisoners – we went to work for the War Agricultural Executive Committee at North Mundham.

Heinz Elfner had been held as a POW in British hands in the Italian city of Modena. 'My turn to be repatriated came in late 1946. We went back to Munsterlager and waited to be set free. A group of British soldiers came and prodded us back on to the train at bayonet point. An officer told us we were going to England, "to help with the harvest".' Heinz and his comrades were taken to Launceston, Cornwall, where they underwent an interrogation. 'I was asked if it would have been better if Germany had won the war and questions like that. Maybe I gave the wrong answers. I was allocated to a Bomb Disposal unit at Huyton, Liverpool. So much for helping with the harvest!

As the weeks and months passed, even some of those prisoners who most resented Germany's defeat saw some faint glimmers of light emerge. Willi Hildemann was experiencing his first winter in the British countryside. It was very different from the desperate situation he had experienced while fighting in northern France:

The first snow fell today. It's glorious outdoors. I've seen so many beautiful things – and I've never been in such close communication with the world of birds. There's a pheasant, and the partridges are mating, the wagtail shows off her colourful plumage, the lapwings are whistling, the wren announces the weather, and the robin trustingly hops up close to me, and brings me merry greetings. The sheep has given birth to a lamb. The young one, a day old, cries for its mother; it's hungry. The elder one fetches the young one and pacifies it. So nature begins to live anew, as we too would wish to begin a new life, and unwind as much as circumstances permit.

*   Munsterlager, the demobilisation camp in the British Zone of Germany – written without an umlaut over the letter 'u' – is near the city of Münster – with an umlaut (ü).

The *Afrika Korps* soldier who, a few weeks previously, had expressed his bitterness at being shipped to England was also sent out to work in the countryside. His diary reflects a dramatic change of mood:

9 April 1946:   Early morning, work outside the camp … Fetching the roller, gathering wood – very harmless. Same in the afternoon. Magnificent. To be able to run round a bit in freedom, to see trees, grass, plants, birds. It makes me happy as a child.

But the requirement to work for the British still rankled with some of those who had been brought to the country from the USA on the false promise that they were going to their homes. 'When we arrived here we were very resentful; we felt we shouldn't be here at all,' Bruno Liebich says. 'We earned 1 shilling a day – 6 shillings a week – and a shilling went on a piece of cake.* [He grins] But we were fed and housed free of charge, so it wasn't *too* bad.'

The pay in Britain was much less than Bruno and the others had received in the United States. And they were paid only one tenth of a British civilian farmworker's wage, although often it was the prisoners who were given the most arduous, repetitive, dirty jobs.

The desperate need for home-grown food during the war had forced British farms to become more productive and to use more mechanisation: but there were still twice as many horses as tractors.** Theo Dengel was sent to work on a farm of about 200 acres:

It was very primitive, a typical small farm. I remember the harvesting of barley and they had one of these old-fashioned harvesting machines you pulled with a tractor, and it tied the barley up into small bundles with string, and we had to run behind and stack it up into sheaves to dry. That was hard work because you were running behind the tractor all the time. When it came to threshing, the first thing was to load the sheaves on to trailers to bring to the threshing machine and then it was a real family do. The wife was there, two daughters, and the two POWs got the job of stacking up the sheaves which had been threshed. It was a very dusty, nasty job. We had to build these great big stacks. It was hard work. But the family really got stuck in, and because the women worked hard you had to work hard yourself. You couldn't slack off, you had no choice, really.

---

*   The cake in question was, according to Arno Christiansen, of a 'particularly virulent shade of yellow', and was made from powdered milk and dried eggs. It did not compare in any way, he says, with the Linzertorte and the 'great slabs of rum-soaked sticky rich fruit cake' that he was used to at home.
**   500,000 horses; 250,000 tractors.

'At the end of the machine were outlets where you hang the sacks,' recalls Eberhard Wendler. 'The noise is terrific and the dust. Each kernel has got a husk on it, the chaff, which is blown very fast into sacks. That was a job for the prisoner of war. It doesn't weigh much, but the dust! And especially with barley, all these needles get in your jacket, your trousers, everywhere, and you're black like soot; it's such dirty, filthy stuff. You'd try to pick the needles out, but you'd go back to the camp and next morning they were still there.'

Theo Dengel adds, 'It was all hard labour – harvesting sugar beet, mangolds or potatoes. That was in November and it was raining, everything was clay and you had to dig the potatoes out and they were full of muck. It was unpleasant and there was no mechanisation whatsoever; it was all manual in those days. The farmer used a tractor to loosen the soil and he had one horse – that was it. It was a hard life for a small farmer in those days, very primitive, still, even in 1946.'

The War Office eventually advised camp commandants that prisoners could be issued with rudimentary protective clothing and waterproof footwear but – as their memo reveals – even a simple matter like this was surrounded by red tape: 'Applications for rubber boots for prisoners of war should be dealt with in accordance with paragraph 5 of Memorandum Serial No. 1600.'

When the farmers had no work to be done, the men were sent out ditching. 'Throughout the war there had been no cleaning up of the ditches at the side of the roads,' Theo Dengel explains. 'Every time it rained there was flooding. Ditching was a fall-back job during the winter, in the off-season and so on. Sometimes there were ten lorry-loads of men. We had a good English ganger. He was responsible for collecting lunches at the camp mess hall, and he made the tea. He was meant to supervise the work but most of the time he sat in the lorry sleeping. Ditching was an amiable, easy job.'

The fact that German prisoners were now being used as a labour force, just as Commander Locker-Lampson had urged, did not prevent him from quizzing his parliamentary colleagues at every opportunity. If anything, his questions took on an increasingly eccentric character. He enquired whether the Minister of Agriculture would consider using prisoners 'to help in gardens and teach them as soon as possible to look after bees and goats'.

He was assured that it would not be in the national interest to divert such labour for training in the care of bees and goats.

'What is the good of capturing Germans, unless we use them?' thundered the Commander. There was no task in his eyes, it seemed, that couldn't be imposed on the POWs. When concerns about harvesting the potato crop were voiced, all eyes turned to Locker-Lampson in expectation.

'Why not employ German prisoners?' he shouted, right on cue.

TABLE 7: TYPES OF WORK BY POWs

Type of Employment	Remarks	Number of POWs
Agriculture	Including camp staffs associated.	163,000
Preparation of Building Sites		22,000
Other useful work		94,000
Not employed	11,000 sick and in detention	46,000
Unemployable	Mainly Officers and Protected Personnel	13,000
	TOTAL	338,000

The numbers quoted reflect the situation in mid-1946: see Hansard, 4 June 1946 (HC).

Associated camp staff: those in German working camps, but not working directly in agriculture, e.g. those engaged in catering, clerical work, etc.

Protected Personnel: chiefly medical work (e.g. assisting the German or British camp doctors).

As Table 7 illustrates, not all German prisoners worked in agriculture, although this was by far the most common job they were employed in. The possibility of using them in coal mines had been considered and ruled out: their lack of skill and experience might endanger British workers, it was claimed. A more likely reason is that the unions would never have allowed it. A representative of the National Union of Mineworkers told a meeting in Tamworth, 'The first day a German goes down a mine is the last day a Britisher goes down.' He emphasised the risk of having 'possible Nazis underground, who could cause immense damage to our men if sabotage were their objective'.

Britain's towns and cities had been severely damaged by German bombing and many people thought it was appropriate that German POWs should be used to make good the damage. To achieve this aim, however, was harder than one might think. To begin with, it would have been an organisational nightmare to match the skills available among the prisoners with the specific tasks to be completed. As a result, POWs were rarely used for the actual reconstruction of houses. Instead, they were employed on site preparation works, such as digging foundations and drains, as labourers assisting skilled British workers, and in the manufacture of building materials.

Fritz Jeltsch was transferred from Tring in Hertfordshire to Nuneaton. 'They were building a big housing estate between Coventry and Birmingham. We worked on the building, mixing cement, carrying the bricks for the bricklayer. From Nuneaton I went to Byfield near Leamington Spa and I worked in a cement factory.'

A further problem in most areas was that, while housing plots were plentiful, materials were in such short supply that building as such could not yet commence. *The Times* reported in April 1946 that brick production was only one quarter of the figure for 1938. Stocks were falling, and shortages were expected when the house-building programme got under way. Bringing the brickworks back into production was no easy matter: they had been 'extensively used by the Government during the war as factories and dispersal dumps for stores,' a *Times* reporter explained. It was German POWs who provided the labour to prepare the brickworks for reopening.

By July 1945, 16,000 new homes were under construction across the country and 24,000 Germans were engaged in preparing the sites for them. At Weston, Bath, prisoners constructed the roads and the drainage network and dug the foundations for 280 new council houses. To the south-east of London, POWs carried out groundworks for the Whitefoot Lane Estate, Bromley, and the Cherry Orchard Estate, off Shooters Hill Road, Greenwich.

Britain in the 1940s suffered from a succession of extremely harsh winters. In early 1946 – less than twelve months after the war had ended – German POWs were employed on snow clearance duties when blizzard conditions hit the south-east. The Kent village of Paddlesworth is located on high ground three miles inland from the Channel coast. In March 1946 the little community was completely isolated by 12ft snowdrifts.

'Eighty German prisoners, after two days' hard digging through drifts, "liberated" Paddlesworth, near Hawkinge, at mid-day on Wednesday, after the village had been cut off since Saturday,' a local reporter wrote. His choice of words is interesting: the village would undoubtedly have been one of the first places in Britain to be occupied if Hitler's army had invaded in 1940, and the inhabitants did not readily associate the word 'liberated' with German troops. On this occasion, though, the POWs in their *Feldgrau* uniforms were a welcome sight to the villagers. 'We were down to our last bit of bread and margarine,' claimed the licensee of the local pub. A photograph accompanying the newspaper report depicts a group of German soldiers making their way between two deep banks of snow. They are carrying a pram with a baby in it, while the child's mother walks on a few steps ahead.

It was a widely held belief that German POWs should undertake mine clearance and the removal of unexploded bombs, even though such activities were strictly contrary to the Geneva Convention. British specialists were already at work on this but progress was hampered, firstly, by a shortage of manpower resulting from demobilisation, and secondly, 'by the loss of beach plans made in 1940' showing where the mines had been planted.

Legendary footballer Bert Trautmann was one of those allocated to this task; he worked in two separate bomb disposal units and is said to have enjoyed these assignments much more than working on a farm. According to Henry Faulk, the POWs concerned were men with suitable training who could handle this type of work comparatively safely, but it is clear that this was not always true. Heinz Elfner's only previous experience in this sphere was a short time he had spent as an artillery mechanic early in his service career. As previously touched upon, Elfner had volunteered to 'help with the harvest' but was assigned instead to bomb disposal. He says:

There were so many unexploded bombs and mines in England that without our help it would have taken years to clear them. It was against the rules to employ POWs on such dangerous work but special permission from the War Department had been obtained for us to do this. Our English officers thought that we were volunteers but this was not true. We did not complain; we just got on with the job hoping we could go home soon. After all, we were fed adequately and had a roof over our heads, whilst at the same time in Germany many people were starving and lived in squalor.

At least three prisoners are believed to have been killed while clearing explosives: one victim, 26-year-old Heinz Lentz, died in 1947 while clearing mines on Selsey Beach near Chichester. Theo Dengel was asked to interpret at the inquest:

I was warned by the Coroner's officer, a police constable, that I wasn't allowed to ask questions, or make comments; my job was strictly to interpret. I sat there absolutely amazed. The Coroner didn't seem at all interested that in a way a war crime was being committed. The verdict was accidental death but they didn't ask any searching questions. The officers were lying. The mind boggles that they would use POWs to clear mines long after the war. It was very, very strange.

Other prisoners were injured or killed while performing less obviously dangerous duties. In September 1947, ten German POWs and two British soldiers were killed when the vehicle they were travelling in collided with a 60-mph express train at a level crossing near Bridlington. A further seventeen POWs were injured. One of the prisoners, Hans Graf, was authorised to drive the truck, but for some reason a British sergeant had taken over at the wheel. It was later revealed that this man held a driving licence only for motorcycles. The government refused to pay compensation to the families of the dead, on the grounds that they were not obliged to do so under the Geneva Convention. However, the general rule was that men who were injured at work through no fault of their own were to be compensated, and would receive half pay until they were fit to return to their jobs.

A relatively small number of POWs worked in industry. Werner Völkner says, 'The depressing thing was that some of my mates and I worked in a factory making barbed wire – and then going back into camp behind barbed wire!' Soon afterwards, Werner was transferred to Surrey to help clear the Wey Navigation Canal.

During the war they hadn't done any maintenance and everything was overgrown. What we had to do was cut down the big trees overhanging the water. Our interpreter overheard the overall boss asking the foreman whether he'd got enough cigarettes and tobacco for the POWs. We'd never had any. But we knew that the foreman used to flog the wood to the nearest houses and got paid for it. So we said, 'Tomorrow all the wood we cut down we burn.' And we burnt all the wood and he did his nut! And our interpreter said, 'You've been withholding the cigarettes from us, so we're burning the wood.' It worked – from then on we got five cigarettes a day.

As Britain gradually eased itself into the post-war era, POW labour helped to put the country back on its feet. Beginning just after VE Day, England and Australia played a series of Victory Tests: in preparation for this, German prisoners were sent to Headingley cricket ground where they 'washed the Bramall Lane benches and put them back in place; and washed the paintwork and whitewashed. There was justice in such work. German bombs in the winter of 1940–41 had half destroyed the stand'.

Although hostilities had ended with the Japanese surrender in September 1945 it was not until the summer of 1946 that Britain held its official victory parade in London. The ceremony had been deliberately held in abeyance until thousands of servicemen overseas could be repatriated. German POWs were used as a labour force to prepare for the celebration and afterwards to clear up tons of rubbish left by the spectators. Among their tasks was the construction of temporary barracks in Kensington Gardens for participating British and Allied servicemen. A newsreel cameraman filmed the POWs as they marched smartly to their place of work wearing a variety of British and German uniforms. It is an incongruous scene. A woman sits on a park bench with a baby next to her in a pram. Within arm's reach eight German soldiers in uniform are uncoiling rolls of barbed wire to form the perimeter fencing. Absorbed in a magazine she is reading, the woman seems completely oblivious of the Germans ... and just what was going through the minds of the prisoners themselves is impossible to fathom.

Around the country, local communities staged their own festivities. In his own dispassionate way, Eberhard Wendler writes:

8 June 1946: Victory Day. Today we didn't work ... in the afternoon we went to the victory celebration.

Prisoners were sometimes required to do tasks they found highly distasteful. Dieter Spring was put to work translating technical documents confiscated from Germany as reparations for the war. He wrote to an acquaintance:

It is a rather awkward situation and I do not like it at all. All the documents are scientific ones of the former Krupp works and other German inventors and scientifists [sic] ... now I entrust you something what I can't say and dare not to say in the circles here. You see all the documents are practically stolen and me as a German they are using me to translate such things and it gives me a few pangs of conscience ... But if I utter here such things they probably send me to a place where I never shall see again South England which I like so much.

Germany had already developed an operational jet fighter plane, and this was an area where Britain lagged behind. Twenty-five German scientists, who were 'leading aeronautical authorities', were brought to the Royal Aircraft Establishment at Farnborough, Hampshire, to 'solve the problems created by the jet engine'. German prisoners of war were detailed to 'wait on' the scientists, who were housed in a special hostel.

Trusted prisoners with specialised skills did important work at British defence installations. Soon after his transfer from Belgium, Robert Frettlöhr, a former electrician, was chosen for these duties. 'A hundred of us, all tradesmen, finished up at RAF station Lindholme. I was in the Motor Transport section, in the electrical department looking after batteries and so on. The lads who used to be there were being demobbed. And eventually the commanding officer said, "You will be in charge of the battery room." So I ran the battery room. And we were snooping around in the music room and out of the hundred men there were five who could play instruments.' Robert himself played piano, having been taught by his aunt, a professional music teacher. He had later learned to play guitar, flute and zither. Then, in the band room at the RAF base, he happened to find a double bass, and took to it immediately. And while he was at the aerodrome Robert met the bassist in the Squadronaires – an Air Force dance band of national renown.

Robert says:

> I still have the book he gave me, on how to play the double bass. Five of us created a band. We had a professional pianist with us, and a professional guitarist. Jimmy played trombone and piano-accordion and another lad was the drummer. Eventually we finished up playing in the NAAFI social club. We knew some of the members of the Squadronaires, but they were getting demobbed and there was no band left except us. And they decided to have *our* band. We rehearsed and rehearsed in the officers' mess. And we had one lad who played guitar and who was a cook in the officers' mess. Well, he couldn't play guitar to save his life, but he got us rashers of bacon, and anything we wanted. And our trumpeter had been a blacksmith and he made a massive frying pan and we had fried potatoes. The RAF officers used to come with their girlfriends and listen to the band and they brought bottles of beer. We were paid 7s 6d and we had a nosh-up in the NAAFI – chips, sausage and beans, and twenty cigarettes.

Bruno Liebich claims that he had the perfect occupation – as a dustman. 'It was the best job in town because as farmworkers we were all on the fields hoeing beetroot, picking potatoes, you don't see a soul. But as a dustman you meet people.' The job offered another distinct advantage. 'There were the little tips you got for taking a broken bike or some extra rubbish. We never had any real money, you see, only coupons from the camp.'

One of the most bizarre schemes involving the POWs was suggested by Martin Lindsay, the MP for Solihull. At the risk of over-simplifying his plan, the basic idea was to use the Germans as breeding stock to enhance the pedigree of the nation. 'We all know how much the United States have gained by the admixture of good, foreign blood,' he said. 'There are, today, in Great Britain no fewer than 200,000 surplus women of marriageable age between 20 and 40 … a number of these would find husbands in due course, if we could get the best of the Germans to remain in this country.' Unconventional as this plan must have seemed at the time, it had something of a prophetic ring to it, as we shall discover.

The Geneva Convention stipulated that officers could not be required to work (though they could be offered work, which many accepted, as it helped pass the time). Whether they worked or not Britain was obliged to pay their regular salaries for the time being. The amount to be paid was also laid down in the Convention – either their own regular rate of pay or that of an equivalent British officer, whichever was the lesser amount. As German officers usually received less than their British counterparts it was the German rate of pay that prevailed. A Lieutenant received £4 16s per month; the pay-scale rose to £16 for the highest-ranking generals, the equivalent of their German army salary of 240 *Reichsmark*. 'Is that all a full general gets in Germany?' asked Lord Wedgwood, 'It seems incredible.'

A rate of exchange, 15 *Reichsmark* to the pound, had been agreed upon by Britain and Germany in 1940. All money paid to the officers by Britain was regarded as an advance that was recoverable from the officers' own government at the end of hostilities. From November 1943, a further reciprocal arrangement had made it possible for officer prisoners to have their credit balance paid out to their families or dependants in Germany if they wished.

When it came to the pay of 'other ranks' (those who were not officers) the situation was less straightforward. The Geneva Convention offered no guidance as to what these men should be paid, merely suggesting that the details should be agreed between the warring governments. As no such agreement had ever been reached, the British Government determined that only 'working pay' would be awarded to prisoners. This was the sum payable to British troops as a supplement to their basic pay when carrying out work that lay outside the scope of their normal duties. According to the regulations, a rate of 1s per day was awarded for 'superior labourer's work calling for more than ordinary intelligence – such as such as concrete work, erecting scaffolding etc.'. The unskilled rate of 6d per day was appropriate to 'ordinary labourers' work', such as digging ditches. (As far as the German POWs were concerned, agricultural work including harvesting and picking vegetables counted as skilled work, while clearing bomb-damaged sites was held to be unskilled.)

The British government insisted that these small amounts were simply 'pocket money' (as they put it) to enable the prisoners to buy everyday items. Their basic pay should be credited to their account by the German military, and handed over to them by Germany upon their return from captivity: 'Prisoners of war are paid or credited, or *should* be credited [author's emphasis], with their rates of pay as soldiers by their own countries,' confirmed Mr. Frederick Bellenger, Financial Secretary to the War Office. 'German, Austrian and Italian prisoners of war will … receive what is due to them from their own Governments when they go back to their own homes.'

It was an astonishing statement for that particular time. Since the German government had ceased to exist, and an Allied military government ruled Germany, Bellenger knew very well that there was no prospect of the soldiers receiving any of their back pay – unless Britain or her allies paid it.

Remuneration for work done was in *Lagergeld* ('camp money' in the form of tokens) since real British currency could have been a help to escapers. Regular searches were made at some camps to ensure that prisoners were not in possession of cash: however, these became less and less frequent as it became clear that few POWs were likely to break out. Camp money could be used to buy goods from the canteen including cigarettes, hair-oil, writing materials, snacks such as cakes, and so on. Profits from the canteen went into the welfare fund and the money was used for the benefit of the prisoners – often on goods such as books, musical instruments and materials for handcrafts. A drawback of camp money was that the paper or plastic tokens could only be used in the camp where they had been issued. Prisoners who were transferred to another camp – which often occurred at short notice – unexpectedly found themselves with 'savings' which were valueless.

The wide disparity between what the farmer paid to the War Agricultural Executive Committee for the services of the POWs and the small amount handed over to the prisoners themselves caused dissatisfaction on all sides. The farmers were paying the going rate and expected the Germans to do a full day's hard work. The prisoners were resentful at their small wages and often did as little as possible. Politicians and public simply wondered what was happening to the balance, which amounted to about £3 15s weekly per prisoner, while the government claimed to be making a loss on the deal, and not a profit. When pressed, they gave vague assurances that the rest of the money was swallowed up in the cost of accommodating, feeding and guarding the prisoners, but they avoided going into further detail by pleading that a 'disproportionate amount of work by hard-pressed staffs' would be required to substantiate their claim. Some sources put the *true* cost of the prisoners' keep at about £1 8s weekly per man – leaving a profit for the government of £2 7s per man per week.

12

Britain Switched Off

By May 1945, when the war between Britain and Germany ended, the two nations had almost destroyed each other. They balanced on a knife edge, teetering between rebirth and ruin. While Germany toppled into economic and social chaos, Britain emerged with 'the psychology of a victor but with her economic circumstances more resembling those of a defeated country'. The 'broad sunlit uplands' that Churchill had promised in 1940 seemed as remote now as ever. The nation's condition was so fragile that even the tiniest mishap could be fatal.

Rubble-filled bomb-sites scarred almost every street in the cities. Some 800,000 houses had been severely damaged or destroyed, and there was insufficient labour to clear the debris, let alone repair or rebuild the homes.

The British Merchant Navy had lost almost 12 million tons of shipping – more than half of its pre-war fleet. Both imports and exports were at a disastrously low level. Industry and agriculture struggled to keep production at survival levels.

From an economic standpoint, the country faced total collapse. During the war the United States had bankrolled Britain to the tune of billions of dollars under the Lend-Lease scheme. The British government assumed that this would continue, at least until the country was back on its feet again. But on 2 September 1945 – the very day of the Japanese surrender, which brought the war to a close – the USA pulled the plug without warning. Clement Attlee, who had succeeded Winston Churchill as Prime Minister in July, told Parliament, 'We had not anticipated that operations under the Lend-Lease Act would continue for any length of time after the defeat of Japan. But we had hoped that the sudden cessation of this great mutual effort, which has contributed so much to victory, would not have been effected without consultation.' He added that the cancellation of Lend-Lease 'puts us in a very serious financial situation'.

For the POWs, though, it was business as usual: 'We didn't know about the money drying up,' says Eberhard Wendler. 'We never got in contact with any civilians – when you're a prisoner of war you don't come into contact with anybody. Nobody told us anything, we had no newspapers, and we wouldn't have been able to read them if we'd had them.'

Egon Schormann, a Lieutenant in the *Wehrmacht*, was also unaware of the difficulties Britain was facing. 'I found out years later that the general situation in England at that time had not improved. We had regarded the coal rationing in the winter of 1946–47 and the miserable low-calorie food in the officers' camp at Llanmartin as unnecessary aggravation.' One of the lecturers sent to address prisoners as part of the re-education effort reported that, 'Some [prisoners] express doubts on the bad economic situation in England. They think it is bad will and a trick to keep Germany down.' It was only the few prisoners with an above-average knowledge of current affairs who appreciated the seriousness of Britain's situation. Writing in *Lagerecho*, one of the German-language camp newspapers, Rudolf Intrau claimed:

> Many people wonder how it is possible that England, as a victorious nation, has been overtaken by such a calamity. We hear repeatedly about a dollar-crisis, but that is not the only reason. England's losses [in the war] have without doubt been on an unimaginable scale. The nation has been impoverished.

In February 1946, Agriculture Minister Tom Williams addressed Parliament on what he called the critical world condition, and mentioned the chilling prospect of a worldwide famine.

'The position created by the ravages of war ... has now developed grievously beyond our fears. ... in this country the need throughout the war to save shipping was preeminent, and for six years we were forced to expand our acreage of grain and potatoes to the utmost of capacity ... The world is now faced with a catastrophic change in the situation ... We simply cannot allow a large fall in tillage in the face of a world famine.' He added that, to combat the shortages, prisoner of war labour would be used to maximum effect, and intimated that cash incentives might be offered to the POWs. There was even a prospect that they might receive the 'going rate' for the job.

As the New Year dawned, Britons wondered whether 1947 would bring better tidings. But they had failed to reckon with the country's erratic climate. January brought false hope: it was cold but free from snow. But then came the worst weather in over half a century. During February, snow fell in some places on twenty-six out of twenty-eight days. The weather – and the chaos it caused – filled the front pages of the daily newspapers:

BRITAIN SWITCHED OFF
Over 2,000,000 will be out of work
The effect of the blizzard on all coalfields and transport has been disastrous ...

As the country struggled for survival, this new threat felt like a deathblow. The impact on coal production was devastating. Coal, in those times, was pivotal to the running of the country. Most homes were still heated – at least in part – by coal fires; without coal there could be no gas supplies; virtually the entire electricity supply was generated in coal-fired power stations. Coal was needed to make steel and many other vital materials, and fuelled railways and shipping.

In a hushed House of Commons the Minister of Fuel and Power, Emanuel Shinwell, broke the grim news to MPs.

1. Seventeen-year-old Theo Dengel at the time of his call-up. (Theo Dengel)

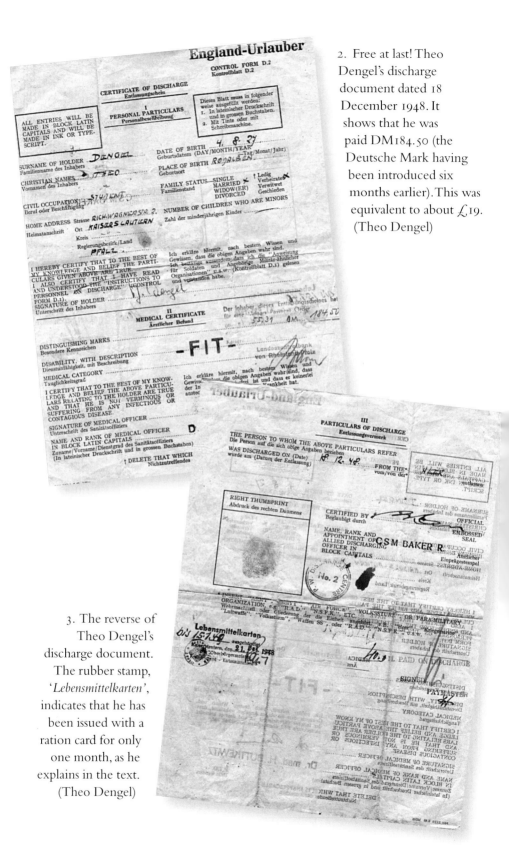

2. Free at last! Theo Dengel's discharge document dated 18 December 1948. It shows that he was paid DM184.50 (the Deutsche Mark having been introduced six months earlier). This was equivalent to about £19. (Theo Dengel)

3. The reverse of Theo Dengel's discharge document. The rubber stamp, *'Lebensmittelkarten'*, indicates that he has been issued with a ration card for only one month, as he explains in the text. (Theo Dengel)

4. Bruno Liebich's official POW 'mugshot', showing his British POW number. (Bruno Liebich)

7. Bruno Liebich with a box he made during his time as a prisoner of war. (Author)

5. Theo and Joan Dengel on the occasion of their engagement in 1948. (Theo Dengel)

8. Werner Völkner. This picture dates from around 1943 when he was serving on the Eastern Front. (Werner Völkner)

6. Bruno and Audrey Liebich. (Bruno Liebich)

9. *Below:* Werner Volkner. (Author)

10. Eberhard Wendler (*left*) with POWs and civilian farm worker. (Eberhard Wendler)

11. Eberhard and Kathleen Wendler. (Author)

12. Eberhard Wendler spent some time in the sickbay at High Garrett POW camp in late 1944. This sketch of him was drawn on the back of a patient's temperature chart by another POW. (Eberhard Wendler)

13. Luftwaffe pilot Ulrich Steinhilper temporarily swaps his Messerschmitt 109 for a motorbike. (Independent Books)

14. German prisoners of war disembark from a Landing Ship (Tank), closely watched by American troops. (After the Battle)

15. The one that got away first! Walter Kurt Reich describes his exploits to an American reporter. (Author's collection)

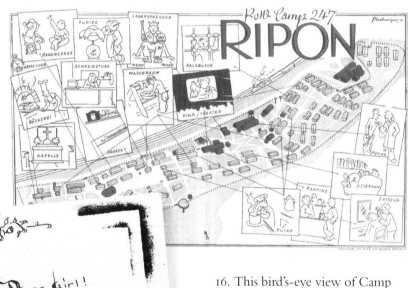

16. This bird's-eye view of Camp 147 (Ripon) was drawn by prisoner Heinz Schneider from Halle, Saxony. (see table, p. 52). (Ingeborg Hellen)

Dear Girl!

It is very wrong from you, that we have a long time nothing seen from you. We are always very glad, when we can see you nicely face. – Dear Girl, we have an ask for you, can you drive now alwaysalong our bus. We are very happy, you allways to see. –

With the hope you can read this letter, and that we can you see allways in the next time, want we to shut.

You happy P. o. W's.

17. This note was thrown by German POWs to a Land Army girl as she cycled to work alongside their lorry (see p. 140). (Imperial War Museum)

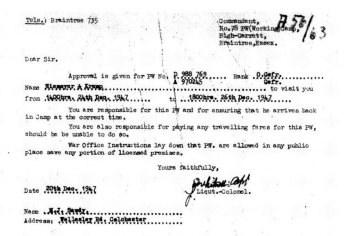

18. Note giving permission for a civilian to accept two POWs from High Garrett Camp near Braintree as guests at Christmas 1947. (Imperial War Museum)

19. Eden Camp at Malton, Yorkshire, remains in near-original condition and is a major visitor attraction today. The brick-built water tower dominates the skyline; at many sites of former POW camps such a tower is all that remains. (Author)

No.	When Married	Name and Surname	Age	Condition	Rank or Profession	Residence at the time of Marriage	Father's Name and Surname	Rank or Profession of Father
75	Eleventh January 1947	Leo Ganter	26 years	Bachelor	Motor Mechanic	6 Clare Road Liverpool 20	Otto Ganter	Post Office Official
		Monica Patricia Cann	21 years	Spinster	P/W 31...	D Camp R.Sd. Donnington Wellington Salop	William Henry Cann	Post Office Official

Married in the *Register Office* according to the Rites and Ceremonies of the _____ by *licence before* by me,

This Marriage was solemnized between us, { *Leo Ganter* / *M. P. Cann* } in the Presence of us, { *D. C. Spence* / *E. E. Bythell* } *A I Manning* Registrar

Robert Gurjoac Superintendent Registrar

20. The marriage certificate of Monica Cann and Hermann Leo Ganter. Monica was fined for 'causing a false statement to be inserted in the marriage register'. When marriage between POWs and British women was made legal, it was decided that the prisoner's 'occupation' was to be given as 'Prisoner of War', followed by the name and address of the POW camp. (General Register Office)

21. The tractor and threshing machine on this Gloucestershire farm fall silent for a short time as German POWs take a break from work. Patrick Barrett, the small boy at the front, thought the Germans were 'smashing' because they played with him. Willy Reuter (the prisoner standing immediately behind Patrick in this photograph) returned to Germany in 1948. Patrick and Willy were finally reunited fifty years later. (Patrick Barrett)

Pits have been blocked; men have been unable to get to the pits; and in some cases men have got to the pits but have been unable to get away from them. There have been blocks on the road … many roads are impassable … The electricity stations are in the grave position of being unable to say whether they will be able to carry on for the next week or ten days.

Domestic consumers went without electricity for hours on end so that industry could struggle on.

'Intensive efforts are being made to clear the main trunk rail and road routes from north to south. Polish troops and German prisoners of war are being used for this work,' *The Times* announced. '2,610 British troops, 2,635 German prisoners of war, and 1,120 Poles have been clearing snow from roads. Nearly 1,000 British troops and many Poles and prisoners of war have been clearing roads for the movement of coal.'

Agriculture was severely affected. Prisoners of war who would normally have been working on the farms were switched to vital snow-clearance tasks. By mid-February the weather had deteriorated still further: Greenwich Observatory recorded the coldest day since 1843.

POW Dieter Hahn recollects:

They sent us out to shovel snow over Shap Fells. It was a waste of time – in places with the snowdrifts all you could see was the tops of the telegraph poles. We had to dig down to find the road. We never cleared the thing. That road, the old A6, was the only main road between England and Scotland over Shap Fells. We shovelled the snow into lorries. We had no extra clothes except maybe some gloves or a scarf.

At Crick, near Rugby, POWs dug out a train which had been trapped by snow drifts. In the Northern Command (as *The Times* put it, lapsing momentarily into the military jargon of the war years) a combined force of 7,000 men – British troops, Poles, and German prisoners – stood shoulder to shoulder clearing the drifts. In desperation, the authorities turned to the most extraordinary solutions. In Leicestershire, two jet engines were mounted upon a Valentine tank in an attempt to melt, or to blow away, 10ft snowdrifts so that miners could reach their workplace, Desford Colliery.

Prisoners from a camp at Skipton, North Yorkshire, were used to clear deep snowdrifts on the windswept Dales. A special train took them to their place of work leaving at 6 a.m. and returning at 5 p.m. each day. It was not unusual for them to arrive, only to find that all of the previous day's work had been undone overnight by the wind and snow. A local man reports that prisoners would often claim to have lost their shovels; to combat this ruse the authorities would issue as many as 100 new ones daily.

The nation was paralysed. A shock headline in the Sunday Express declared:

GAS SUPPLY CRITICAL – 'GRAVE CONCERN' ABOUT FOOD.

Newspaper photographs depict German prisoners rescuing stranded sheep. Then, in March, the blizzard conditions returned. In Staffordshire:

> Two hundred men dug through to the principal village on the route, only to have to dig their way back at the end of the day. Before this road could be finally opened, 20ft drifts had to be cut. On other roads ice has been the greatest obstacle. Even 13-ton bulldozers made practically no impression on ice formations. The report from this area concludes: 'Five thousand men, including prisoners of war, have been employed at night when necessary and under terrible conditions.'

A million sheep died and in some places carrion crows descended on the carcasses of the animals and devoured them. Werner Völkner – having been moved yet again and now working on a Surrey farm – remembers huge flocks of pigeons descending on the fields in search of food. His boss told the foreman, 'You take the Jerries and put them out in the field, they were soldiers, they are supposed to be good shots. Let them shoot some pigeons.' And so it was that squads of German POWs were sent out into the fields of England armed with shotguns.

After three months of Arctic conditions, milder weather arrived. But the crisis was not yet over. 'When the thaw came there were terrible floods, and near Littleport in the Fens a dam burst, causing huge floods,' recalls Ray Rudolf, a POW at a camp near Mildenhall, Suffolk. As the cold spell drew to a close he and other prisoners were sent to deal with flooding just over the county border in Cambridgeshire. 'We helped by transporting sandbags, and formed a chain gang to pass them along to a fireman who chucked them into the water to stop the gap in the embankment where the water was flooding out.'

Peter Roth was also involved in this emergency work. 'I was at a camp in Cambridgeshire at the time and the Wash got flooded. They were afraid that the dykes would break and they came to the camp and asked for help.' In spite of his lifelong commitment to outwitting anyone in authority, he volunteered.

'When anything like this happened we *would* help,' he says meekly.

When the worst of the crisis was over, the government was forced to reassess its use of POW labour – particularly in agriculture. It was clear that large squads of prisoners under armed supervision could be a viable labour force for the bigger farms. As many as twenty-five or thirty POWs could be transported to the fields and could work there until the job was completed, returning several days in a row, if needed. But a considerable amount of time was wasted just in travelling to and from work. Farmers complained that the Germans turned up at 9 a.m. and left at 4.30 p.m. These hours were dictated not by the needs of farmers but by the minutiae of camp routine – morning and evening roll calls, meal times and so on. Consequently, the German labour force was not being used as efficiently as it might have been.

Satellite camps were therefore set up so that the men could live closer to where they worked. The base camps could have as many as ten satellites, but four or five was a more typical number. Still smaller outposts – 'hostels' – were also established. A base camp could have a maximum of six such hostels, and these would normally be situated within a 30-mile radius.

The nation depended on its many smaller farms, too, and these urgently needed labourers, but in far smaller numbers. In mid-1945, John Profumo – having returned to Westminster after his distinguished military career – asked the Minister of Agriculture whether he would ensure that German prisoners were made available in *small* numbers in view of the shortage of labour to bring in the harvest.

The large squads were first divided in half. Later, these groups were further subdivided. A confidential memo dated 18 January 1945, now in the National Archives, states that whereas gangs of German prisoners had normally been taken to work on the fields under the supervision of armed military guards, it was now proposed – 'as an experiment' – that, 'Prisoners will be taken out under escort and small parties, up to a maximum of *four* per party, will be dropped off at individual farms; the farmer will then be held responsible for the supervision and safe custody of the prisoners until the escort collects them at the end of the day.' The memo expresses the hope that this approach will prove to be more efficient.

Erwin Hettwer was invited to participate in one of these squads:

> When asked who could speak English, I did not raise my hand, following the old army rule never to volunteer. But others were saying, "You went to high school, you should be able to speak English." So I was assigned with two others to work on a farm. It was time to bring in the hay … We were driven to work in the back of a lorry with two guards armed with rifles. I noticed one of the guards, a young soldier, was constantly moving his jaws. I did not know whether he was grinding his teeth or had some other affliction. I asked the other guard what was wrong with him. He looked and started to laugh, pulled out a small package and handed it to me. And that was the first time I had a piece of chewing gum.

A marked contrast was seen between the quality of the work done by large gangs of men who never met their employer, and that carried out by much smaller groups under the farmer's direct supervision. Arno Christiansen says that when harvesting potatoes on a large, impersonal farm, they 'picked up one potato [and] trod two into the ground'.

In what was a surprisingly bold move for the War Office, 'selected German prisoners' would be allowed to drive the lorries. Needless to say, a number of conditions were imposed: 'prisoner-drivers' (as they were to be known) must be accompanied by an armed guard; on arrival they had to work with the other POWs; the lorries were to be only part-filled with petrol, to minimise the risk of their being used to escape; and the War Office would arrange driving tests for the selected prisoners.

A letter printed in *The Times* makes it evident that these stipulations were not always faithfully adhered to:

> When driving my car around a bend, a lorry filled with prisoners of war suddenly turned head-on towards me, and a collision was only averted by my having to mount the grass verge. The lorry continued but the incident seemed so extraordinary that I turned round and, eventually overtaking the lorry, stopped it. To my amazement I found the lorry full of German prisoners, none of whom could speak English, including the driver, who had with him three other men in the cab. Fortunately, my wife, who was with me, could speak German, and was informed by the driver that he had been driving in this country only four days, and he explained that in Germany they drive on the other side of the road and it was easy to make a mistake. He produced a paper which authorized him to drive, signed by an executive of the war agricultural committee, and which also gave a telephone number to be referred to in case of difficulty … It appears to me to be quite wrong that German prisoners of war are allowed to drive vehicles in this country.

Not content with having his letter published in *The Times*, the motorist contacted his Member of Parliament too, and the matter was duly raised in the House. 'Selected men are permitted to drive lorries subject to restrictions,' the Minister of Transport answered; POWs were never given driving licences, as such. And the paper issued by the War Agricultural Executive Committee was, he added somewhat lamely, just 'an authority to the prisoner of war to make a particular journey'.

Other prisoners, whose workplaces were within easy reach of camp, were allowed to cycle there and were issued with army bikes which sometimes – to their undoubted surprise – were brand new. The ability to move around like this was a welcome development, as Arno Christiansen remembers. 'To prisoners who had been locked behind barbed wire, and only taken out under guard, for such a long time, it was almost freedom! The sensation of not being watched over was almost a physical thing, like the shifting of a weight.'

The Government banned farmers from giving the prisoners any form of reward or incentive for good work. Giving the prisoners money could help them to escape, while it also 'reduces the availability of commodities to British citizens', officials claimed. But like the fraternisation rules, this regulation promptly came to be more honoured in the breach than in the observance, especially on small farms. Arno Christiansen says that occasionally the POWs 'were asked to stay on to work a bit late, perhaps to finish a job, or help with a bit of clearing up. On such nights the farmer would notify the camp that they would be late, and they would always be provided with a good meal before they set off on their cycle ride, often a packet of cigarettes as well.' Farmers began to invite the prisoners into their homes, and the Germans often encountered a welcoming atmosphere which was very different from the regimen they had experienced while in the camps.

Even so, the German prisoners were not universally welcomed. Theo Dengel encountered hostility at a farm where he worked:

> The farmer, a man in his late 50s was quite an unpleasant character, very off-hand, always complaining. When it came to meal break at 10.00, 12.00 and 3.00, he came out with a basket with tea and sandwiches. And at lunchtime it was a huge meal. I'll never forget, one day he said 'Don't think I agree with this – I bloody well hate it. This is Auntie's doing.' Well, I discovered eventually that there was an old aunt in her 70s who felt sorry for these young POWs and it was she who made the sandwiches and baked the cakes just for us. And it didn't go down at all well with the farmer, he grumbled about it. He hated the Germans, full-stop.

Children, perhaps inevitably, had fewer preconceptions. Patrick Barrett lived with his parents on a farm overlooking Cheltenham racecourse: he was 6 years old when the prisoners arrived. 'I thought all the German POWs were smashing because they had time to play with me.' (See plate no. 21)

One woman recalls:

> I was only about nine or ten, but I remember them well. A lorry used to bring them and they'd help with any jobs on the farm. Anyone could hire them, you know, for jobs that had to be done. They brought food with them and my mother used to supplement it sometimes with potatoes and things like that. Two of them, Ernst and Heinz, used to come for tea on Sundays. My parents invited them, and they came on their own without any guards – it was after the war ended by this time. They were only young men – boys, really. I can't remember seeing them as 'the enemy' or being frightened of them. I was quite friendly with them. There wasn't any animosity at all, because we're not a family like that. They played with me and once they gave me a wooden sewing box they'd made, with carving on the lid. They made me toys, too – they were very good at making things like that out of wood.

'I remember so well the German prisoners "spud bashing" on the common,' says Roger Clark. 'As young children we were placed on top of a pile of baskets and had to say "*Heil Hitler*" three times to be let down.'

Malcolm Whitaker, born in 1932, remembers four POWs coming to the family farm near Stow-on-the-Wold. Three of them were amiable, while the fourth 'swore at our planes and threw a stone on to the roof and broke a tile.' Before long, the other Germans 'had had enough of him and one of them gave him a good hiding. He never came back'.

The Germans themselves began to view farm work as a challenge. 'Although our backs got increasingly sore, we worked competitively,' Hans Reckel asserts. 'We drove each other on with words of encouragement.' Eberhard Wendler emphasises that he never had any misgivings about working for the British: 'To be quite honest, right at the beginning when I first had to go to work when the war was on, all I thought was "Let's go harvesting, let's help here, let's get it going, let's build it up." We just felt, "Let's get on with it". I always worked hard. The English were our cousins. We're related.'

The Germans' diligence soon earned the farmers' respect. A newspaperman wrote a glowing account of POWs deployed in Northumberland. 'Some farmers report that they are the best prisoner-workers they have had,' he enthused (making a thinly veiled jibe at the Italians). Time and motion experts later measured the relative efficiency of the two groups scientifically, and concluded that 1 German was equal to 3.77 Italians as far as work output was concerned.

Bruno Liebich remembers the long hours spent hoeing lines of beetroot:

> the most boring job of all. Even though we hated it we still did it. I think the general idea for us Germans is, "If you're going to do a job, do it well." We didn't want to be obstinate. We pinched this and that but we didn't damage machinery. That's different. We're used to obeying orders from whoever's in charge of what we're doing – in a job, in the army, or as prisoners. So it was natural. I don't want to boast about it, but it was sort of ingrained, inborn almost.

'We didn't mind the farm work,' claims Henry Metelmann. 'We felt that working is good for you. We met the farmers, we met English people and liked them as human beings and there were often really friendly relationships. And we didn't want to let the farmers down so we worked hard.'

'Saturday was pay day,' Werner Völkner relates. 'On one occasion another prisoner and I were using a push-hoe – we wanted to get the job finished before the weekend, and we carried on working until it was done. So we were late collecting our money. The farmer said, "You won't get a British worker doing that."' Werner believes that this was a cultural difference. 'It caused some resentment among the Brits when they saw the "Jerries" working so hard.'

In early 1945, *The Times* had been able to report that 70 per cent of the nation's war-time diet was being grown on home soil. This was due, in part, to farmers being able to draw on additional labour by Italian and, subsequently, German POWs, as well as the Women's Land Army. When harvest time came around that summer, demand for labour had reached a peak. The government called for members of the public to come forward and lend a hand: however, farmers soon reported that 'Voluntary workers … have lost interest and several other correspondents say that the Italian prisoners are even less assiduous than they were a year ago. They have more faith in the German prisoners, who keep discipline and take some pride in their work.'

'I have seen a good many Italians lying about in the sun and whistling at the girls as they go by; I have not seen Germans doing that,' Mrs Leah Manning, MP for Epping, told the House. 'I think they have done a very good job on the land and we could not do without them.'

A Lincolnshire farmer quoted in *The Times* complained that British workers on piece-work were too expensive. 'If it were not for a few prisoners of war we should not be able to get the odd jobs on the farm done.' The report stated, 'The Germans continue to earn the good opinion of farmers, who find them steady workers, keeping at the job from the time they arrive at 8 a.m. until 6 p.m., and even cutting their dinner hour in order to earn an extra penny or two.'*

Across Britain as a whole, German prisoners of war accounted for one-third of all agricultural labour – and considerably more in some areas, such as Leicestershire, where the proportion in 1946 rose to 50 per cent. 'What is going to happen when the prisoners go away?' demanded Lord Cornwallis early the next year. 'How long are we going to have them? We must have answers to those questions. In my county [Kent] we cannot even man the threshing machines without them now.'

The widespread adoption of piecework frequently led to difficulties. Civilian labourers were often paid in this way, receiving a set amount for every item produced or unit of work carried out. When working alongside German POWs, who were on a much lower rate of pay and were unaccustomed to the work, they found that the POWs hindered them by working too slowly.

Erwin Hettwer and another German POW found a way around this obstacle when they were employed at a stone quarry alongside British labourers who were on piecework. He recalls:

> The quarry workers ... were paid by the number of lorries they loaded. While the worker would look at the rock, turn it, hit it with the hammer once and it broke into pieces, we would just chip corners off and nearly break our backs doing it ... but it made us think. Why could we not work as a team, he would break and we would load the stones. The lorries still went up, two credited to him and two to us. But of course his output went up, because two people load faster than one and he did not have to switch from breaking to loading ... He was happy because his pay went up. The system worked just fine for him and us.

More flexible working practices had resulted in the improved productivity the government was looking for. But these developments also marked a significant turning point in the relationship between the prisoners and the British public. The non-fraternisation rule, which had never been strictly adhered to anyway, became irrelevant when the POWs, no longer under strict discipline, increasingly began to socialise with the farmer, his family, and his civilian workers. The easing of restrictions for men on

---

* Working pay was calculated at 1½d per hour: i.e. 1s per eight-hour day. Those normally working fewer than eight hours could increase their earnings by not taking any time off for meal breaks. It was not possible to earn more than 1s per day, however, as the regulations stipulated that daily working pay was capped at that amount.

the farms was matched by a relaxation of discipline within the camps where weekend roll calls became less frequent or, in some cases, were abolished entirely. In early 1946, it was announced that German POWs could live on the farms where they worked with the farmer and his family. (This was already a common practice with Italian prisoners.) Nine thousand Italians and roughly 5,500 Germans were already living and working as 'billetees' and every Italian POW would eventually be replaced by a German.

The changeover was completed by February 1947. Lord Strabolgi announced, 'We have sent all the Italians back, although a lot of them would have liked to stay here – to the great relief of the remaining gamekeepers in the country, they were not allowed to – and many would like to return.'

Arrangements for billeting the Germans did not always run smoothly. A Devon farmer, recently demobilised from the services himself, said he had two German prisoners working at his farm and complained that now he would only be allowed to retain them if he provided them with accommodation. 'Our farmhouse is in a state of reconstruction,' he wrote, 'and in spite of all permits [we] are still not possessed of a bath. We managed, however, to clear a room for two men to live as family.' He claimed that the inspector who had come to view the facilities informed him that he would have to drive the prisoners 8 miles to their camp every Sunday so that they could have a bath. The farmer would have to use his own petrol ration for this. And, to add insult to injury, he lamented that, 'The Germans get the agricultural cheese ration [while] the owner of the farm does not.' In most cases, though, the POWs were warmly welcomed. 'Most of the farmers who employed us for a shilling a day were very happy to see us there because they were short of labour,' says Eduard Winkler. 'Generally speaking, the Germans were good workers. There were quite a few farmworkers among us.'

Eberhard Wendler became one of the 'billetees' and his diary entries at that time illustrate the interdependency between billet and base camp.

> **16 May 1946**: At 8 A.M. three of us left camp for the last time and went to our farm … In the evening our things were brought over. Including a bunk-bed. We cut it up with a saw and pushed it through the window – a troublesome task.
> **25 May 1946**: Walked to the camp and exchanged my trousers for a new pair.
> **29 June 1946**: Cycled to the camp, had my hair cut, and exchanged a shirt and a towel for new ones.
> **3 August 1946**: In the camp for a haircut.
> **25 August 1946**: Went to the camp to be interrogated and photographed.

Waffen-SS member Karl-Heinz Decker had been brought back to England following the closure of the camps in Belgium and was held at a camp in Cheshire. Unexpectedly, a request came for men who could handle horses. Karl-Heinz had attended agricultural college before the war and this was right up his street. Decker recalls:

> There were three of us and we said, 'Let's get out of here.' We went to groom horses for Major-General Sir Brian Horrocks, the chief of Western Command – a very nice

gentleman.* In his book he said he didn't like the SS, but he had all *Waffen*-SS on his staff! The cook, the grooms – I don't know whether he realised it or not. We had a wonderful time until we were told one day we had to move from there. And Sir Brian said, 'If I can help you in any way, let me know.' And they sent us to Presteigne, Radnorshire, where we had roll call in the morning, roll call at lunchtime and roll call at night – just like when the war was on. We didn't like it, so we wrote to Sir Brian. After a few weeks we were called to the commandant of the camp and he said, 'I've got a letter here naming you three to be returned to Chester. How did the War Office know that you were here?' And we said, 'We don't know.' And they sent us back to Chester by train, escorted by a guard with a gun.

Joseph Kox, a prisoner at Purfleet, Essex, was informed that he would be billeted out. An officer drove him to a pig farm at Theydon Bois, where he met Arthur, another German POW, who was already living there. Josef was shown around by his new friend, and was impressed to see that the accommodation had electric light, a radio, a stove and clean white sheets.

But what really amazed him was the tray he was given that evening, laden with cheese on toast, bread, butter, jam, tea, cocoa and cigarettes.

'How long does that have to last?' he asked.

'Oh, that's for now,' Arthur replied, 'tomorrow we get more.'

Not all POWs enjoyed such luxurious conditions. 'Where I was in lodgings,' Eberhard Wendler recalls, 'they had no running water inside – no electric – the toilet was a tiny hut in the garden with a bucket. And when that was full we took it to the top garden and dug it in. I'd never known anything so primitive.'

In some areas, though, the authorities seem to have made it their business to ensure that the POWs were well treated. Prisoner labour was withdrawn from a cattle farmer in Dorset – the aptly-named Mr Bullock – because of his 'unsatisfactory behaviour to the prisoners over a long period. Complaints were made by the prisoners themselves, by their camp leader and by the British non-commissioned officer in charge of the prisoners.' Elsewhere, prisoners were treated as if they were part of the family. 'The treatment by the farmers was very good, because we were good workers,' says Gunther Wulff. 'Well, I was a farmer's son and knew what I was doing. I did work for Mr Brown in Donnington, and his family almost cried when I left.'

Two men, who had been sent to a farm on a daily basis, state that at first they were required to take their meals in the barn. Later they were invited into the house to eat with the farmer and his household. Five weeks after first arriving they became permanent billetees. 'We worked for our food and a bed to sleep in … We ate at the table with the farmer and his wife as if we were their own sons.'

---

* Sir Brian Horrocks participated in Market Garden, the operation depicted in the film *A Bridge Too Far*, mentioned elsewhere. His character was played by Edward Fox.

13

An Affair of the Heart

Although some prisoners were now living in the midst of British families, the rules against fraternisation still dictated that officially it was illegal for civilians to speak to POWs (except in connection with their work) or offer them food, cigarettes or any other gift, however small.

Werner Völkner recalls the factory where he worked just after the war. 'The women in the factory weren't supposed to fraternise so they couldn't give you a cigarette. But they lit one up for us and put it where we'd see it and pick it up because we were not allowed to have matches or anything like that. Some of them had a sandwich and they'd push it towards you and walk away.' It was not until late 1946 that an easing of these restrictions would take place, and even then any form of 'amorous liaison' was strictly outlawed. But there were many instances where the rules were broken.

In March 1945, while Britain and Germany were still at war, two nursing sisters and three nurses at the Florence Nightingale Hospital in Bury were put on trial for sending letters, 'otherwise than by post', to POWs, and sending cigarettes and an article of clothing. They had met when the Germans had been admitted to hospital for treatment. Detective-Sergeant Stansfield explained that the police had suspected an escape plot at first, but conceded that letters written by 21-year-old defendant Ivy Knott – he coyly described them as 'rather warm' – were of a romantic nature and harmless. Winnie Cunnane, 31 years old, from County Mayo, said, 'Rudolph proposed marriage to me. I didn't answer him, but I didn't refuse.' She explained that she had sent letters and cigarettes to him in the same way as she had to British soldiers who had been patients. She had become attached to the prisoner and admitted to 'a little kissing in the kitchen'.

Sister Margaret Mulvenna told the court, 'I had a high regard for Erich which overcame my better judgement. I hope the consequences will not affect my career.' But they did. She and the others were dismissed from their posts. The two sisters were fined the hefty sum of £15 and two of the nurses were fined smaller amounts.

In September 1946, three women were convicted for giving German POWs articles 'likely to facilitate escape'. One of the women was a German national; another had been a German national prior to her marriage. They had sent a prisoner two parcels containing cigarettes, sweets, chocolates, coffee, cocoa, razor blades, scissors and other seemingly innocent items. The conviction was obtained with the help of evidence from an intelligence officer from the POW camp: with the air of someone divulging the most secret information, he disclosed that 'chocolate was a most important thing to an escaping prisoner'.

Even the smallest displays of friendship could be punished. In May 1946, a woman in Chatham, Kent, was fined £1 for throwing a piece of cake over the wire fence around a POW camp to one of the inmates. To most observers, penalties like these seemed petty and disproportionate. Question were asked in the House of Commons when, in March 1946, another woman received a penalty of £5 for fraternising with a German. The war was over, and since it was no longer an offence for British servicemen to fraternise with German women, why should it be a crime for a woman in Britain to fraternise with a POW?

Lord Nathan told the House of Lords:

> I see in to-day's *Daily Mail* that in a single column there are given, by some curious chance, two instances of fraternization. In one case it is said that the men throw kisses to the young ladies, and great complaint is apparently made about that. In the other case, it is said that the young ladies throw kisses at the men, and there is complaint about that. Indeed, a member of the local council in one of these cases says it is intolerable that this behaviour by Germans should be allowed to go on, and it is time it was stopped.

Whatever the rules said, it was inevitable that sparks would fly when the all-male German POWs ran up against all-female organisations such as the Women's Land Army and the ATS (Auxiliary Territorial Service – the women's branch of the military).*

'We weren't supposed to speak to them, but we did,' says Peter Roth with a twinkle in his eye. After his time in Glen Mill and other transit camps he had been transferred to a farm in Cambridgeshire where the POWs had to dig up and bag carrots. On one occasion Peter was sent over to another group of workers to fetch more sacks. This other group comprised three British men, three Italians and two British women, one of whom was Margaret Stratton. She and Peter were instantly attracted to each other. In camp the next day, Peter picked the six remaining flowers in the tiny garden next to his hut and presented them to Margaret. She in turn gave him a piece of cake and a cigarette, and a clandestine relationship began.

In early 1945, he was sent to a satellite camp at Manea.** This subcamp was unusual in that it was located right in the centre of the village and consequently the prisoners came into more frequent contact with the villagers than at other, more distant POW camps. Peter recalls:

---

*   By the end of the war this organisation had almost 200,000 members who included the Prime Minister's daughter, Mary Churchill, and Princess Elizabeth, the future Queen Elizabeth II.

** The name of the village rhymes with 'rainy'.

The people in Manea were always good to us. We conversed as well as we could. There were always people who tried to be good to you by giving us cigarettes, things like that. When there was a wedding on in the village hall next to the camp and there was food left over they gave it to us. And the women there were crackers over us. They used any excuse to come and bring us some food.

In Gloucestershire, Margaret Stone – a member of the Women's Land Army – cycled every day to her place of work in Andoversford. She often saw a squad of POWs as their lorry passed her on the road, and they used to wave to her.

Conscious of the anti-fraternisation laws, she deliberately avoided them for a time: but finally she decided that there could be no harm in waving back. Next time they saw her, the POWs responded by throwing a note to her. (See plate no. 17)

Some encounters led to headline-grabbing stories. Doris Blake, 25 years of age, had been married to a Twickenham postman for the last five years and had two children. But the marriage was not a happy one and they had separated some time ago. Newspapers would later describe her as 'dark and attractive' – a description borne out by the photographs of her which adorned their pages. She had a 'craving for romantic adventure', it was alleged.

Doris went to live in the country and found a job picking fruit at the Chivers's fruit farm near Haddenham, Cambridgeshire. There she encountered a POW, ex-*Afrika Korps* soldier Alexander Todt. Apparently they had met before the war at either a dance or a tennis match – accounts differ – and recognised each other again straight away. Doris withdrew her life savings of £70 from a Post Office savings account and went with her new boyfriend to London, where they had a 'wonderful time'. They then made for the south-east coast and spent a 'glorious week' in Ramsgate, before travelling to Dover in search of a boat. There in the harbour they espied a gleaming, white, 30ft racing yacht, the *Lalun*. Alexander cut the mooring rope and they set sail for Germany.

'Every ship in the Dover Patrol was yesterday sweeping the Strait for a fast, all-white yacht, in which German prisoners are believed to be heading for the continent,' reported the *Daily Mail*. As more details became known, newspaper editors thought their lucky day had come. 'Dark, attractive' Doris had eloped with an escaped prisoner said to be none other than the handsome son of Fritz Todt, Hitler's Minister of Works, the man responsible for building the Siegfried Line. (This made a good story even better but was untrue. Fritz Todt's only son, a Luftwaffe pilot, had been killed in action during the war.)

As the yacht neared the French coast, Doris and Alexander ran into difficulties and made an unscheduled stop at Calais. By now, news of their escape from Britain had reached the French authorities and, as they tried to leave the port again, they were arrested. Doris was taken to the police station in Boulogne where an enterprising reporter from the *Daily Mirror* interviewed her.

'I'm not sorry for what I've done, I'm only sorry I was caught,' she told him with disarming candour.

French officials dismissed the matter with a Gallic shrug. 'It is not a very serious affair – an affair of the heart,' a police official said. 'You know how we look upon these things in France.'

But Doris and Alexander were about to discover how the authorities looked upon these things in Britain. The owner of the yacht, a retired Trinity House pilot, told Dover Magistrates' Court that the vessel was 'irreplaceable in these days'. Doris maintained that she had intended to send money to the owner to reimburse him.

'It may sound crazy but it's true,' she said. The prosecution agreed with the first part of that assertion but not the second. Firstly, she had no money to pay for the yacht, which was worth £500. Secondly, she did not even know the identity or address of the owner.

She was found guilty of stealing the boat and was also convicted under an obscure wartime regulation forbidding British civilians from leaving the country without authorisation. She received a one-month prison sentence in Holloway jail. Todt was court-martialled for fraternising with Mrs Blake and for his part in the theft of the yacht.

Escapades such as these in no way diminished the surge of public sympathy for the German prisoners. In fact, the POWs came to be seen as ordinary people with all the usual human needs, failings and aspirations. With less than a month to go before Christmas, Tom Skeffington-Lodge, MP for Bedford, asked whether special arrangements could be made for German prisoners to spend Christmas Day in British homes if they were invited to do so.

'I do not at present contemplate any relaxation of the current rules,' Frederick Bellenger replied.

Bellenger had recently been promoted to the post of Secretary of State for War. He had served in the British army of occupation in Germany after the First World War and was married to a German woman, Marion Theresa Stollwerck, daughter of one of Germany's principal chocolate manufacturers. And as his colleagues were all too aware, he had narrowly escaped being taken prisoner himself at Dunkirk. Fearing, perhaps, that others might accuse him of being too soft with the German prisoners, he adopted a fair, but noticeably firm stance towards them.

Skeffington-Lodge pressed his point home:

'Will the right honourable gentleman bear in mind that it is important to return our prisoners of war to Germany as an example of our British way and purpose, and that the suggestion in my question will do very much to achieve that end?'

'We are certainly doing a lot towards that end, but I am afraid that I cannot add anything to the answer I have given.'

Although the government would not allow any relaxation in the rules, in late 1946 it did introduce improvements in the way POWs were paid for their work. Prisoners whose output was good were to receive a bonus equal to their base pay. Those who consistently showed themselves to be good workers were given a further 3s.

Basic pay	6s
Productivity bonus	6s
Consistent good work bonus	3s
TOTAL	15s

The prisoners' wages were thus increased by up to 150 per cent, although they were still paid only in token money, not in cash. The bonus element would not be available to the prisoner to spend in Britain but would be credited to his account; the money would be handed to him in German currency upon repatriation. Alternatively, it could be remitted straight away to family or dependants in Germany, this being the first time that prisoners were allowed to send money home.

As Christmas drew near, Bellenger announced a last-minute U-turn. 'Arrangements are being made to allow well-conducted prisoners of war to take unescorted walks within a radius of five miles of their camp or billet until lighting-up time, to converse with members of the public, and, subject to permission from their commandant, to accept invitations to private houses within the 5-mile radius.' (See plate no. 18) However, the POWs were still forbidden to enter shops, cafés, cinemas, pubs or other public premises.

Richard Stokes asked whether this was just for Christmas.

'It deals not only with Christmas time, but after Christmas,' Bellenger replied. 'I think those honourable gentlemen who have a sense of proportion will admit that this is a considerable advance.'

Unfortunately, for some POWs this proclamation came too late to be of any use. Theo Dengel says:

> It was a complete fiasco. Typical War Office! It was announced just before Christmas and the camp commandant was furious about the way they'd handled it. He got the instructions on 21 December – he knew it was coming, but he hadn't got the details. The rule was that the British family had to write to him and apply for permission to have a named POW to stay the weekend with them, and the Commandant had to write back and confirm. Well, there just wasn't time. In the camp of 500 people nobody went. The only ones to benefit were about 100 POWs who were living with farmers.

Moreover, the new rules were little use to POWs whose camp was more than 5 miles from the nearest village or town. In those places where the scheme did come to fruition, though, the event was a moving, heartwarming one. On Christmas Day 'queues of cars' formed outside the camps as British families came to collect a prisoner whose name they had been given, but whom they had never met. The War Office insisted on doing everything by the book and hosts were required to sign a receipt for 'one live body' before taking the POW with them to their homes. Two thousand Germans were invited by the Dean and Chapter of Peterborough Cathedral to a special service in German, and POWs up and down the country attended local church services near their camps. In Walderslade, Kent, where local residents had at first protested on learning that a POW camp would be sited near their homes, there was a distinct change of heart: 'Prisoners will share the family fireside and a joint church service will be held.'

Theo Dengel relates that Bishop Bell (the Bishop of Chichester) invited all of the POWs at North Mundham Camp to a special Christmas service at the Cathedral. However, Chichester Council, despite the lifting of restrictions generally, had banned POWs from the city. The men were not even allowed to march as a unit the three miles to the Cathedral and, as no transport could be arranged in time, the invitation had to be reluctantly declined.

On the other hand, Bruno Liebich still enjoys vivid memories of that Christmas:

We were told, 'If you want to go and visit somebody you can be invited. It will help if you speak English.' Sometimes someone in the family spoke German, but usually it was the other way round. My best friend, Horst, spoke good English and said, 'Yes, I'll go,' and he finished up in Harpenden with Mr and Mrs Herbert and their two teenage daughters. Horst had a good time and they asked him whether he had a friend to go with him – and that was me. Next time I went, too. I was very shy at the time and didn't speak much English. But I was curious; I was all for it. I wanted to meet the locals, you see. So I was invited for dinner in an English home – 110 Station Road, Harpenden, I still remember that. It was the first time in a British house. We wore British army uniform dyed a reddish colour. That's the best we had; we had nothing else. We went in and all shook hands. I think in a way I was scared in case I put my foot wrong or something. But it was a great event to have happened – not many people can claim that, being invited to a British home as a prisoner. And I carried on having a connection with Mary Herbert for quite a while until she passed away.

Eberhard Wendler's diary records his own experiences of the day:

25 December 1946:   We celebrated Christmas under the flickering light of the Christmas tree, far from our homes. In the afternoon we were invited to tea with Mr Frank Smy.

For Eberhard, too, it was the first time he had set foot in a house since leaving his family home in January 1944, almost three years previously:

The farm where I was billeted was very remote and the only civilians I came into contact with were the farm manager and, very occasionally, the farmer. Mr Smy was the farm manager's son-in-law; his job was to deliver coal with a horse and cart. I only knew him slightly. I went with two others from the camp. I was shy and apprehensive, but in fact we got on well. They made us feel at home.

Josef Kox was asked by the farmer on whose farm he was billeted to join the family on Christmas Day. Josef and his comrade demurred, feeling that the farmer was simply being polite and would much rather have spent the time alone with his wife and children. 'You're going to have Christmas dinner with us,' the farmer insisted. 'You are two of the family.'

Heinz Elfner says:

It was a wonderful act of generosity and we all appreciated it. However, there were not enough Germans to go round! We were not allowed on public transport so our English officer had to drive us. I can hardly describe my feelings when we were invited to sit at the table for the Christmas meal. There was still food rationing, but it was evident that these people had made a special effort. The master of the house was carving the turkey and saw to it that their guests received an extra large portion. I was close to tears when I started to eat. This act of human kindness shown to me by those few people represented the general feeling of the majority of the entire nation at that time. I shall never forget this to my dying days.

It was a truly memorable Christmas for 20-year-old Horst Rossberg, too. He says:

As we entered the house we stopped and then something unbelievable happened – the two daughters, Reené and Margot came up to us and greeted us with a kiss. We did not know what was happening and I think we had very red faces because for both of us it was the first time in our lives that a girl had kissed us.

Prisoners in some areas showed their appreciation by making gifts for their hosts. In Colchester, POWs made 1,000 carved toys out of scrap material for distribution to children.

Although the arrangements had been left too late to benefit some POWs, as Theo Dengel indicated, a similar scheme was operated the next year. 'At Christmas 1947 more than half the camp went. By that time, restrictions had been eased – you didn't need to apply for permission, you just said to the commandant, or his clerk, "I've got an invitation, I'll be out on such and such days." That was it.'

Wilhelm Kranefeld wrote a letter to *The Times*:

I am one of the German prisoners of war who have been invited by an English family for Christmas Day. 'My' family … gave me a written invitation; they gave me the money for the fare; they told me it wouldn't be Christmas for them if I wouldn't be with them. The Commandant of our camp granted my application at once … the staff of the railway company was kind and helpful … and all the people in the trains. No sign of hatred, of curiosity, only smiles, politeness, hearty conversation, a lot of small gifts – I cannot express my feelings about this. But in no way was I prepared for what was done for me during Christmas Day by the family. I was like a dear part of it. Where they were, I was too, what they had I had too, and where they went, I went too. It was like a fairy dream.

At Morpeth Congregational Church a choir of POWs gave a choral recital. 'The tunes in many instances were familiar if the words were sung in their native language and, without exception, those privileged to be present were loud in their praise of the rendering of *Silent Night, Holy Night*.'

In contrast to these peaceful scenes, civilians in Germany were undergoing great deprivation. On Christmas Eve, *The Times* included a piece on the situation there:

HUNGER AND DESPAIR IN GERMANY

Major Lloyd described the picture in Germany as extremely grim. It was almost impossible, he said, to exaggerate how utterly shattered was the economy and how complete the collapse of morale in the German people. He saw no evidence of direct starvation, but there was unquestionably great hunger and great despair. The people were desperately short of shoes ... The whole economy of the country seemed to be based on a cigarette barter system; with a few dozen cigarettes one could buy anything.

As the Minister of War had explained, the dispensations granted to the POWs were intended to remain permanently in force after Christmas. Prisoners would be able to roam freely within five miles of their camp and visit civilians. They did not have to return to camp until 10 p.m. They were now permitted to correspond by post with civilians (including the Member of Parliament for their area), but were not supposed to write to newspapers, government departments or businesses (though some evidently did so). They could visit local sights and go into churches.

Now that the men were 'on parade', as it were, outside the camp, one commandant had a large mirror placed near the main exit as a not-so-subtle hint that he expected 'his' prisoners to look smart when mingling with the public.

Immediately after Christmas, Werner Völkner decided to take advantage of the new concessions. As a young man in Germany he had enjoyed reading detective novels set in the Home Counties of England. Some featured a character named Lady Maude, who served dainty cucumber sandwiches to her guests in the parlour. One day, he dreamed, he would travel to England to see these stately homes and castles, and witness this genteel lifestyle for himself. Now his chance had come in the most unexpected way. As a prisoner near Guildford, he was only a stone's throw from some of the towns mentioned in the novels.

He put on his best uniform. The prisoners had all managed to 'acquire' two uniforms – one for ordinary wear and another which they kept for 'best' (though this still had patches in a contrasting colour to identify them as POWs). They would press their outfit by placing it under the straw mattress on their bed. To get a good, sharp crease an old army trick was employed – first they applied soap to the inside of the trouser legs before pressing them.

These preparations completed, he made the short journey to Woking with three comrades who spoke some English. Werner says:

> We were walking along near the station and were looking at all the suits in a tailor's shop window, when somebody shouted, 'Hey, Jerries!' We said to one another, 'Shall we go?' and we decided to go and see what he had to say. And the Englishman said, 'Well, where did you serve?' and one of the POWs said '*Afrika Korps*'. The Englishman had a stiff leg – he said 'Africa? – that's where I was wounded, come on, come on in.'
>
> So we went in and had a cup of tea and – guess what – cucumber sandwich. It was such a disappointment, nothing like I'd imagined. But these poor people lived on ration cards and that was the only thing they could offer. He got out a packet of cigarettes and they were talking together in English, and he turned to me and said, 'You speak English?' and I said, 'Yes, I smoke.' It was all I could think of. It was the first time I'd been in an English home – 'Come into the parlour,' you know. It was more than a surprise – and then I thought, 'Why did we fight?' It was something unusual and very much appreciated by the four of us to be invited into somebody's home, and there was quite a conversation when we told everyone in the camp.

At the farm where Werner was employed, a representative of the Surrey War Agricultural Executive Committee recognised the value of Werner's military training. 'I told him I was in a tank division and he said, "All right, you can drive the tractor." So I was driving the tractor and the others were loading the things up, and at first I had quite a job trying to reverse with a trailer.'

Werner was later sent to work at a market garden, where he and his British workmates became firm friends. He says:

> There was a chap, Mr Adams, who had lost both legs in the First World War at Gallipoli, and he wheeled himself in a little three-wheeled vehicle. He lived on the farm and made the boxes for the vegetables. All the others we called by their first names. Bill Huggett from Kent, was the top tractor driver; he'd also been in the First World War. Then there was Nobby, the foreman. We had another chap whose name was Bob; he'd been a sergeant in the RAF. One day when we were having dinner Bob said, 'You *bloody* Jerries, you're full of bleeding tricks!

Bob, it seems, had somehow acquired a German BMW motorbike, a remnant from the war. He said, 'I got on it, I was driving it, changed gear and gave it full throttle and the damned thing went backwards!'

Werner continues:

> Bob had a young brother, Dick, who was about seventeen or eighteen, who said, 'Look at me, my boots are falling to bits and because of the rationing I can't get any decent clothing to wear.' So our interpreter said, 'Clean your boots up really nicely and put a good shine on them, give them to me and I'll get you another pair.' So we went back to the clothing store in camp and we said, 'We can't work in this. We need new boots and clothes.' And we were given a new pair of boots and a British battledress.

Dick was delighted with this 'new' outfit and didn't even seem to notice the telltale patches of a POW uniform.

'We watched young Dick as he got on to a bus, and the driver said, "You f****** German get off this f****** bus! I'm not having any bloody Jerries on *my* bus." And young Dick wasn't short on swear words either, and told the bus driver where to go. And we all stood there laughing, and he said to us, "Haven't you got a bloody jacket without bloody patches?" It was wonderful.'

Some bus drivers made a point of refusing to carry POWs – even after the Germans were officially allowed to use public transport. Other passengers on the bus would frequently protest at this discrimination, and in the face of public pressure the driver would sometimes back down.

Eduard Winkler experienced contrasting impressions of British civilians. At first he had been held at a camp near Leicester. 'We only went out of the camp twice. The population there was rather anti-German. They spat on us and threw stones, which was rather disconcerting.' But he was later transferred to a camp at Caperby in rural North Yorkshire. He goes on:

> We used to go up on the moors and sometimes the farmer took a gun and we'd shoot rabbits. Once the farmer handed me the gun while he stopped for a cup of tea. I saw a rabbit and shot it and he said, 'You *can* shoot!' And I said, 'I was in the German army!' From then on he brought an overcoat for me [to conceal the POW uniform] and another gun and we both used to shoot rabbits. To our surprise, most of us were invited to tea by the inhabitants of the village. The people were very friendly. It was completely different from Leicester. I've no idea why it was so different. Perhaps they were bombed heavily in Leicester.

Bombing was only part of the story. While people in the cities and towns were deprived of food, those in the country often had direct access to unrationed eggs, milk, meat and vegetables. The effects of the German U-boat blockade were, as a consequence, much less keenly felt in rural areas. It may also be that the slower pace of rural life simply made village dwellers more tolerant than their urban counterparts.

14

Brush Up Your English

Within the camps, the men organised some sports and pastimes for themselves, while other activities were arranged by the authorities. In most camps a hut was set aside as a combined cinema and theatre, with projectors and other equipment provided by bodies such as the Red Cross and the YMCA.

The British camp administration supplied the films to be shown, but finding appropriate material was never easy. To begin with, unless the film was in German the majority of the prisoners would not understand the dialogue. But the difficulty with pictures made in Germany was that film production had come under the direct control of Josef Goebbels, Hitler's Minister for Propaganda: the material, especially from the early war years, carried a strong pro-Nazi message that was entirely unsuitable for the British to show to the POWs.

However, as the tide of the war had turned against Germany, and public morale there reached a low point – particularly after the setbacks in Russia – film-makers endeavoured to make lighter, more entertaining movies. As a young German woman recalls, 'After Stalingrad, theatres were closed, but cinemas stayed open because they showed a lot of revue and variety films to keep the populace happy. They were films that had nothing to do with politics – I remember films about Mozart and Schumann – they were rather anodyne and harmless, just for entertainment.' Many of these productions were set in a distant, more romantic era; audiences could allow themselves to be distracted, if only for a short time, from the concerns and fears of wartime.

And so it was that these movies – designed for an entirely different purpose – proved to be ideal fare for POWs. Eberhard Wendler's diary shows that he visited the camp cinema just before and just after the end of the war:

22 April 1945: a film was shown in the dining hall (Friedrich Schiller).

6 May 1945: we had another film (Alexander Röscher).

4 June 1945: another film: *Ich vertraue Dir meine Frau an* [I Trust to You my Wife], with Heinz Rühmann and Lil Adina.*

---

* Heinz Rühmann was one of Germany's most popular entertainers. When the Nazi party came to power he divorced his wife because she was Jewish, and joined the National Socialist Party. *I Trust to You my Wife*, a 1943 musical comedy, was the only German film in which the Czech film actress Adina Mandlová appeared. Her name was deemed by the Nazi regime to be too Slavic and was altered for the purpose to Lil Adina. Another of Heinz Rühmann's films, *Die Feuerzangenbowle* [The Punch Bowl], is also known to have been shown in British camps: in Germany it has a cult following to this day.

Eberhard's diary does not show him attending any other films at High Garrett camp: the reason for this is unknown, but quite possibly the limited supply of suitable material simply ran out.

Britain's attempts to use films as part of the re-education process, however, fell flat. The prisoners immediately realised that they were being 'brainwashed'; the government-produced films were, in any case, of poor quality, and audiences quickly dwindled away.

The Germans are a musical people. Choirs and orchestras engaged the prisoners' attention in a way that films could not. 'You'd be surprised at the talent that was in the camp,' says Eberhard Wendler. 'A concert was staged. The commandant attended and sat at the front – he seemed to enjoy the show. The singing! The choir sang songs about home and many of us had tears in our eyes. We bought musical instruments. One of the satellite camps nearby had an orchestra which went around and gave performances to the British public.' Funds for the instruments were usually provided out of the camp welfare fund, bankrolled with the profits from the canteen. The Red Cross, the YMCA and other organisations also provided sheet music and instruments, as well as writing materials, books, magazines and craft tools.

Plays, musical comedies and even operas were presented. Theo Dengel, in his memoir, *D is for Destiny*, describes the set-up at North Mundham Camp around 1947:

> The excellent facilities provided by the large theatre/recreation building were now being well used. When there were no organised film shows or lectures, the hall was used by the men in the evenings or at weekends, to play cards, chess or dominoes; there was even a dartboard – although I am not sure how well that was used, as the Germans were not familiar with this game … Captain Brill took great care to ensure that these areas were always well-decorated and furnished. He put Willi Sauer in charge of organising the use of the theatre; he could not have found a more suitable man for this task. Willi's official job was that of camp painter and decorator. Before the war he had been a professional artist, and had a real flair for organising events in the theatre. Early in 1947, with the help and encouragement of Captain Brill, Willi had obtained the loan of gramophone records and a set of large puppets, together with the appropriate scenery, of the opera *Madame Butterfly*. With some volunteer helpers he eventually put on a performance of the full opera using the puppets; first for the POWs, then to an invited audience of villagers and their friends. It was a huge success; the whole presentation was very professionally performed. We had a photographer from Chichester to take photos of the performance, and the local reporter from the *Chichester Observer* produced an appreciative write-up.

In some camps, when the prisoners put on a dramatic performance in the camp theatre, they made all the costumes and props themselves. 'The members of the orchestra wore "dinner jackets" – uniforms dyed black. The only thing we couldn't make ourselves was women's shoes – those we had to cadge from civilians!'

Prisoners with the necessary skills, such as tailors, watchmakers and shoemakers, could sell their services to other prisoners, as mentioned. Thus, from the beginning, many activities were not so much pastimes as small-scale commercial undertakings. POWs carried out useful tasks within the camp in exchange for welcome money (in the form of tokens) or cigarettes. When contact with the public became a possibility – predominantly after Christmas 1946 – the sale of home-made items took off and their production was transformed into a business. Trade with the civilian sector brought in some real money – something the POWs had not had before, and their purchasing power thus increased significantly in terms of the range and quantities of goods they could acquire.

While working on the land, the men tied the bales of straw with twine, and soon found alternative uses for this handy product, as Werner Völkner describes:

> We nicked lengths of twine that were left over and took them back to camp. We hammered a nail into the wooden door and started plaiting the twine, and somebody had a sack needle and we made all sorts of things – slippers, handbags and shopping bags. And then we used to sell them. Somebody had the idea of producing them in red and green. By then we had connections with the outside and you could get little tubs of coloured dyes made by Dylon.* We had tin cans with a fire underneath, boiling the water, and we'd put the Dylon in there and then the plaits so we could then sell handbags with colour in them, which brought in even more money.
>
> One man had been in the *Afrika Korps* and still had some Egyptian pounds. And one day he asked through the interpreter, 'Is it possible to get them changed into English money?' and the boss changed them for him at the bank. And because we knew they might be spotted at the camp he rolled up the bundle of British banknotes and hid them in the handlebars of the bicycle. They never looked in there! Another ruse the prisoners of war got up to!**

Some prisoners had been assigned to the task of dismantling old or badly damaged aircraft with a view to recycling the materials. Otto Funk served in this capacity, and recalled that the POWs interpreted the concept of 'recycling' to suit their own ends. Using scrap metal, they fabricated cages for rabbits and sold these to local civilians. Toys were made out of wood and metal. This unofficial business was conducted with Germanic efficiency, the prisoners being divided into specialist teams: one man was responsible for scrounging the materials; others would fabricate the products; a further group sold the finished products to the public.

At Christmas 1946, POWs had asked permission to donate handmade toys to be placed around the Christmas tree in Durham Cathedral for later distribution to

---

*   Dylon was a new product which had been introduced in 1946.
** See also p.155 for rules governing cash holdings.

children in local hospitals. They met with a Scrooge-like response from Frederick Bellenger. 'Free distribution on a large scale of toys made by German prisoners is open to considerable objection while the output of the British toy industry is restricted,' he told the House of Commons.

'The manufacture of a few toys in a camp workshop cannot, by any stretch of the imagination, affect the toy industry,' another MP retorted.

A few months later, Richard Stokes exhorted Bellenger to encourage the production of goods, not just as gifts, but as an opportunity for the Germans to use their skills to earn more than the pitiful pay they were given for agricultural work. 'Many of these men are good craftsmen and something ought to be done to enable them to dispose of the things they produce. There is no reason why those things should not be sold, bearing in mind the shortages in this country. They make beautiful toys which could be sold, and the money could go to them individually – or a portion of it could go to them and the rest go for the benefit of the camp.' (This proposal was never adopted: not officially, at any rate.)

A report commissioned by the German government after the war praises the 'satisfactory' and at times 'outstanding' facilities provided in British camps for sport and games. Helmut Bantz had been an accomplished footballer and gymnast in pre-war Germany, and even after he had been taken prisoner his passion for sport was undiminished. 'We played a lot of sport in the camp, especially football and athletics. We built a sandpit in our garden for the long jump and erected high jump stands … It was so good even our English guards were thrilled.'

The popularity of camp entertainments and pastimes had declined, however, when prisoners began to work on farms. Work gave them an outlet for their energy and they returned to camp in the evenings often too tired to participate in anything strenuous. Finally, the introduction of satellite camps, hostels and billeting meant that up to half of all POWs were living at some distance from the main camp, making it harder still for them to use sporting and other facilities.

Pastimes *within* the camp suffered a further decline in popularity when the Germans were granted new concessions, such as permission to travel more widely. The attractions of mixing with members of the local community greatly outweighed anything that could be provided within the confines of a barbed wire compound. Theo Dengel describes how these changes evolved:

The civilian Camp Labour Officer [Ted Page]… held regular, well-attended weekly meetings in the recreation room to discuss any topic the men might raise, in particular about the British way of life, the working of democracy in people's everyday life, etc. The Camp Commandant's clerk and interpreter, who had been to the study course at Wilton Park assisted … [In 1947] attendance declined rapidly; men preferred to relax in the evenings and enjoy the exceptional summer weather; at weekends most had found a gardening job to earn some English money. Others were busy meeting their girlfriends. Erwin used every opportunity to meet up with his Land Army girlfriend … and Karl, camp duties permitting, had a weekend job in a Batchmere nursery; in the evenings, when he was free, he cycled to Batchmere to discuss philosophical and religious topics with the owners, Eunice and Ron Clark. Talks in the camp had to take second place. During the late autumn months, participation in discussion groups declined further; there were constant changes with many men being transferred to Billingshurst to await repatriation or transfer to another camp. The Foreign Office reporters appeared unaware of the real reasons why their 're-education programme' faltered.

By enrolling in study groups the prisoners could pass the time while furthering their education. By far the most popular classes were those in the English language: large numbers of prisoners realised that one advantage of being a POW in Britain was the opportunity to learn a language which was spoken in many parts of the world. (Significant numbers of prisoners, especially those who had had a glimpse of life in North America, conjured with the prospect of emigrating to English-speaking countries such as the USA and Canada upon their release, while South Africa, Australia and New Zealand may have also come into their reckoning.)

One day at the camp guardhouse Eberhard Wendler noticed a red fire bucket hanging on a hook. He turned to a friend who spoke some English and pointed at the stencilled lettering.

'What's that word?'

'Fire,' the friend replied. It was pronounced like the German word, *Feier*, which means 'festival' or 'celebration'.

Eberhard shook his head. 'How can I possibly learn the language of a people who don't even use the letters of the alphabet properly?'

But he was keen to try, and enrolled in a class organised within the camp. The instructors were, in fact, other German POWs who had to pass a test before the British authorities allowed them to teach others. Eberhard attended what appears to have been his first tuition in the language in early November 1944, less than two months after arriving at his permanent camp. The class later became a twice-weekly event. He purchased several study aids, as his diary shows:

15 March 1945: Bought myself the book *Englisch in ein paar Tagen* [English in a Few Days] – both volumes – for four shillings.

15 April 1945: Ordered an English textbook.

14 May 1945: Bought a book – *Brush up your English* – for 3s 6d.

16 June 1945: Received from our English teacher the book, *Kleine Englische Sprachlehre* [Pocket English Grammar].

Unfortunately the prisoner who was teaching English was transferred elsewhere and the lessons ended abruptly. From that point onward, Eberhard studied on his own initiative and gradually learned the language by himself.

Arthur Riegel attended Norton Camp in Nottinghamshire where a training establishment for teachers had been set up with the assistance of the YMCA. 'Norton offered me more opportunities than I could possibly have dreamed of as a POW,' he later wrote. While there, he also improved his language abilities and his skills in electronics. The library contained 20,000 books on every imaginable subject, and the camp administration deliberately avoided filling the huts to capacity so that the prisoners had more room to study. The YMCA later announced that 600 POWs had graduated from this academy and would go on to teach in Germany; another 200 took their *Abitur* in preparation for attending a German university after their release.*

A special academy was formed in association with the University of Hamburg so that prisoners could study in Britain for their medical degree. German doctors within the camps found that with low incidences of sickness – only one in 500 prisoners was ill – they had little to occupy themselves, and asked for books on specialised areas of medicine such as paediatrics to study in advance of their eventual return to Germany.

The men's spiritual needs were administered to by clergymen who had been conscripted into the *Wehrmacht* and were themselves prisoners of war. (In the later stages of the war, Hitler did not allow chaplains, as such, in the field: they therefore joined the forces as soldiers, ostensibly in support roles such as catering.)

Churches near the camps also tried to help, despite the language barrier. Among Eberhard Wendler's diary entries are:

28 January 1945: I attended Catholic worship. There was a German priest from London.

16 June 1946: We went to chapel for the first time by car.

19 October 1946: An English priest visited us at our farm and gave each of us *The New Testament* in German.

When attending local churches, the prisoners were surprised to hear the hymn 'Glorious Things of Thee are Spoken' being sung to the same tune as the German national anthem, 'Deutschland, Deutschland Über Alles'. But the impression left by the Germans on the British churchgoers could be equally profound. Julian Barrett recalls the morning of Christmas Day 1945:

* The *Abitur* is roughly equivalent to Britain's A-levels. Young people's education in Germany was severely disrupted by the war and by the requirement to take part in Hitler Youth, *Arbeitsdienst* and similar duties. A certificate was given to those engaged in such activities, entitling them to take an accelerated course of studies after the war, leading to the *Abitur*. However, this certificate was not recognised by the post-war government, and students wishing to take the examination were obliged to start again.

We arrived at the church and discovered that these prisoners were also at the Mass. This was a surprise. After all, weren't these the agents of the devil as we'd been led to believe? They were seated at the back under guard. Later, during the distribution of communion, they stood up and gave the most beautiful and moving rendition of 'Silent Night' (in German naturally) I had ever heard or have heard since … it taught me a lesson about the utter waste and futility of war, that we are all human beings, and all of the same race.

At harvest time the next year over 1,000 POWs attended 'a thanksgiving service in Durham Cathedral in recognition of their assistance with the harvest. The dean (Dr C.A. Alington) in a message of welcome said they had worked splendidly.'

The POWs were helped in many ways by bodies such as the Society of Friends (Quakers), the Salvation Army, and other churches and religious organisations. Dr Bell, the Bishop of Chichester, campaigned for better conditions and early repatriation for the prisoners: as a result of his strenuous and forceful efforts he was often branded 'a thorn in the side' of the government.

As with most other activities, however, the amount of time spent by the prisoners on religious study and worship decreased once the stricter regulations and rules were repealed. When the prisoners were free to go outside the camps and to mix with civilians, attendances at services declined noticeably.

The factors which shaped the experience of officer POWs differed from those affecting the enlisted men. Significantly, officers could not be forced to work, although some chose to do so. Thus they were spared the backbreaking agricultural labour which the other ranks had to endure and either did no work at all or carried out tasks of a physically undemanding nature. Some improved their English; one began to learn Chinese and eventually became highly proficient in the language. A team of officers at Featherstone Park Camp helped British experts undertake valuable archaeological work on the nearby Hadrian's Wall and on a Roman bridge on the River Tyne.

The Bishop of Sheffield cited a camp in his diocese where an architectural school was established by prisoners:

About fourteen or fifteen of them are qualified professional architects, and they are employing their time in training younger fellows in the elements of the profession. Some have been prisoners for a very long time. They have to try to make jobs for themselves. I was allowed by the camp commandant, who is immensely proud of his school in the camp, to set a specific task. This they did, and did with a degree of competence and ability which won the unqualified admiration of one or two of the most distinguished architects in our country.

It was, he added, a great pity that such talent was going to waste.

Improved incentives for working prisoners were introduced in June 1947. Those working a minimum of 40 hours per week who qualified for the previously announced bonuses would receive 3 shillings of the bonus in token money instead of as a credit. 'Prisoners of war who work satisfactorily' could now change 50 per cent of their token money into sterling: this meant that, for the first time, they could legally have cash in their possession, although this was limited to £2 for security reasons.

	TOKEN MONEY	BONUS CREDIT
Previous arrangement	6s	9s
New arrangement	9s*	6s

(*of which 4s 6d was convertible into cash)

Along with the improved pay and bonuses came a further easing of discipline. German prisoners were increasingly encouraged to integrate with local communities – even in Chichester, where the council had formerly banned them from the city, as Theo Dengel explains:

It was somewhat ironic that in February or March 1947 Chichester City Council officials needed to telephone the Commandant to request the help of a contingent of prisoners to clear the city's main streets of the heavy snow which had effectively blocked all traffic through the town … about 200 men were issued with shovels, provided by the City Council, to clear the central thoroughfares: South and North Street, East and West Street around the old Market Cross. I recall 3–4-ft-high walls of snow piled up at the edge of the pavements. Perhaps this action helped to persuade the city fathers to become a little more friendly, as within a few weeks the restrictions concerning POWs visiting Chichester were lifted by the Council.

While the terrible weather persisted well into March, the government's attitude towards the prisoners thawed a little, with the announcement of yet more concessions. POW uniforms with patches were to be phased out and replaced by standard British uniforms dyed a chocolate brown colour. (This took rather longer than hoped because of a shortage of cloth.) Individual commandants were given the authority to allow prisoners to travel beyond the previous 5-mile limit, but only 'to reach a special amenity, such as a town, otherwise out of bounds'. However, prisoners 'of exemplary character' would be allowed to go further than this. The men could now enter private homes, if invited, without seeking their commandant's consent. They could go to football matches in organised parties at the invitation of the organisers. Attendance at approved educational courses outside the camps would now be permitted. And POW bands could 'entertain their friends in return for hospitality', though following a protest from the Musicians' Union they could not charge for admission to such performances. German prisoners had given a charity concert in aid of an East Grinstead children's home but when they announced their intention to give a second performance in a nearby village, the Union had vigorously objected. Local MP, Colonel Sir Ralph Clarke, raised the matter in Parliament.

'Of course, while we are not in the hands of the Musicians' Union or any other union,' replied Emanuel Shinwell MP, 'we must pay due regard to their representations.'

Colonel Clarke drily retorted, 'Does the Minister realise that a charity concert at which there is no charge for admission is of very little use?'

The prisoners of war had previously been banned from going into cinemas. But Eduard Winkler circumvented this rule. 'I met various people in Withernsea,' he recalls. 'There used to be a picture-house manager who was a member of the International Lions Club, and the first time I went into the town he invited me to his house for tea. He used to keep a raincoat in the foyer of the cinema and I used to put it on to go and see the pictures.'

When the new rules came in, such ploys were no longer necessary. POWs would henceforth be permitted to use shops, cinemas, restaurants and public transport within five miles of their camp, though the ban on visiting pubs never was lifted. Theo Dengel remembers that it took a while for the public to get used to these changes. 'Some shops and cafés, and for a short time the Odeon cinema, displayed signs: "Germans not welcome". Well, that was their privilege, but eventually, by mid-summer 1947 all these signs had also disappeared.'

When two POWs reached the front of the cinema queue in Spalding, Lincolnshire, only to discover that they did not have enough cash for tickets, local citizens in the queue did a 'whip-round' and gave them the necessary money. Karl-Heinz Decker took advantage of the new dispensations to visit his local cinema with another POW. In those days there was, of course, no smoking ban and the two Germans each lit one of the special cigarettes issued to POWs by the War Office. These were of such a special and distinctive blend that questions had been asked about them in Parliament. Major Beamish asked Mr Bellenger 'of what tobacco *or other ingredients* these cigarettes are made'? [Author's emphasis.]

'They are made of a good blend of Greek and Turkish tobaccos and nothing else,' replied the Secretary of State for War.

'They were absolutely diabolical,' Karl-Heinz remembers. 'There was no name on them and we don't know what they were.' As soon as they had lit up, someone in the audience tapped Karl-Heinz on the shoulder and asked him if he would mind very much extinguishing his cigarette, as the smell was causing distress to those present.

For some time now, Theo Dengel's relationship with his parents had come under a certain amount of strain. He had disagreed with his father as to how his education and career would unfold once he returned to Germany. If he wanted a good job he would have to go back to square one and study again for his *Abitur* but, having spent so long in the army and as a POW, he was already in his early twenties. 'Initially I had quite a hang-up about it. I was very upset with the whole situation because I didn't fancy going back to grammar school for three years before university. And my father was nearing retirement age and I couldn't see how he could finance four or five years at university.'

Despite these disagreements Theo wrote home regularly and at length. It dawned on him that by typing his letters he could get more words on to each sheet of paper, and so he came to an understanding with one of the clerks. 'Hermann used to let me in to the Labour Office. I did some typing there and generally sat around.' During one of these unofficial visits Theo bumped into the camp's Chief Labour Officer, Ted Page, who had been sent there in late 1945 or early 1946, when North Mundham had been converted into a satellite camp for the ever-increasing numbers of German POWs. He lived at the camp, where he was the only civilian. Theo says:

> I had a lot of respect for him and he became a very good friend. The camp had been built for the Canadian Air Force and the commandant and all the Brits lived right in the middle of the camp. It was most extraordinary for a POW camp, but that was the atmosphere there. The commandant, Captain Brill, had a beautiful bungalow and had his own batman there and Ted Page shared living quarters with him. But the Captain never spoke to him and when I got a bit more friendly with Ted I asked him what was wrong between him and Captain Brill. He told me, 'I'm a conscientious objector and he's a regular army officer.'

Ted got to know the men well and knew how to get the best out of them. Hermann and another clerk, Kurt, 'were anxious to please,' Ted wrote, 'and I knew immediately that it would go easily'. At length, Theo was interviewed for one of the clerk's jobs and joined the team as Labour Organiser under Ted Page's supervision.

When POWs were sent to work on a farm, the farmer had to fill in a timesheet, which he returned to the Labour Office. One of Theo's first duties was to check these papers. He was also expected to answer the telephone and deal with the many comments, queries and complaints which came into the Labour Office:

> The farmers wanted cheap labour. If you went to a particular farm as one of a small group, the understanding was that the farmer would provide a drink at lunchtime. Some did and some didn't. When they didn't it caused a lot of ill feeling. And a lot of the work was traditionally regarded as piecework in the farming world. Hoeing sugar beet, weeding, lifting potatoes and beet. The farmers expected POWs to do that and weren't prepared to pay extra. POWs only received 1s per day when the average farmworker's wages were £4 a week. A shilling only bought you about four cigarettes in the canteen, so there was no incentive whatsoever to work hard. And Ted Page got a lot of complaints – it got so bad at one stage that I refused to answer the telephone. He spent half his time fending off farmers. He said, 'Look, be sensible.

If you want the chaps to work piecework make an arrangement – quite unofficially – that you pay them a bit extra. It's between you and the men whatever private arrangement you make.' Some listened and they got excellent results and the men worked really hard. But there were big farmers – what I call millionaire farmers – with thousands of acres. They never talked to a POW – all the communications were through their foreman. But they were the first to complain and they were quite unpleasant on the telephone. I refused to speak to them and handed the phone to Ted Page. The Chief Labour Officer in Chichester gave them some blunt speaking and said, 'You can't expect these chaps to work when they get paid 1s a day. It's not my decision to pay that, it's the War Office.' But the big farmers would never consider a secondary payment. If a POW had to go there he'd have a long face and he'd say, 'I don't want to go there.' And I'd tell him to go for a day and if they chucked him out we'd find him another job next day. In small farms, though, there was a much better relationship.

In Theo's area of Sussex, two retired First World War officers – both in their late 60s – represented the War Agricultural Executive Committee. Theo recalls:

They went around talking to farmers and listening to complaints and so on. These fellows had a strict routine. They went around in a car in the morning visiting farms. I used to warn the gangers that the Major was coming so they were looking out for the car coming. If the men were working at clearing a ditch, for example, they'd probably only done about a yard! The inspectors knew that there was this grapevine, but they didn't care. At lunchtime the old gentlemen retired to a pub, had a meal and a pint or two. By that time they were sleepy, being in their sixties, and by half-past-two they were on their way home.

When a farmer first phoned to ask for prisoner of war labourers, Theo would pass the enquiry on to the two elderly men, who went to visit the farmer. The negotiations completed, they would pass the details back to Theo so that he could arrange the labour. Theo says:

The problem I had with these two charming men – they used to come into the office, usually on their way home – they'd say, 'We want two men to go to such-and-such farm.' We had a huge map in the office, but names of farms weren't often shown. And of course there were no postcodes, no sat-nav, and no mobile phones. So the old gents would say, 'You drive up to the White Horse and turn left – go on for 2 miles till you get to the Green Wagon, turn left there, another 2 miles to the Coach and Horses …' Now, I was supposed to give those directions to a lorry driver! It was totally impossible. There were continuous problems trying to relate to where the hell they were talking about.

Generally speaking, people contacting the office spoke to me. Very often, Ted Page was out so they had no choice. If it was a real complaint, I told them I'd get the supervisor to contact them. It wasn't for me to sort it out. If it was just a case of 'We didn't like that man,' I'd just say, 'Fine, I'll send someone else.' The farmers never remembered the chap's surname, they just asked for 'Heinz' – and I'd say, 'I've got about a hundred chaps called Heinz here! I'm sorry; you'll have to be a bit more specific.

It was impossible to keep records of who had worked at each farm, but sometimes Theo *did* remember who had been where:

'One day, Ted Page was in the office and a very posh 1930s car drove up outside. I looked out and told Ted there was an elderly chap in a suit, collar and tie coming. There was a knock at the door and Ted said, "Come in!"'

'Is it all right for me to come in with all these prisoners?' the elderly man asked. ('He was *very* suspicious because there were two of us POWs there,' Theo recalls.)

'Yes come in, they won't bite,' Ted Page said cheerily.

'I'm Major Dallyn. I need two men.'

'That's no problem,' Ted replied. 'Theo, who have you got that you can send to Major Dallyn?'

Theo reeled off a couple of names.

'Yes! How did you know that?' the Major said, momentarily caught off-guard. He turned to Ted. 'It *is* all right for me to speak to a POW?'

Theo shakes his head and laughs at the memory. 'He was so old-fashioned. And of course when he went we roared with laughter. Two years later his daughter married a POW! [This was Willi Sauer, the camp artist, who had designed the sets for the prisoners' theatrical productions.] I was best man at the wedding. And the two lived happily ever after. The comedy – that the old man was afraid of POWs and then his daughter married one of them! It was so amusing.'

Although the Labour Office was located within a POW camp, it was responsible for other workers as well as prisoners. 'We had about three or four Land Army hostels with about thirty or forty girls and we controlled where they went. Otherwise we had no contact with them. And they all worked invariably as milkers and returned to the hostel at night,' Theo recalls:

Near Selsey the government had erected hundreds of glasshouses in the 1920s and '30s to ease unemployment. They grew mainly tomatoes and cucumbers and this was jolly hard work. They invariably had just one POW because they couldn't afford more than that – always the same man. These chaps used to cycle there. Then there were the small farmers – some came to collect their men, some POWs cycled or were taken there by lorry. The big farms, on the other hand, would have a gang of fifteen to twenty men.

Only a few weeks after I had arrived in the Labour Office, Mr Page asked for my parents' address because he was arranging for them to receive a food parcel through members of the Society of Friends in Horsham. I was amazed at his kindness and the desire to ease the suffering of some of the people in post-war Germany … The first parcel arrived at home in March 1947 to the utter amazement of my parents, who were rather bewildered that their preconceived impression of England could be so wrong.

Charlotte Hagen, the recipient of another package, wrote to Ted Page from Gremmelsbach in the Black Forest in March 1947: 'You have brought great joy to me and to my children. We thank you from the bottom of our hearts for your love and understanding.'

Under new rules introduced that year, the prisoners themselves were permitted for the first time to send packages to Germany. One postage-free parcel could be sent every three months. And provided the prisoner paid for the postage stamps, he could also send an additional food parcel and a gift parcel each month at normal postal rates. As a further concession, at Christmas time he could send one extra postage-free gift parcel. As always, the government imposed a number of petty restrictions: a bewildering catalogue of items which could not be sent included: 'candles and night-lights, sheets, tablecloths and postage stamps'. Understandably, 'guns and ammunition' were also prohibited.

While the prisoners had previously had nothing to send, and no money to buy gifts, things were now a little easier, as Theo Dengel recalls:

> Someone sold me a dozen nearly new American army raincoats; I quickly resold them all in the camp at a handsome profit. I was always in need of money to help pay for the regular parcels of food and household items I was sending home; little things my mother asked for, such as sewing cottons, shoe laces, shoe polish, and condiments such as pepper, cinnamon, mustard seeds, baking powder, vanilla essence and cocoa, wheat flour, etc. I received a parcel from home containing two bottles of German wine: a Riesling Kabinett from the Pfalz. I managed to sell the wine for £3 and that helped to pay for another parcel.

In December 1947, Theo and a POW named Hermann Nötzold were invited to spend Christmas with the Wellcome family who lived in a small and ancient cottage with their three children: Mary, a primary school teacher; Harry, who was training for a job; and Joan, who was still at grammar school. Afterwards, Hermann wrote to them saying, 'After many years of continuous soldier and prisoner of war life I first gained an insight into family life again, felt then, how long I have been deprived of love, understanding and happiness, which one can only find amidst one's family.'

The 'British family' of a POW at Harperley received a letter from his mother thanking them for looking after her son and expressing her happiness that he was 'getting on so well' in England.

At North Mundham, Theo Dengel noticed a subtle change in the relationship between Captain Brill and Ted Page: curiously, this seemed to coincide with the more relaxed regimen which had been introduced for the prisoners. 'All of a sudden they became colleagues – not friends but colleagues. And they worked together in a very relaxed way. The commandant would come into our office and he'd joke sometimes – but Ted never went into his office, never. A very strange relationship you will observe – the dirty word still was conscientious objector.'

By mid-1947, the public were used to seeing German prisoners in their communities. Most people now viewed them as decent, respectable human beings, especially after the appearance of several high-profile news stories which portrayed them in a favourable light. The accident at Bodiam Bridge (described in the prologue to this book) was front-page news in the *Daily Herald* and the *Daily Express*, and was mentioned in most of the other newspapers as well. In a separate incident, 22-year-old POW Heinz Kroll saw an 8-year-old girl, Joan Robson, fall into a river at Chelmsford. He vaulted a 5ft fence and dived in to rescue her, even though he was a non-swimmer. He then dragged her from the water and successfully administered artificial respiration.

On the other side of the coin, the kindness extended to the POWs by the British often took the Germans by surprise. A sick prisoner had a two-week stay in a Tunbridge Wells hospital. On hearing that he would lose a fortnight's pay, the other patients held a collection and handed him 24s 11d. 'This feeling is different from what it was when we first came to England as prisoners,' he wrote in a letter of thanks. 'Then we had all sorts of wrong ideas about the English and they had the same about us, but since we have been allowed to move out and go into the people's homes, the feeling on both sides has changed to friendliness.'

By mid-year, the nation was basking in what today we might call a 'feel-good factor'. The dreadful winter was over and forgotten; against the backdrop of a glorious summer and the excitement over Princess Elizabeth's engagement to Prince Philip, even the country's economic woes were pushed to the back of people's minds.

Old alliances were ending and new ones beginning. Britain's relationship with its former ally, Russia, took on a distinctly unfriendly timbre, with many historians citing 1947 as the beginning of the Cold War. From this point on, the Soviet Union was a potential new enemy, and Britain and the USA would set about winning as many friends as they could in Germany – or at least in the Western sector of that nation.

Some POWs could barely suppress a sense of 'we told you so'. Werner Völkner echoes the earlier statement of fighter ace Gunther Rall, who had foreseen the possibility of Britain and Germany uniting against a common enemy. 'There were rumours going round that the Americans were going to rearm Germany and we would fight with them against the Russians,' says Werner. 'They were *just* rumours, but I think the Americans and British would have found the Germans to be very good allies because we knew how the Russians fought and what their weak points were. But unfortunately they didn't do it!'

15

'What Are You Doing with a German?'

By Christmas 1947, almost all restrictions on prisoners' movements had been lifted and the POWs could now visit civilian homes up to 100 miles from the camp. The few regulations which remained were often ignored and many commandants had long turned a blind eye to the prisoners' skulduggery. Arthur Riegel was an occupant of a Surrey camp, and as early as the autumn of 1946, in spite of the rules, he and the other prisoners were routinely leaving the camp through a gap in the wire, to be picked up by their English friends who were in the habit of taking them to London for the evening, and returning them to camp in the early morning. On one occasion Arthur had been appointed temporary interpreter and was unofficially left in charge. However, the War Office decided to make a spot check at the camp that very evening, leaving Arthur with some awkward explanations to make.

'I tried to placate the British officer by assuring him that the missing men would definitely be back in the morning, and that there was no need for him to give himself so much anxiety. But he didn't seem to accept my protestations.'

Hans Teske finished up at Hill Hall, near Epping, Essex. Most prisoners in this camp worked at nearby smallholdings and market gardens. He says:

We were very fortunate as we had a camp commandant, an ex-combatant who had fought on the Japanese front. His name was Lieutenant Blumenthal, he was Jewish, and he was like a friend to us. We were actively assisted by him in a number of things which he shouldn't have done. He didn't see this; he didn't see that; he didn't see when I went out of the camp. He knew I went out and that he could rely on me. If there was a roll call in the morning I would be there. I had civilian clothes, which we weren't supposed to have, and the commandant knew I had them. I went to London and to different parts of Essex – to the seaside at Southend – but my commandant could rely on me being there.

In our Nissen hut there was a stove which was going non-stop. Not that we had the normal ration of coal – we 'borrowed' that on 'long-term loan' from different nurseries. On one occasion a farmer reported to headquarters that a bag of coal was missing and that POWs had put it on to the lorry they were travelling in. Members of the Women's Land Army overheard that there was a plan to stop and search the lorry.

The girls cycled toward the lorry and said, 'Whatever you have on there, drop it, because they're going to search you.' And as they were passing Waltham Abbey cemetery they just lifted it over the wall and dumped it. When the lorry was searched they couldn't find anything. And the farmer who'd reported it felt an absolute Charlie because there was nothing. It was one of many occasions where there was a good collaboration between German prisoners and the Women's Land Army.

A small number of regulations continued to be rigidly enforced. Any sort of amorous or sexual relationship with a woman remained strictly *verboten*. To enter a pub was also against the rules. To many Germans the two transgressions were of much the same kind, because in Nazi Germany the phrase 'public house' (*öffentliches Haus*) was a euphemism for 'brothel'. On hearing of this rule, groups of POWs took to prowling around tranquil villages near their camps at night, searching in vain for the local red-light district.

In some instances they didn't need to go that far. A former guard remembered that, 'A couple of females had set up an establishment in a tent not far from the back of the camp. The going rate was a shilling a time.' And the *Manchester Guardian* reported that, 'It is an almost universal complaint from camps in populated districts that girls make a nuisance of themselves and one group of German prisoners petitioned a commandant to protect it from two young women in one area.'

However, women and girls in general felt that with so many young British men still in the services they had no one to go out with. And they found the German POWs attractive in a way that the locals were not. A 1947 report quoted a young woman as saying:

We grew up with the lads in the village and know them like brothers. That's not interesting any more. And it's too dangerous to go steady. Everyone knows about it and thinks there's going to be a wedding. So you have to watch it. But no one takes the prisoners seriously. That's just being friendly. Besides, you want to know what they're like.

Needless to say, 'amorous relationships' *did* occur, regardless of the rules, the regulations and the barbed wire. Peter Roth says:

My wife-to-be was very brave. Twice a week she came to see me on the bus, stayed for two hours and then went home again. And she brought me everything I wanted. I had a plan to escape. There was an Irish guard in English uniform and he hated the British – the love between the English and Irish was never very great. And he offered to take me up to Stranraer – well, I didn't even know where Stranraer was. But when Margaret came on the scene I changed my attitude. If it hadn't been for Margaret I wouldn't have stayed.

Even though Peter gave up all thoughts of a permanent escape, he still used to abscond for a short time for secret meetings with Margaret. 'There were two entrances to the camp, front and back. At the back entrance was a gate where the rubbish was put out. Beside it was a sentry hut. So I had to find a place to cut the wire to get out, but it had to be invisible, because the guards went round every day to check.' When the sentries patrolled the perimeter, Peter noticed, they never went right into the corner of the camp. He 'borrowed' a pair of wire cutters, cut the barbed wire, and made a hook-and-eye arrangement so that he could open and re-fasten the wire. 'One night I came back to the camp and I thought, "bloody hell, I've left my cap behind".' He had marked the cap in a way which made it instantly identifiable. 'I had to go back for it or they'd have found it outside the wire next day and they'd have known exactly who it was.'

On another occasion his evening tryst with Margaret was almost at an end when the alarm was sounded in the camp. The British guards must have suspected an escape attempt. 'Sometimes the British had an alert and they went out and searched the whole area. I was close to the wire and I could see them running around.' He laughs at the memory. This time he and Margaret would have to take a different route to the bus stop. 'They'd made a dyke along the back of the camp. Well, with all this activity I couldn't take Margaret the way we normally went so I took her across this dyke – I had to carry her through the water and got her up the other side and I dropped her over the wall into the farmyard! And I pointed her towards the way out and said "You walk out of there and catch a bus". She nearly had kittens! [But] they never catch me.'

Karl-Heinz Decker remembers it being quite easy to 'fix' the roll call so that they could slip out of the camp – a useful trick, as he had a girlfriend in Chester. 'The lads back in camp covered for us. While the men were being counted, one man in the front row waited until they started to count the second row, then he slipped back into the second row. That way the count was always correct. And we used to go to Chester Castle. Prisoners of war were kept there so we stayed there too and then made our way back again. We did some silly things,' he adds, laughing.

Werner Völkner recalls how a fellow prisoner's romantic adventures got the whole camp into trouble:

One of the chaps spoke a little English, and somehow he made a date with a Land Girl. He went out of the camp, which was quite easy, but every so often there were roll calls without warning and we were told to assemble in the square. One man who played the trumpet in the camp orchestra went on top of the Nissen hut and blew the German signal for 'alarm'. And the chap who was out with the Land Girl heard this and made his way back to camp, but he was intercepted by a policeman. He was wearing POW clothes and the policeman grabbed him by the collar, but his battledress was undone and he slipped it off and ran. So the policeman was standing with this battledress and he came to the camp. The camp commandant was Polish and he'd fought in the First World War on the German side and spoke German – so there was a kind of sympathy there. And when the copper said, 'One of your prisoners was outside the camp,' the commandant replied, 'Oh, no, *my* boys wouldn't escape'. We were 'his boys'. But on the insistence of the policeman we had a check on our equipment and of course everybody had extra clothing, which was all confiscated.

Some POWs found themselves in more serious trouble. In 1947, Hans Joachim Müller, formerly of the Luftwaffe, was court-martialled in Shropshire for 'conduct prejudicial to good order and discipline in that he improperly consorted and associated with' a girl from the ATS.

Twenty or so prisoners crowded into the courtroom at Sheriff Hales, Shropshire, to hear the proceedings. The chairman, noticing them in the gallery, told them that they were welcome to attend as members of the public. 'There is nothing done in secret and behind closed doors in England,' he added pointedly.

The court heard that during a search Müller had been discovered sitting on his bed and that the girl was hiding beneath the bed under a blanket. Captain Wilson, defending Müller, said the accused spoke good English and had the opportunity to meet his opposite number in the ATS. He had been a prisoner since 1944 and had been 'given encouragement by an attractive Irish girl'.

Not long afterwards, Sir Ralph Glyn, MP for Abingdon, acknowledged that:

> we have very rightly given German prisoners greater liberty now, and they are able to go into our towns on restricted leave. It is only natural, I am afraid, that in some cases they have relations with English girls, and I have had cases in my own constituency, where I am trying to get authority for those Germans who wish to marry our girls to do so … How much longer are we going on with Germans walking about our streets and these things happening, without any possibility of a girl being able to marry a German if she wishes to do so? It seems to me to be complete nonsense, to be immoral and utterly wrong.

By concidence the 'test case' on this matter involved another ATS girl, and once again the setting was Shropshire. Twenty-one-year-old Sergeant Monica Patricia Cann was an accomplished shorthand typist based at Donnington Camp, Wellington. She also spoke fluent German and was sent to a local POW camp to give English lessons. One of her pupils was Hermann Leo Ganter, formerly of the *Afrika Korps*. Hermann, whose father had been mayor of a small German town, was five years her senior.

'He looked so lonely and dejected,' she later told a journalist.

Monica and Hermann fell in love and decided to marry despite the rules. She bought a civilian suit for him, booked a marriage at Wellington Register Office, and dragged two strangers in off the street to witness the ceremony. To avoid awkward questions, Hermann gave his middle name, Leo, as it sounded more English – or, at any rate, less German. For his place of residence he gave Monica's parents' address in Liverpool. (See plate no. 20)

A few weeks later Monica confessed to the 'crime', almost certainly unaware of the publicity she would attract. The headline said:

ATS GIRL WHO WED GERMAN SAYS: I'D DO IT AGAIN

'We often went for walks together, always after dark,' Monica told a *Sunday Express* reporter. 'On one of the after-dark walks Ganter asked me to marry him. I was prepared to lose everything for him. I still am.' She explained that she had felt compelled to make the truth known, so she had informed the authorities about the marriage. 'I felt I had to make this a test case for others similarly placed. So I went to the camp commandant and disclosed everything.'

Monica was brought before Wellington Magistrates' Court. Significantly, no charges were brought against her in respect of her earlier fraternisation with Ganter or her marriage to him. Instead, she was charged with the technical offences of 'signing a false notice of marriage' and 'causing a false statement to be inserted in the marriage register'. She pleaded guilty and was fined £2 on each count. Hermann was sent to another camp. News of the marriage spread through the various POW camps up and down the country, and *Pflugschar,* the prisoners' magazine at New Malton Camp, carried a long, humorous account of the affair in verse. The last two stanzas of this are as follows:

> Her punishment was not too grave:
> One pound was cheap to pay
> For such a lovely union
> With Leo on that day.
>
> For Monica I understand,
> Your fame has spread to all ears,
> And every prisoner raves of you,
> For you love — without frontiers!

On 10 June 1947, Mr John Freeman* was asked in Parliament how many requests, both official and unofficial, had been received from British women wishing to marry German POWs. He replied that fifty-four such applications had been received and hastily added, 'No disciplinary action has been taken against any of these prisoners of war on the basis of information contained in letters of inquiry received.' Buried among the rhetoric was the message that the government was reassessing its position in the light of public opinion. If as many as fifty-four people had made written applications, there must be many more wanting to marry who hadn't yet come forward.

This was confirmed when an even more scandalous story hit the headlines. A young prisoner, Werner Vetter, had begun a relationship with a 21-year-old Chingford

* John Freeman had replaced Frederick Bellenger as Financial Secretary to the War Office. He had been awarded an MBE for his conduct during the British advance on Tunis and was later, according to legend, the staff officer who escorted the German generals to the signing of the surrender document at Reims. He is perhaps best remembered as a presenter of the BBC television programme *Panorama* and as the interviewer on *Face to Face*.

laundress, Olive Reynolds. In June 1947, she had given birth to a baby girl, and a military court in Droitwich sentenced Werner to twelve months' imprisonment. The news spread to Germany where the magazine *Der Spiegel* reported that Olive's workmates had signed a petition asking for Werner's release.

The case provoked a parliamentary debate:

In view of Vetter's youth and good record, would this 'disgraceful' sentence be reviewed?

Would he be able to marry the mother of his child?

Would the regulations be changed for *all* POWs?

George Oliver, Under-Secretary of State for the Home Department, confirmed that from now on German POWs *would* be allowed to marry British women.

MPs cheered at the news.

Oliver emphasised the potential pitfalls: the couple could not live together, as the POW would have to remain in a camp or hostel; there was no guarantee that he would be allowed to stay in Britain when his turn came for repatriation.

'The woman, if British, will as the law stands lose her nationality and become an alien.' And when the POW was repatriated the woman might not easily be able to join him in Germany as she 'would not be entitled to a British passport and for travel purposes would have to obtain a Home Office certificate of identity of the type provided for aliens'. (However, as a British-born subject the woman *was* allowed to stay in Britain.) Oliver said that these implications would be made clear to the couples concerned: and if they still wanted to go ahead no obstacle would be placed in their way.

Two weeks later the government said that Vetter's case – and all similar cases – would be reviewed. Vetter and twenty-four other POWs who had been found guilty under the previous regulations now had their sentences overturned.

Heinz Elfner later revealed that the Ganter marriage 'had a huge impact on the German POWs'. Democracy and freedom of speech were still viewed with some scepticism by the prisoners, who saw these concepts as Allied propaganda. 'When he realised that public opinion had forced the government to back down over Cann-Ganter, he began to believe that democratic systems could work.'

Within a short period, 796 marriages took place between POWs and British women. Many more followed later, but by then no one was counting any more. The news couldn't have come at a better time for 18-year-old Southampton girl June Tull. In late January 1947, she had met 25-year-old Heinz Fellbrich. She told a reporter:

A couple of my girlfriends were seeing German POWs and one day I cycled to the camp with them. While they were chatting over the fence to their boyfriends, I saw Heinz and said to my friend Amy, 'He's a bit of all right.' Amy's boyfriend brought Heinz over. He was incredibly handsome and tall with wavy hair. He could hardly speak any English, but there was a spark between us.

The relationship had flourished and after four months she discovered she was pregnant. 'I was scared stiff. Falling pregnant outside marriage was bad enough – but with a German POW!' Thanks to the new rules, they were married on 14 August

1947 in what may have been the first 'legal' marriage between a British woman and
a German prisoner following the easing of restrictions. A German band played at the
wedding reception. 'The bridegroom wore his normal chocolate-coloured uniform,
with a white flower in his buttonhole,' a local newspaper reported. Heinz had to be
back in camp by 10 p.m., and it was another six months before he could live with June.

A notice in *The Times* on 5 June 1947 announced the engagement of Mr Nicholas
Richard Gold and Miss Frances Prudence Russell. The groom, it was stated, was
the son of a certain Captain Gold, who resided in the Avenue Bosquet, Paris – a
swish address in the 7th arrondissement. The bride lived near Frome, Somerset, at
Beckington Abbey – a stately home dating from around 1500. Her father, Geoffrey
Phillip Russell, was a retired naval commander; her mother was the daughter of a naval
officer, granddaughter of an Admiral of the Fleet and great-granddaughter of a general
who had fought with Wellington at Waterloo.

Announcements of this kind were not uncommon. However, not everything was as
it seemed. 'Nicholas Richard Gold' was, in fact, a 28-year-old German POW named
Klaus Barth, 'a striking young man, 6ft tall, with fair hair'. He had been an inmate at
the White House Camp (now the site of the Mendip Lodge Hotel) and was one of
a group of prisoners from the camp who had been carrying out decorating works
to Beckington Abbey. While there, he became friendly with 24-year-old Frances.
Subsequently he escaped from the camp. '[He] was working as a prisoner of war at our
house doing the ceilings,' Frances recalled. 'We fell madly in love, and a few days after
he escaped he came to the house nicely dressed. Mother and Father did not recognise
him and I introduced him as a friend of mine. Father asked him his religion and
interviewed him in a room while mother and I listened at the door.'

Mrs Russell remembered her daughter bringing a 'good-looking, well-dressed
young man' to the house and saying, 'Mummy, this is my fiancé.'

'I was very astonished indeed,' Mrs Russell later testified. Visitors to the house
claimed that the young man was introduced 'by various names and forms of
introduction'. One was told he was a Dane; to another guest he was introduced as 'an
Irishman with a Gaelic accent'. Sometimes Mrs Russell presented him as her son, at
other times as her daughter's fiancé. After a few months, Frances was pregnant with his
child and the announcement of their engagement was hurriedly placed in *The Times*.
They married in July – as Mr and Mrs Gold – at the parish church in Milford-on-Sea.
A local newspaper said that the bridegroom had been wounded while serving in the
RAF during the war. Their baby was born six months later.

Suspicions were inevitably aroused: a Mrs Voyle, who worked at the abbey for about
a year, knew that one of the POWs who decorated the house had later escaped. 'A
long time after,' she recalled, 'I went to a bedroom and he opened the door. I was that
flabbergasted I didn't know what to say.' In the spring of 1948, Captain Stanley de
Courcey Ireland, RN, who had purchased part of the Abbey to live in, met Nicholas
Gold, who was introduced as a Dane whose mother was a Danish princess. He was told

that Gold had served in a parachute regiment and been seriously wounded. Another visitor said they all had tea together. 'I sat next to him, but he would not speak to me when I spoke to him. He never said a word.'

Finally, in mid-January 1949, a police constable went to investigate. The suspect produced an identity card in the name of Russell but the constable arrested him and took him to the police station at Frome.

'Obviously he had not registered for national service,' a police superintendant later said. 'When asked what unit he had served in he said "parachutes", and said he was a sergeant but later admitted he was a POW.'

Gold appeared before Frome magistrates a week later charged under the Aliens Act 1920 with failing to produce a passport and failing to register. Frances and her parents were each charged with harbouring him.

But on the day of the hearing a dramatic turn of events unfolded. The prosecuting counsel admitted that there was considerable doubt whether Gold was, technically, an alien. He stated that when a prisoner married a British subject the Home Office issued him with a certificate: in Gold's case this had been prepared and was ready to be issued. It was only then that his status would change from prisoner of war to alien. 'I am informed that in all cases where a German prisoner of war has married a British subject the question of deportation is carefully considered, and I understand that in this case he will not be deported but will be treated as an alien in this country.'

The magistrates agreed to drop the charge against Gold. They also accepted that Captain Russell had not been present when the prisoners had been decorating Beckington Abbey, and therefore had no way of knowing that Gold was a German, and the charge against him was dismissed. Frances and her mother were not so lucky. They were each fined £75 for harbouring an escaped prisoner.

In America we couldn't talk to anybody – just the guards,' Bruno Liebich asserts.

> We were kept away from the public but in England it was different. Contact with people was possible. Myself and another POW had joined two English civilians to work the dustcart in St Albans. We were in Jack's Café one morning and the two English dustmen bought us a cup of tea while they had breakfast. I remember this girl, a waitress, coming downstairs from the restaurant. I winked at her and a gentle smile from her signalled acknowledgement.
>
> I scribbled her a note asking if we could meet and gave this to one of the English dustmen to pass on to her. We'd been starved of female company for three years so any contact with a girl was something tremendous.

In a roundabout way, it was through his work in the Labour Office at North Mundham that Theo Dengel met his future wife, too. With several fellow POWs he had gone one evening to the annual Sloe Fair in Chichester. 'By chance we met a group of pretty girls who worked at the local telephone exchange. It did not take long to discover that

I had been speaking regularly to most of the girls when I was making my daily round of telephone calls to the various camps in the area.'

Joan Warriner was one of the telephonists. 'We were never short of boyfriends. We got chatted up and asked to dances and so on,' she says. 'Theo and I were introduced at the fair and we had a rapport immediately – in fact, that's *why* we were introduced. The telephone exchange wasn't fully automated so more or less every call came through the operators – and he used to chat to the girls.'

After this first rendezvous Theo suggested meeting again and Joan agreed. He told her, 'I need to have a word with your father and get his permission first.'

Joan replied that formalities of that kind weren't necessary in Britain in that day and age, but 'being German and slightly "proper" he thought that was the right thing to do,' she explains.

Joan's parents had separated during the war. When Joan was 16 her father had met someone else, and Joan had gone to live with them. 'I was the eldest of four and I was always the one who had to do everything at home, so I jumped at the chance. So I was a bit independent – at least I thought I was. Besides, I thought if it didn't work out by the time I was eighteen I could go into the forces, and no one could stop me.'

Joan's father had served in the RAF and spent some time in France soon after D-Day before moving into Belgium and then Holland. He had just been de-mobbed when Joan asked him if he approved of her seeing Theo.

He said yes, but he wasn't very keen, and he didn't think it should be serious, but if we wanted to be friends that would be fine. And we said that was all right and that was what would happen, but of course we knew quite well it wouldn't. It was a little bit difficult because some people looked down on us. There were two Fleet Air Arm stations, an RAF station, and an army barracks nearby: the usual comment was, 'With all these Englishmen around, what are you doing with a German?' There's no real answer to that, is there? If there's an attraction there's an attraction. Theo and I became very attached to each other and Theo said he would like to get married – something I hadn't yet given any thought to. Well, he was twenty and I was eighteen. And Theo said, 'I *must* go and see your father.' He insisted that was the correct thing to do.

At that time Chichester was a very old-fashioned city with a lot of little old ladies wearing plenty of lace walking around with their little mittens, and my stepmother knew a lot of them. And they'd say, 'I saw your daughter with a German.' She didn't like that side of it very much. My parents didn't think he had any prospects and they were also beginning to suspect I was getting a bit wayward, perhaps. I think it *was* partly because he was German, because there were never any problems if I went out with a British soldier.

While Joan's father and stepmother were, at best, lukewarm about the relationship, Theo's parents were definitely antagonistic. He explains:

When I told my parents I was getting engaged, I got a long tirade about loose girls who only wanted to marry me for my money [he laughs] and I received a letter from my brother-in-law saying, 'Who is her father, what money has he got? What endowment has she got?' It was really offensive and he got a mouthful back. There was a very lengthy lecture from my mother about the disastrous consequences of not getting married in the Catholic Church. Then, a few days later, an ultimatum: if I did not get married in the Church all future contact with the parental home would cease.

Joan's employers, the Post Office, advised her that as a married woman she would no longer be allowed to work full-time. They also reminded her that she had signed the Official Secrets Act upon taking the job as a telephonist and warned her not to divulge any secrets to her 'enemy alien' husband.

While prisoners of war who had entered into a contract with a farmer would eventually be allowed to stay in the country permanently, those directly employed by the War Agricultural Executive Committees, such as Theo, were to be compulsorily sent home by the end of 1948.* However, an exception could be made for men who had married British women and who wished to stay. The individuals concerned had to be married by October to qualify.

'We had about three weeks in which to arrange the wedding,' Joan Dengel recalls. 'My parents were preparing to buy a shop in Lymington and move there, so I had nowhere to live. And Theo and I had no money.'

They decided to go ahead anyway.

Robert Frettlöhr and the POW band he had formed were enjoying considerable success playing in the NAAFI social club at RAF Lindholme rear Doncaster. He says:

One night this girl walked across the dancefloor, and I nudged Jimmy and I said, 'Jimmy, I'm having her.' Little did I know, this young lady had already seen me marching in the mornings. And I was on the carpet in front of the commanding officer not once but a few times because of the non-fraternisation rules. He said, 'Is it serious?' And I said, 'Yes, sir.' And he said, 'Well, I give up.' [He laughs.]

Dieter Hahn was employed by the Ministry of Works to dismantle aircraft in the Lake District. He recalls:

I remember going to Lake Windermere where they made the Sunderland flying boat – we had to dismantle those and salvage the seats, the wooden propellers and so on.

* The WAECs were abolished in late October. Having dictated to farmers how to go about their business for the duration of the war, the government suddenly decided to hand the initiative back to those who probably knew best. From now on, farmers were encouraged to recruit and manage workers for themselves.

That's where I met my wife, Marjorie. That absolutely changed my life. My wife worked in a bakery in Kendal and her grandmother lived in a small cottage not far from our warehouse and in the back was an old yard – Kendal in those days was riddled with little yards – and that's where we met. We got on well straight away – my being German wasn't any problem. Fraternisation was still forbidden but we couldn't care less. I remember there was a little paper shop at the corner of the street and every morning the owner came and knocked on the door and gave us a little paper packet with five Woodbine cigarettes inside. Every morning he brought them, but he hid them so no one saw. I remember that. Marjorie and I fell in love and I had to go to her parents to ask permission to marry her. I don't think her father was very impressed – he'd been badly wounded in the First World War. But we got on in the end, no problem. I was still a prisoner when we got married. I still lived in the camp and she lived at home because we didn't have anywhere to live.

By now Dieter's employment had changed again:

I worked on a farm where I had two shire horses which I thoroughly enjoyed because they were magnificent beasts. I remember their names – one was called Tommy and the other was called Prince. I took them out ploughing, pulling a roller and things like that. And there was a tractor which I occasionally drove, which I quite enjoyed.

Karl-Heinz Decker was transferred again – this time to St Asaph, Denbighshire:

One of the POWs was going out with a girl there, and her mother invited us for tea. And one day she said, 'Now, boys, you're going to the dance!'

'First of all, we *can't* dance, and who would want to dance with a prisoner of war?'

'Don't worry; I'll organise it,' she said.

That was *really* good, that was – we went to St Asaph, not far from the cathedral, it was. It was old-time dancing and it was fantastic! Well, in the end I went old-time dancing wherever there was something going on. I had a pushbike then. I went as far as the mental hospital in Denbigh. And I met my wife, Gladys, who was waiting for a divorce – it had been one of these war marriages that don't last.

Fritz Zimmermann, formerly a soldier in the Panzer Division of the *Afrika Korps*, worked at a farm in Shropshire, and fell in love with a Land Girl named Lilian. The farmer asked for Fritz to be billeted at the farm, and this was sanctioned; however, when the camp commandant later discovered that Lilian, an unmarried young woman, was also resident there he sentenced Fritz to twenty-eight days in the 'calaboose'. In Fritz's words, Lilian 'went to London to see somebody at the War Office … The following day, the law about fraternisation was changed. Lilian always said this was due to her! Our wedding was on 2 September 1947. I was one of the first POWs to marry a British woman.'

16

Home in Time for Christmas

'When are we going home?' That was the question on every POW's lips. A German-language camp newspaper put into words what every captive already knew. 'Repatriation: this word explains most, if not everything, the POW thinks about.'

'We wondered, "How long are we going to be here, how many years?"' Eberhard Wendler reflects. 'The war had gone on and on and on, then when it was over we were never told when we would be repatriated – whether it would be in a year's time or two years.'

The prisoners realised that Britain's overwhelming motivation for keeping them was its desperate shortage of labour. 'They needed farmworkers because many British workers were still in uniform,' explains Henry Metelmann, 'and we had to accept that "Might is right".'

Shipping problems alone dictated that the rate at which Britain's own men were brought back would inevitably be slow. And even when all the British troops had been demobbed there was no certainty that the 45,000 who had worked on the land before the war would return to farming afterwards. Many returning soldiers had seen a bit of the world and, their minds suitably broadened, dreamed of a better living than agriculture could ever provide, and better conditions, too. Farmworkers' cottages were often primitive relics of the Victorian era. In the county of Norfolk alone, over 400 parishes had no mains water supply, while almost three-quarters of British farms had no electricity supply of any kind.

In any case, demobilisation was no solution, at least in the short term; the global situation meant that for the present every time one man was discharged another was recruited.

An argument also voiced was that sending 400,000 POWs back to Germany would place an insupportable strain on that country's shattered infrastructure. 'We conquered Germany. We met furious, insane resistance from the Nazis,' Philip Noel-Baker reminded Members of Parliament in 1946. 'To break that resistance, we had to smash the production and transport systems of Germany *as no country has ever been smashed before*. The administration of the nation completely collapsed. It fell into chaos.' [Author's emphasis.] Some 92 per cent of railway traffic was out of action, he claimed; in the British zone 3.5 million out of 5.5 million homes were severely damaged or destroyed; civilians, including children and the elderly, had no fuel during the winter. To send the men back to a country in such turmoil made little sense.

The Bishop of Lichfield, faced with a similar argument in the House of Lords, had replied that POWs 'say that they would give anything just to be with their people, however bad the conditions in Germany. All they ask is simply that they should be allowed to go there and share whatever conditions there are.'

But a feeling remained that Germany owed the victors some compensation for the damage it had caused during the war. 'It is not unreasonable,' Noel-Baker asserted, 'that when the war is over some prisoners of war may be held for a certain time longer than the [Geneva] Convention might have contemplated originally, as some form of reparation. Certainly there has never been a war in which there has been such a great physical destruction on the territories of other countries, for which reparation was required.'

Richard Stokes returned to this theme a few months later: why, he demanded, should POWs carry the entire burden? 'If there is to be slave labour – that is what it is – enforced as reparations, clearly it should be levied on the nation as a whole, and not merely on the people who accidentally found themselves prisoners of war when hostilities ceased.'

It was in the area of repatriation that the Geneva Convention proved to be most inadequate. When its authors drafted it in 1929 they had been influenced by the First World War a decade earlier, and could not have predicted how another world war might unfold. With hindsight, the weaknesses in the section on repatriation quickly become apparent:

> When belligerents conclude an armistice convention, they shall normally cause to be included therein provisions concerning the repatriation of prisoners of war. If it has not been possible to insert in that convention such stipulations, the belligerents shall, nevertheless, enter into communication with each other on the question as soon as possible. In any case, the repatriation of prisoners shall be effected as soon as possible after the conclusion of peace.

To begin with, there *was* no armistice. There had been no handshakes, no negotiations, no horse-trading; no haggling over this or that piece of territory; no squabbling about where frontiers would run; no arguments about the disposal of weapons; no quid pro quo; no terms, no conditions.

Instead, Germany had surrendered unconditionally.

Furthermore, the Allies and Germany could not 'enter into communication with each other' because Germany, as a sovereign state, had ceased to exist. It had no government, no leadership, and no representatives to bargain or negotiate on its behalf. Instead, it lay completely under the control of the Allied powers.

Finally, turning to the last sentence, the Allies could argue – with some justification – that there had not yet been a 'conclusion of peace' with Germany. There was no real prospect of a formal peace treaty being signed: to begin with, there was no one to sign for Germany; secondly, in respect of East Germany, the relationship between the Western Allies and the Soviet Union had soured to such a degree that there was little likelihood that all parties would ever reach mutually acceptable terms. Without such a treaty, the victors could – under a strict interpretation of the Geneva Convention – hold their prisoners of war for as long as they wanted.

Although the government claimed that its actions were technically legal, many people felt that, from a moral standpoint, they were wrong. In a letter to *The Times* the Duke of Bedford claimed, 'We have, with more adroitness than honour, sidestepped the letter of the law in regard to the early return of [the] prisoners. If we continue to violate the spirit of the Convention's ruling, for our own convenience, we have but little claim to act as judges of criminals charged with breaches of international law.' Popular opinion on this issue – perhaps surprisingly – tended to be in favour of returning the Germans to their homes as quickly as possible. A Scottish laird wrote from his castle in Brechin:

> Whatever his faults, a German soldier is a human being and has his family and home to return to like other men, and it would reflect a great deal more credit on those responsible for his return if they were to admit that he also has rights as a human being and send him back to create, if not a friendly Germany, at least a cooperative one.

In a Commons debate on 27 March 1946, Richard Stokes protested that Allied governments were 'doing some of the very things for which we are trying the war criminals at Nuremberg, such as forcible detention and slave labour – because it is nothing else when German nationals are detained as they are here.'

The prisoners of war themselves took issue with the unfair way in which even the Nazis among the SEPs in Germany had been set free after a very short time, while none of the POWs held in Britain had any idea when they would be released. Henry Faulk – the officer in charge of re-education – writes that the prisoners' view was, 'Give us something to look forward to. Tell us how long we must stay. We want certainty even if it means ten years.' Other injustices came to light, as well: Erwin Hettwer tells of a prisoner billeted on a farm who became very close to the farmer's daughter. The problem was that she was not quite sixteen. The POW was charged with having intercourse with a minor. 'A British officer was appointed as his defence counsel,' Hettwer explains. 'He pleaded guilty and received a "severe" punishment. They ordered him to be deported to Germany. It meant that he was sent home, while we stayed imprisoned for another three years.'

There had admittedly been some instances – even during the war – where prisoners were repatriated under special circumstances. In December 1944, all men over the age of 60 had been sent home under a scheme operated by the Red Cross. The next month, in a swap arranged by the Protecting Power, approximately 1,000 wounded German prisoners were repatriated in exchange for a similar number of British POWs held by the Germans. Beginning in 1946, about 2,000 prisoners with specialised skills were sent back to help rebuild Germany under a scheme code-named Oberon. Eberhard Wendler recalls men being removed from the camp where he was being held:

> Those who were anti-Nazis – and there weren't many – they would be taken first. Then if you were the *Bürgermeister* (Mayor) of somewhere you would be needed. Then

they needed miners. All the mines had been smashed and they had nothing to burn at all. You saw pictures where people had come out at night with a saw and cut down all the trees beside the road and taken the wood. So miners and people in the building trade went first. They went before people like us were even considered.

For these remaining prisoners, it seemed, there was no prospect of a quick release.

'You normally have plans and aims for your life: I'm going to do this and that's going to happen. But we had nothing to look forward to, because of where we were. You *really* felt you had no hope. And it's terrible when you live without hope. You felt homesick. You knew it was all wrong.'

Churchmen such as Bishop Bell of Chichester, politicians including Richard Stokes and others, and a multitude of individuals all kept up the pressure on the government to release the Germans. Some 900 prominent people put their names to a letter to the Prime Minister; in Germany no fewer than ten million women signed a petition. The *Daily Mirror* made a plea: 'Criminals at least know the length of their sentences, and it is high time the Government made up its mind on the question of repatriation. Tell the prisoners they can go by a certain date if they work well and behave themselves.'

A ray of hope finally appeared. To ease the critical labour shortage, Britain had turned its gaze towards the millions of displaced persons currently leading an impoverished life in Europe. Plans were put in place for some 90,000 people – mainly from the Ukraine, Poland and Latvia – to be brought to Britain as predominantly unskilled workers under the designation 'European Voluntary Workers' (EVWs). At the same time, a similar number of Poles who had served as members of the British forces were transferred into the Polish Resettlement Corps, which acted as a halfway house between leaving military service and entering civilian employment. Both sources of labour were expected to come on stream during 1946, and thus the possibility that the Germans might be repatriated came a step nearer.

As Parliament went into its traditional summer recess in early August there was still no word about repatriation. But on 4 September, Prime Minister Clement Attlee's cabinet met at 10 Downing Street: one of the principal topics under discussion was the release of the Germans. Local elections were being held in Germany on 15 September and 13 October and to allow the prisoners the opportunity to vote it was 'important that as many as possible of them should be repatriated during the current month and also that an announcement of the repatriation scheme should, if possible, be made before 15 September.'* Even at this stage, the Cabinet did not think it necessary to take the prisoners entirely into their confidence, as the minutes of the meeting reveal:

* Quite how the Cabinet imagined the prisoners could return to Germany, settle at an address, and register in time to vote, even by the later of the two dates, is a mystery. A more plausible reason for choosing this moment to begin repatriation is that the last few Italian POWs would be leaving Britain around the end of September: from then on, troopships would be available to transport the Germans.

As regards the form of the public announcement of the scheme it was preferable that this should not go into such detail about the release dates of the various groups that every prisoner would be able to calculate when he was due for repatriation. The main need was to satisfy British public opinion and the prisoners themselves that an orderly scheme had been devised for the progressive repatriation of all prisoners save the senior officers and ardent Nazis.

Downing Street duly released a communiqué on 15 September announcing that repatriation would commence almost immediately. Constant pressure from all sides seems to have had an effect, and the anticipated availability of EVWs and Polish workers would allow the Germans to be replaced over a period of time.

Under the government's plan, prisoners would be repatriated at an initial rate of 15,000 per month. First to leave would be those who had displayed 'a positive democratic attitude' and who were 'likely to play a useful part in the rehabilitation of Germany'. The length of time spent in captivity would be taken into consideration. Priority would also be given to those with industrial or other qualifications needed in Germany. Cases where there were 'exceptional compassionate circumstances' would for the first time receive preferential consideration. And agreement with the other Allied powers was being sought so that prisoners repatriated under the scheme could return to their own zone, British, American, Russian or French. The great majority of prisoners, some 394,000 in number, would be eligible for a place in the repatriation queue.

It was proposed that a modest start would be made the next month, October 1946, but in practice the programme began even sooner: some 2,500 men were returned to Germany before the end of September, and in October, the first full month of the scheme, the projected monthly quota of 15,000 was very nearly attained. Even so, at this rate it would take twenty-six months – effectively until the end of 1948 – to return all of the POWs, though the hope was expressed that the process could be accelerated when more shipping became available.

With the exception of the special cases, prisoners would be repatriated on a 'first in, first out' basis: that is to say, they were assigned to numbered groups according to length of captivity. The system was very similar to the one governing the demobilisation of British personnel in the forces, and in all likelihood was based upon it. No priority in the repatriation queue was given to married men.

The newly introduced compassionate release was a uniquely British concept: no other nation in World War Two repatriated its prisoners on humanitarian grounds. Initially, it was planned that 500 compassionate cases per month would be considered, but in practice the number was higher. At first, the application process for compassionate release appears to have been typically bureaucratic and convoluted. The prisoner himself could not submit an application: this had to be done by his relatives in Germany. The family had to complete a form which was submitted first to the local district council and then to the regional authorities for assessment. If their case was approved it was forwarded to the Control Commission in Germany who sent it on to the War Office in London.

The first POWs to receive this dispensation left Britain at the end of February 1947 – some six months after the scheme was announced, which perhaps gives a clue to the long-windedness of the procedure.

Prisoner Paul Becker was badly injured in a traffic accident in June 1946 and had both legs amputated. Eight months later he was still in hospital. One of his children had died of starvation two years previously, and there was another child, 7 years old. He was in the first group to be allowed to go home to Germany under the compassionate release scheme, presumably qualifying as both wounded and a compassionate case.

The principle that compassionate release depended on an application being received from the prisoner's family in Germany was found to be unsatisfactory and prisoners were later allowed to apply themselves. Frederick Bellenger explained this volte-face by insisting that unusual circumstances demanded 'rough and ready' solutions. The time between a POW making an application and his return to Germany was eventually reduced to one month.

Lagerecho, the camp magazine at Hardwick Heath, Suffolk, offered the following advice in its issue for 31 August 1947:

> It has been announced that in many cases prisoners of war receive reports of their wives having extra-marital relationships with other men. Until now it has not been permitted for the POW to seek early release in such cases on the grounds of family problems. It has been decided that applications on the above grounds will, from now on, be looked into. Such applications must however be accompanied in every instance by an official confirmation that the couple's children are suffering as a result of the wife's bad conduct.

Between the time of the announcement and the end of 1946, only those POWs who had been graded 'A' were allowed home (except 'special cases' of one kind or another). In 1947, some 'B's were released as well, but those with a 'C' grade were not even given a repatriation date at this stage. The make-up of each group varied from month to month. In April 1947, for example, the quota of 15,000 prisoners was met, and the group was constituted as follows:

Grade 'A'	1,859
Grade 'B'	7,950
Sick and wounded	2,083
'Economic' grounds (i.e. rebuilding of Germany)	1,247
Compassionate grounds	997
Special cases	1,379
TOTAL	**15,515**

As the House of Commons had been in recess when the repatriation scheme had been announced, it was not until 8 October that John Freeman, newly appointed as Financial Secretary to the War Office, had an opportunity to explain the scheme to Parliament:

> The position of the Government is perfectly clear. We cannot – and the House and the country would not wish us to – treat the German prisoners of war with such consideration, or with such softness, as to deprive the people of this country of what they need, or hamper the reconstruction of this country. But we do believe that they should be treated with humanity, and with the dignity and decency which they deserve as human beings, and which we Socialists on this side of the House at any rate have always striven for and held in the greatest respect.

There were rare instances where POWs who had been given a repatriation date had this brought forward.

On 19 September – barely a week after Britain announced its repatriation policy – 25-year-old Flight Lieutenant Dominic ('Nic') Page and his navigator, Francis Ashworth, climbed into a Mosquito aircraft and took off on a routine photo-reconnaissance training flight. Page had been an RAF pilot since he was 20, but he was shot down soon after qualifying and was imprisoned in German POW camp Stalag Luft III. While he was there, seventy-six of his comrades escaped through a tunnel they had dug (the inspiration for the film, *The Great Escape*). Page, though, was not one of the escapers: he remained in confinement until the war had ended and resumed his flying duties after returning to the UK.

As Page and Ashworth flew overhead, three POWs from Camp 106 – Ulrich Wolf, Fritz Oeder and Josef Schönsteiner – were at work on a Lincolnshire farm. They probably took no notice when they heard yet another aircraft approaching: the field where they were employed was close to the RAF airfield at Wittering and flights came and went all the time. Suddenly, though, there was a distinct change in the engine note.

'I heard a roar and then a bang,' said Wolf. 'I noticed that one of the wings had come off the plane and small pieces of the aircraft were falling. The aircraft went into a spin and then went out of view behind some trees. I rushed to the crash and found a fire raging. With the help of two comrades we pulled the occupants out but they were dead.'

At the inquest into the deaths of the two RAF men, the coroner commended the conduct of the prisoners. News of their exploit eventually filtered through to Germany, where a report about the incident appeared in the first-ever edition of the weekly news magazine, *Der Spiegel*. When asked whether the three prisoners of war would be repatriated early as a reward for their bravery, War Secretary Frederick Bellenger affirmed that the men in question would be home in time for Christmas.

17

Please Come Back!

To many POWs it felt as if the repatriation scheme had been introduced too late, and that the two-year wait facing some prisoners was excessive. A few men took matters into their own hands.

Almost every day newspapers reported escapes. Prisoners felt that virtually any risk was worth taking to extract themselves from the camps and somehow reach Germany. In particular, those who had been in captivity in the United States and then been brought to Britain must have believed that escape from Britain was a distinct possibility, whereas in America it would have been futile.

'In America where would you go?' says Hans Behrens. 'The camps were always in the desert or somewhere very remote. You had no chance of survival in the heat with no food, no water, and if you met somebody outside they were very hostile.'

In Britain it was indeed a different story. The camps were by this time largely unguarded and prisoners were, broadly speaking, able to come and go as they wished. In fact, it was not so much a question of escaping as simply leaving the camp and failing to return. And, unlike in America, there were no very great distances to be covered. To those who had crossed the Atlantic Ocean, the English Channel must have seemed an easily surmountable obstacle.

Even after the government had unveiled its repatriation plans there were, therefore, several escape attempts. Some POWs, perhaps, had chewed over the official proposals and decided that they couldn't wait for such a long time. Lothar Schulte escaped from the camp where he was being detained near Aylesbury, Buckinghamshire. He was seen getting off a bus outside the Savoy Hotel in the Strand. 'His brown trousers, blue and green jacket and blond hair' caught the attention of an onlooker and he was promptly recaptured. Two prisoners who had fled from a camp in Staffordshire on 1 September were at large for ten days during which time they made their way to London. The suspicions of a lavatory attendant were aroused by the pair and he locked them in a cubicle until police arrived.

The previous October, *Feldwebel* Klaus Rehaag had escaped from a camp in Surrey and made his way to Piccadilly, London, where he approached a man selling fruit from a barrow and asked him for a job. It is rumoured that Rehaag had been a teacher of languages before the war, and it may be that he spoke English well enough not to arouse suspicions. In any event, the street trader took him on and it was only after a day or two that Rehaag admitted to being an escaped POW. The police arrived soon afterwards, arrested the prisoner and returned him to captivity. It seems that in 1946 Rehaag escaped for a second time. This time he was never traced, and his name was placed on a list of escapers who were still 'wanted' by the authorities.

With hindsight, it seems probable that many 'escape attempts' were little more than pranks devised by the prisoners to relieve the tedium of captivity. Easy as it was to leave the camp, few prisoners got much further than the coast. The *Dover Express* reported that Ernst Gehrke had escaped from a camp at Nuneaton and stolen a yacht. But he had been overcome by seasickness and was rescued and taken back to his camp.

In August 1946, two naval ratings, Heinz Bartsch and Walther Spindler, were reported as having escaped from Glen Mill Camp. From there they somehow made their way back to Germany, but were recaptured there. Legend has it that a prisoner named Müller, together with two comrades, absconded while working on an Essex farm and stowed away on a ship bound for Germany. While his two companions disappeared without trace, Müller was at liberty for a year, staying for a time with his grandmother in Dresden. But without the appropriate papers he found it impossible to survive: finally he stowed away on a ship sailing back to Britain, returned to Colchester, and gave himself up.

Four prisoners escaped from a camp at West Malling, Kent, and made their way toward the Channel coast. They arrived on 16 September at the village of Kingsdown, 6 miles from Dover in the shadow of the famous white cliffs. The main road through Kingsdown runs along the foot of the cliffs, and a turning, North Road, leads towards the sea. The last building before the beach, they discovered, was a pub – the Victory – 'nestling only a few yards from where the waves lap the shingle'. Here the POWs spotted what they were looking for – a boat, the kind the locals call a 'punt' – not the sort favoured by Oxford and Cambridge students, but a sturdy vessel about 25ft in length with a large lug sail and a much smaller sail at the stern. It could also be rowed using three sets of oars.

The prisoners determined to steal it: but if they had known its owner, the publican, they might have had second thoughts, for he was no ordinary person. If ever a man had seawater running in his veins it was George Arnold, the licensee of the Victory, a local man through and through. His father, Richard, had been master of a sailing vessel at the age of 18: George had followed in his father's footsteps, sailing on a fishing boat as a 12-year-old boy, learning how to cure bloaters, serving in the local lifeboat crew. George 'knew what it was like to shudder with fright as the craft was tossed like a cork on mountainous wave'. At one point he had exchanged his career as a fisherman for the tough life of a policeman in the East End of London. But in 1939 he and his wife returned to Kingsdown and he became a fisherman once more and joined the local police reserves. After the war he took over The Victory pub.

When necessary, boats like George Arnold's would go to the rescue of other vessels stranded on the Goodwin Sands, some 6 miles out to sea. But to cross the 22-mile-wide

Channel – one of the most perilous stretches of water surrounding Britain – was something that even he would have balked at.

With a fresh westerly wind behind them, the prisoners' voyage started well enough; but as they neared the French coast they ran into difficulties. Joseph Agez, the skipper of a French trawler, was fishing off Gravelines, between Calais and Dunkirk, when he spotted the small boat and was alerted by the prisoners' distress signals. He took the Germans into port, where they were formally arrested and taken to the jail at Dunkirk. They were returned to Britain a few days later.

To determine which prisoners were suitable for repatriation, a further process of screening was introduced. Interpreter Officer Harry Grenville explains:

> They each had an interview which was conducted by a chap from the Foreign Office who came down to the camp. I sat in on the interviews at his request and after a while he said "You've heard enough of these interviews; you can do your own from now on." The POWs graded 'A' were the ones we reckoned you could rely on to play a part in the emerging German administration on the other side and they got preferential repatriation. The 'B's were the vast majority of over 90 per cent who you might regard as non-political – they were repatriated strictly in accordance with their date of capture: first in, first out. And the 'C's were the unrepentant Nazis who still had traces and wouldn't shake them off. I only discovered two of them. I got those two transferred to a special camp in the very north of Scotland within 24 hours of interviewing them.

Theo Dengel considers the grading to have been arbitrary. He says:

> In early 1947, three or four chaps from MI5 came and interviewed everybody, ostensibly to obtain their political convictions, and to prepare a schedule of anticipated repatriation dates. I was graded 'C2' [the lowest sub-division of the 'C' grade] – I was hopping mad! I was as anti-Nazi in my experience as I could get because I detested the whole thing. They asked questions such as, 'Were you in the Hitler Youth?' – 'Yes.' But you had to – there was no choice. They asked loaded questions and every time I tried to explain they told me to shut up. They awarded grades, as it were, to comply with quotas. It was as if the authorities had determined in advance what proportion would belong to 'A', 'B' or 'C', and juggled the results to make them fit. I came out pretty disgusted and complained to the officer.

Hans Teske had been a paratrooper and, as such, could not yet be given a place in the repatriation queue. He still had to undergo a perfunctory grilling, though. He recalls that:

Whitehall 'bowlers' came to interrogate and classify us into groups. This man from Whitehall came in mufti. There was a Nissen hut in total darkness except a light shining in my face once I got there. I couldn't see his face. He asked me two questions. The first question was 'What do you think of South Africa?' I said, 'I've never been in South Africa, I've been in North Africa.' The other question was also negative and he didn't want to hear any more and finished the interview. Next day, we were given the result of our interrogations – I was classified as 'C'. In other words, I could not be repatriated. It turned out that all former parachutists and all submariners in captivity had been classified 'C' – so there was nothing to worry about.

The subjective nature of the screening process attracted criticism, not only from the POWs but from politicians and members of the public. Savvy prisoners could manipulate the conversation and get the interviewer to upgrade them; less cunning but more truthful men could be unfairly downgraded. However objective the process was intended to be, inevitably the interviewer's personal hunches, preconceptions and prejudices would creep in. Even Herbert Sulzbach, generally regarded as a paragon of objectivity, remarked in his notes that one German was 'not too nice (cat-lover!)' And, as POW Alf Eiserbeck succinctly put it, 'How could a man who didn't know you and who saw you for three or four minutes tell what you were?'

Theo Dengel remarks:

The camp leader was a former SS man with a smooth tongue. He was given an 'A1' grading! But the commandant saw through this and made sure he was repatriated later. He didn't want to go back anyway. There was still a de-Nazification process in Germany in those days and I can't see how this chap could have got past this process. He was known in his own locality as an SS officer. He was a *very* unpleasant person; somebody boasting two years after the war about medical experiments – that takes a thick skin, doesn't it?

In a Gloucestershire camp, former SS guard Eduard Issel committed suicide when told he would soon be called to be questioned by officials. He apparently feared the outcome of such an interview, particularly as the SS had been declared an illegal organisation, and was unaware that the meeting was simply to determine whether he could be considered for repatriation.

At first, like all of his comrades, Peter Roth simply wanted to be set free. 'If they asked me a question I gave them the answer they wanted. What I think in my mind is up to me isn't it?' But his strategy backfired:

The man who interviewed me asked three questions: one was what I thought about the Danzig 'corridor' – there was always a dispute about it. [A disagreement over this strip of land was one of the reasons Germany gave for starting the war.] I told him that the corridor was German territory and that we should have had access to the Baltic. But instead of taking up arms they should have should have thrashed it out around a conference table. So he said, 'I give you grade 'A'. You'll be sent back to Germany. In a fortnight or three weeks you'll be home.' But I didn't *want* to go. Not because I hadn't got a home to go to but because of Margaret. I asked him if I could speak with him confidentially and asked him to promise that what I said would remain between him and me. I gave him a bit of bullshit and said, "I've been told by my father that an Englishman never breaks his word …'

I told him about Margaret and explained that I wanted to stop here. So instead of giving me 'A' and sending me home, he gave me 'B-plus'. And those lads who tried to be snotty with them, they gave them 'C'.

It soon became apparent that screening was likely to delay the repatriation process. Only twenty-seven interviewers had been assigned to the task – fewer if some sources are to be believed. As each interview was supposed to last fifteen minutes it would have taken at least two years to carry out all of the screening, not allowing for travelling to the hundreds of camps up and down the country.

The Bishop of Chichester raised the issue in the House of Lords: 'I would urge that the evidence necessary for a real judgement of political reliability can only be found gradually in Germany and by Germans.' Men who were under 28 years of age were being classified as 'C', he pointed out, whereas in Germany – where a parallel scheme of screening and grading was in force – it was policy for such young prisoners never to be graded 'C'. These young men would be 'treated as at worst minor offenders'. He pleaded for repatriation to be completed by the end of that year (1947).

In retrospect, it is evident that the grading system was cumbersome. At the top and bottom of the scale there were relatively few 'A's and 'C's, while well over three-quarters of prisoners fell into the catch-all designation of 'B' ('grey'). In early 1947, when many of the 'A's had already been repatriated, the totals were approximately:

'A'   2 per cent
'B'   85 per cent
'C'   12 per cent

Prisoners with a 'B' grade were not defined by any particular characteristics, merely that they were neither 'A' nor 'C'. They didn't know whether they were near the top of the scale – where a little effort to improve their grade could have led to early repatriation – or whether they were at the bottom of the range, in which case there was little point in trying. At first, prisoners were not even told their grade, but, in answer to a question in the House, John Freeman later stated, 'Every prisoner of war now screened is being informed perfectly clearly what his grade is. He has ample opportunity to appeal against his grading if he thinks fit.'

Lord Pakenham stated that screening had originally been introduced for a completely different purpose: 'to separate the strong anti-Nazis from the rest, in the interests of the anti-Nazis themselves, to make sure that they were not being persecuted by the others'. Was this same system really appropriate for the purpose of choosing which prisoners were to be allowed to go home? Lord Pakenham thought that, on balance, it was. While admitting that screening had 'inevitably been rather hasty' he felt that the procedure now in force would produce satisfactory results.

There remained, however, the prisoners graded 'C'. Since they were not yet included in the general repatriation programme at all, what was to be their fate? Would they be detained forever? The government seemed always to duck the question.

Finally, on 18 February 1947, Richard Stokes demanded to know why U-boat commanders and chief engineers had been told that 'they cannot be included, proportionately, amongst the 15,000 prisoners of war who are being repatriated monthly to Germany'. Mr Bellenger explained that these men were 'included in the categories, which, under the demilitarisation laws, are subject to special screening'. The numbers involved, as it turned out, were not very large. Out of 133 men who had already been screened only four had been excluded from the repatriation process. A further 227 still awaited screening.

However, it was clear that the process of repatriation in general had to be speeded up. When a 21-year-old POW hanged himself at a camp in Surrey, the coroner said, 'In my view this continual confinement as prisoners may have had something to do with this unfortunate thing, a boy of 21 taking the extreme course of hanging himself. It is to be hoped, as many of us think, that these German prisoners of war will be returned to their own country with the greatest possible speed.'

Henry Faulk makes the astonishing assertion that 'There were no reported cases of men missing a repatriation transport because of a 'C' grading.' This being the case, one cannot help wondering why screening and grading were undertaken in the first place. The government at last responded to the criticisms. One interpreter claims that he was urged to 'grade up the blacks into grey if you can'. 'The general idea,' he says, 'was to try and upgrade them and get them home.'

Eventually, at the end of June 1947, the authorities abandoned the screening process.

Bruno Liebich, who had originally been given a 'B' grade, was subsequently upgraded to an 'A'. He was duly repatriated in October 1947, but this caused him a serious problem, as he had just met Audrey and they had fallen in love.

'Audrey wanted me to stay because I *could* have stayed. But I said, "No I must find my mother and my brother, my sister, my people. I have to go." It was a delicate situation and caused many a tear.' He had already established contact with his mother while in the POW camp in the United States. Since then, the Russians had expelled his family from their home to another part of the Soviet Zone while Bruno had been transferred from America to Britain. Despite everything, they had kept in touch and now Bruno desperately wanted to see his family. 'I didn't want to be released to my mother's new abode because of fear of being taken away by the Russians for unlimited slave labour in Siberia, and so on. My own brother died there in a similar way.'

Usually, prisoners were repatriated to the zone in which their home was situated. But when this was in Soviet territory they were not forced to go if they did not wish to: instead, they could ask to be returned to whichever sector they chose. Bruno opted for the American Zone. He explains:

I used an address of homeland friends near Frankfurt, and after finding my cousin's address in Bavaria I moved there. During my time in Bavaria I risked travelling by rail to see my mother and other relatives in the Soviet Zone and my mother also came to visit me once. And meanwhile my girl was saying, 'Come back, please come back.' I knew I had a girl here who loved me and I loved her and we wanted to be together. In 1947–48, the situation in Germany was extremely bad and this made it easier for me to make the decision to return.

He applied for permission to re-enter Britain but soon afterwards – quite unexpectedly – he was offered a job in Germany. He says:

I actually worked for the American military government because my English was reasonable. It was a re-education job, showing films in the schools. But for me it was just a job. Now, in Bavaria the farmers all had AC or DC supplies – some were 110 volt, some 150 volt. I had to reorganise everything and get all these converters and rectifiers. And the Americans always found the stuff I wanted.

So now it looked as if he would be staying in Germany after all.

18

Next Stop Germany

At the Moscow Conference of April 1947, the Allies had agreed to repatriate all of their prisoners of war by the end of 1948. The USA had, of course, already released all of its POWs, though many of them were still in captivity in Britain and France. Russia, on the other hand, still had about 1 million German servicemen as prisoners of war – often in the most deplorable conditions.*

The British Foreign Office wanted the Soviet Union to release its German prisoners but could not apply any pressure on the Russians until all of Britain's own POWs had been repatriated. Demands to send the Germans home came from other quarters, too. In September 1947, the prominent publisher Victor Gollancz and 2,000 other 'leading citizens' had signed a letter to the Prime Minister himself expressing concerns over the slow rate of repatriation. Attlee replied, 'It would be wrong to give the prisoners the impression that they could hope for a change in our present programme, particularly now that our need for agricultural manpower has so greatly increased, and while transport difficulties remain as acute as ever.' The only shred of hope that he offered was that the situation would be reviewed after that year's harvest was completed. But at Christmas 1947, long after the harvest had been gathered in, the International Committee of the Red Cross felt compelled to issue a further statement, much stronger in tone than its earlier communiqués. It protested about the state of limbo in which prisoners of war were still being held:

> Although the forces of which they were members no longer exist, they still wear uniform, are deprived of any kind of private life, and are considered only in the light of the work they are compelled to do, as a rule for extremely low wages. In short, they are kept beyond the pale of human society.

To its credit, the government seems to have made some effort to accelerate the process. In December 1947 alone, 35,000 prisoners were repatriated – more than double the originally projected quota. Theo Dengel says, 'By December 1947, 50 per cent of the

---

* Russian troops and civilians alike had suffered appallingly during Hitler's occupation of their country. The Soviet Union no doubt considered that its actions towards German prisoners were justified and reflected public sentiment within their country.

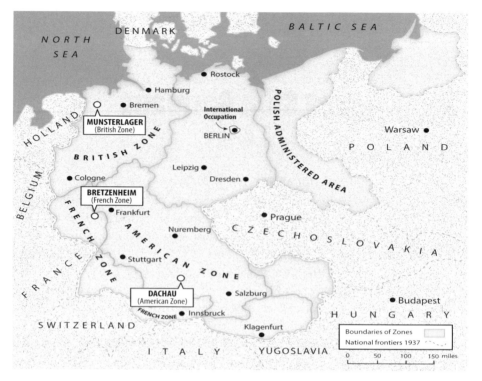

Germany, showing the occupation zones (as of July 1945) and the discharge camps for German prisoners of war.

chaps had gone. European Voluntary Workers came flooding in from Germany. The camps filled up with Ukrainians, Serbs, Croats.'

As far as the prisoners were concerned – especially those likely to be repatriated last of all – the deadline agreed in Moscow still seemed a long way off. But events suddenly took an unexpected turn. In 1939, London had won the right to host the 1944 Summer Olympic Games. The war prevented the Games being held that year, but at the end of hostilities Britain was invited to stage the 1948 Olympics instead. Amid rationing and financial meltdown, the government hesitated: the cost of staging such a major event could easily have tipped the nation into bankruptcy.

But King George VI perceived the Games as a means of restoring Britain's morale after the deprivations of wartime. He urged the government to accept the invitation and they agreed. Now London would be in the spotlight on a world stage. 'The British government realised they would have to release all the prisoners sooner or later, and at the latest before the Olympic Games,' claims Hans Teske, the former paratrooper, who had expected to be one of the last to be freed. 'They were not allowed to keep prisoners of war while the Olympics were on, so [now] we could count on a fairly early release.'

Teske's belief that the International Olympic Committee had pressured Britain to repatriate all of its prisoners was widely held, but was not strictly accurate. When questioned by the author, the IOC stated that it had never imposed a condition of this kind upon Britain. Nevertheless, the nation would receive the most intense scrutiny during the Games, and the continued detention of war prisoners would have been likely to provoke international condemnation. The government therefore felt obliged to return the POWs to their homes several months earlier than they might otherwise have done.

In fact, repatriation began with such haste that some prisoners were taken unawares. One man, a prisoner of seven-and-a-half years, was given only three hours' notice before his departure. It was these prisoners, the ones who had been in captivity the longest, who would be allowed home first. All were assigned to groups identified by a number, from which they could estimate, roughly, when they were likely to be repatriated – something they had been unable to do previously.

Date of capture	Group(s)
Up to December 1941	1–3
January 1942–December 1944	4–24
January 1945–May 1945	25–29

As their repatriation dates approached, the POWs amassed as much food and as many cigarettes as they could, since both commodities were highly valued in Germany. Flints for cigarette lighters were sought after as they had long been unobtainable, and one POW recalls taking a large quantity of these back to his father, who then sold them on the black market.

In typical fashion, the British authorities issued a bewildering list of dos and don'ts concerning the goods which POWs could (or could not) take or send home. 'Rationed goods, including cycling capes and hoses' were banned in prisoners' luggage, as were 'foodstuffs, (except military rations, canteen goods or bona fide presents in reasonable quantities), uncensored mail, British or Allied government property, English currency or securities'.

'Private goods may be taken home,' the regulations stated (but only if 'legally obtained'). The prisoners were given the same baggage allowance as British troops – three kitbags or suitcases with a maximum weight of 56lb in total (112lb for officers), plus a parcel of books, and 'small kit'. Any extra baggage could be sent home by parcel post, but larger possessions – such as gramophones – often had to be left behind to be shared among comrades still awaiting repatriation.

As they stocked up with goods for the second time, the men who had been detained in the USA and Canada and been promised repatriation once before must have felt a sense of déjà vu – perhaps tinged with a suspicion that once again the Allies would break their promise.

But at last the moment came to leave their camps for the last time. First they would spend up to a week* at a transit camp near the port of embarkation. One man states, disbelievingly, that none of his property was pilfered by the guards during his stay at this camp.

More form-filling awaited the prisoners, including a lengthy questionnaire relating to de-Nazification. This document, in German and English, was headed:

MILITARY GOVERNMENT OF GERMANY
PERSONNEL QUESTIONNAIRE

Prisoners were required to answer a number of questions about their past, for example:

Have you ever been a member of the NSDAP? Yes/No? Dates?

Other questions asked what publications the prisoner had contributed to from 1923 to the present. The POWs were also required to list any political speeches they had made, to provide full details of their work history and of their time in the armed forces. An intelligence officer compared this form with the one they had filled in at the beginning of their captivity: if any inconsistencies were noticed between the two sets of answers, particularly in the sections on membership of Nazi organisations, the prisoner's repatriation was likely to be postponed.

Upon repatriation, the prisoners could be transferred back to Germany via several different routes, including, typically:

Transit Camp	Port of Departure	Destination
Quorn, Leicestershire	Hull	Cuxhaven
Berechurch Hall, Colchester	Harwich	Hook of Holland
or Camp 7, Brent, Middlesex	..	.. .. ..

Other transit camps and routes were used in addition to those indicated. In typical War Office tradition, one man held at North Mundham Camp near Chichester is known to have been sent first to the local base camp at Billingshurst, and from there, two days later, to a discharge camp near Bristol. He was kept there for just over two weeks before undergoing an eight-hour journey to Hull, followed by the sea crossing to Cuxhaven.

NEXT STOP – GERMANY

* Later reduced to about two days as the procedure became more efficient.

the headlines declared, '500 POWs go home'. The drab, rust-streaked sides of the troopship towered above the quayside at Hull, that Thursday 26 September 1946. Like many troopships used by the British government this one belonged to the Empire class – a jumbled assortment of merchant vessels which had been hurriedly pressed into wartime service.*

The *Empire Spearhead* was an Infantry Landing Ship which had played a role in the invasion of Normandy in 1944: it's even possible that some of the Germans boarding her this day may have sailed on her earlier in their time as prisoners.

The *Daily Mirror* suggested that most of the men were 'sorry to leave Britain because they had been treated kindly here. Lance-Corporal Rudolf Ernst, 26, said he intended to meet his blonde fiancée, Gerda, in Bremen and would like to bring her to Britain after they married.' The anti-German attitudes of the war years appear to have melted away entirely: instead, the journalist seemed to be caught up in the POWs' jubilation.

A newspaper photograph of a subsequent departure is captioned, 'Light-hearted German prisoners arriving in Hull today to embark at Riverside Quay on the vessel that will take them home'. POWs wore 'battledress of various hues' – mottled green, or brown, or black – having been allowed to dye their uniforms to their own personal taste during the last few days before repatriation to their country. Heinz Lothe was on his way home to Celle. In 'perfect English', he informed a reporter that he had been taken prisoner in Holland in 1944. A married man with two children, he was hoping to resume his pre-war occupation as the Rotterdam representative of a British shipping firm. Raising his voice above the clamour of the men waiting their turn to board the ship, another ex-prisoner pointed to his luggage and said, 'I'm taking home some tea for my wife and cocoa for my two little girls, aged 5 and 6. The people here have been kind to us on the farms, and now we're going back to build up our own land again.'

'We were on deck as the ship left the harbour,' a prisoner remembers. 'I, along with many others, found tears in my eyes. After such a long time it was not easy to leave, and now we were going into an unknown future.' Most of the prisoners on the early repatriation crossings hadn't seen their country for six or seven years. 'Germany is still my home, even though it's so terribly destroyed and reviled by so many people,' one declared.

'My wife and young daughter are waiting for me at home in Bergedorf [a district of Hamburg],' a former naval pilot said as he disembarked at a German port a few days later. 'I was a motor mechanic before the war and I hope to take up that trade again.' It was, he explained, seven years and one day since he had been taken prisoner.

---

* Probably the most famous of these was the *Empire Windrush* – a former German passenger liner which had been used as a Wehrmacht troopship in the war, before finally being seized by the British. In 1948, the *Empire Windrush* brought some 500 West Indian migrants to Tilbury, thus opening a new chapter in Britain's history.

The crossing from Hull to Cuxhaven took around twenty-four hours. On arrival the POWs were greeted with something of a hero's welcome. Several former prisoners mention the high quality of the catering both en route and on reaching port on the other side of the North Sea. On the quayside at Cuxhaven, German Red Cross nurses served the prisoners with hot coffee and sandwiches. ('Very good quality and sufficient in quantity,' one prisoner noted.) An ex-POW whose journey took him via the Hook of Holland spoke of the moment when they crossed the Dutch-German frontier, and were greeted with flowers. But the men were haunted by concerns about their shattered country. Hans Sievert had been a prisoner for six years. 'None of us feels like shouting or cheering now,' he said on arrival at Cuxhaven.

From here they went by train to the demobilisation camp at Munsterlager. The barracks had been used as a POW camp for captured British troops in the First World War. Now it was the other way round: following the German capitulation in 1945 the British army had taken over the establishment. It became the demob centre for all POWs who had been in British captivity, and for those who had been held by other powers and whose homes were in the British sector. Returning German prisoners poured into Munsterlager from all directions. 'The suntanned men with the supposedly white tropical caps have come from the Middle East ... those in dark-brown battledress are from England: they are very self-confident and unflinching ... and then there are the ones from the East! They are taciturn and shy.'

'We met ex-POWs returning from Russia,' an eyewitness adds. 'They were very sick and undernourished. The difference between them and the POWs from England is like night and day.'

In a letter to a comrade who was still waiting to be released, one man wrote of his experiences at Munsterlager:

> We arrived at 2 a.m. The organisation there was very good. We received hot food again but the accommodation wasn't so rosy (straw and a single blanket). On the same day we were taken through the demobilisation channel – a well-organised procedure. So have no fear of Munsterlager. They try it on in every way but a hardened POW doesn't allow himself to be intimidated ... the British really are very well organised, not only on the island [Britain] but on the mainland [Germany] as well. Anyone who says otherwise is lying. And you don't get the same kindness from the German authorities. You'll find that out when you get here.

Disturbing rumours reached some ears that other Germans were stealing from the returning prisoners. Laden down with cigarettes, food and other commodities of enormous value on the black market, the men were targets for thieves and confidence tricksters in a country where many people had no wealth whatsoever. Arthur Riegel says, 'We heard a rumour in England that in the Munsterlager discharge centre German "comrades" were helping themselves to the personal property of the returning POWs. The British put a stop to this deplorable state of affairs, and made this known throughout the camps.'

Before the men left Munsterlager, their discharge papers were signed and stamped by a British Sergeant-Major, and they were paid off. The exact procedure depended on whether the man concerned was an officer or not.

Officers received an amount in German currency equivalent to their full back pay. One man writes of his surprise at receiving £54 which, when converted, came to 810 *Reichsmark*. An additional 80 *Reichsmark* were paid as *Entlassungsgeld* (discharge pay).

For the ordinary soldier the calculations were different. Although Germany should have been crediting their military pay to their account while they were prisoners, the collapse of the German state meant that alternative arrangements now applied. The British gave each man the token sum of 40 *Reichsmark* – again in German currency – as discharge pay. In addition, POWs received any bonus they might have earned for 'consistent good work', and this would have been credited to their account awaiting their repatriation. Under this scheme, it was theoretically possible to receive as much as £40. Theo Dengel pocketed the equivalent of £19 and this was probably typical. As he drily points out, though, it was not much for four years service in the *Wehrmacht*.

A source of resentment among the prisoners was the rate of exchange used when calculating these payments. Since the collapse of the German economy there was no official rate. Britain recognised that the *Reichsmark* had lost much of its value, and allowed its own occupation troops a preferential deal at 40 *Reichsmark* to the pound. But when it came to the POWs, the much less favourable pre-war figure of 15 *Reichsmark* to the pound was used. Richard Stokes, MP, accused the government of 'sweating' the prisoners in Britain and 'swindling' them in Germany. Frederick Bellenger replied, 'I do not think it is in my power to reconsider the matter, which was agreed between our government and the German government.'

As soon as he had said this, Bellenger must have realised the trap he had stumbled into. In defence of its protracted detention of the German prisoners, Britain's excuse had always been that it could not conclude a peace treaty with a non-existent German government. Yet Bellenger was now claiming that an agreement made six years earlier with the same defunct German government was inviolable.

Captain Harry Crookshank, MP for Gainsborough, quickly took advantage of the slip. 'May I ask to what German government the right honourable gentleman is referring, because if there is one at the moment it has escaped most people's notice?'

The exchange rate controversy reached the House of Lords. 'Most of them [the Germans] have worked pretty hard here,' Lord Strabolgi asserted. 'I have had good accounts of them and I do not think you should let them go back feeling they have been swindled, so to speak, because of an out-of-date agreement made with their former government.' But these pleas were ignored.

A British sergeant major signed the release form. A rubber stamp thumped down on to the document. In the blink of an eye a man's service in the German forces was over. And in the same instant his stint as a prisoner in British captivity also came to an end. Those whose home lay in the British Zone were issued with civilian clothing and documents – an identity card and a ration book. They were then released and could go straight home.

The former prisoners stepped outside into the civilian world, finally at liberty. Like creatures emerging from a long hibernation they looked all around at their surroundings, blinking in the bright glare of freedom. For Karl-Heinz Decker it was a disorientating experience. 'After I was de-mobbed at Munsterlager I stood outside the gates looking around me and I said, "Where the hell am I? I'm in a strange country." Then I had to look for my parents – I knew where they lived now but I'd never been there in my life.'

On the outside, the POWs found an anarchical situation. 'Black marketeers were thriving,' Siegfried Bandelow recalls. 'This was our first impression at Hanover station. We had to guard our luggage so that it was not stolen. The black marketeers could see at a glance that we had come from England and naturally wanted to cheat us.'

Men whose domicile was in the French, American or Soviet sectors had to travel next to their respective zones where they received civilian documents valid within that area. The discharge camp for the American Zone was the former concentration camp, Dachau, near Munich: in selecting this site the Americans clearly wanted to make a statement, though one POW at least seems to have missed the point. 'We were taken in a cattle truck (without straw or blankets) for two days and two nights to the discharge camp in the American Zone – "Dachau" … The organisation was poor, the accommodation very bad (400 men in one of the huts of the former concentration camp). Food mediocre.'

Kurt Engelhard returned to life as a civilian via the French discharge camp at Bretzenheim. 'I was a free man again after four and a half years. I arrived at Saarbrücken next morning and you can well imagine my mother's joy when suddenly she saw me standing in front of her.'

But Johannes Zimmermann, the survivor of the *Bismarck* who had been rescued from the sea by HMS *Dorsetshire*, remembered his promise to the friend who had drowned. 'It was a lousy, hard job to go to his parents and tell them what had happened. His mum had said to my mum, "Why is it that your boy's coming back and mine isn't?" It had caused a bit of trouble between them.'

The repatriates now had to adapt to a country they scarcely recognised and to a new life. Former POW Peter Scholzen wrote in a letter to Ted Page:

I arrived safely and I found my family well. Present conditions in Germany are so bad as one could not imagine in England. I knew that I was going to meet bad things, but I could not foresee the real state of affairs. My wife, my three children and my parents have not had potatoes for three weeks … My best thank [sic] for all you have done to me and above all for the good treatment I enjoyed. All the best to you and Captain Brill.

The prospect of repatriation was not always a happy one. A British clergyman said one prisoner he knew would 'go back to the broken remains of his demolished home and live there in the hope that one day his wife and two daughters would return to it'.

Some prisoners decided that home was the last place they wanted to be. The *Sunday Express* reported that whereas German POWs had previously escaped in an attempt to get back to Germany, 'Lately they have been escaping to avoid repatriation.'

A 27-year-old wrote in his diary, 'It is bitter to feel that I get no pleasure from repatriation. Ten years is a long time. My whole life seems to be messed up and stark realities begin now. Oh unhappy me! I have no future in Germany. I wish my captivity could begin all over again.' He hanged himself in the toilet of the train which was taking him to Harwich for his onward passage to Germany.

Leo Ganter – whose marriage to Monica Cann had caused such a sensation – was informed that he would be sent home on 22 July 1947. Monica was herself demobilised from the ATS that month and went to the camp in Sudbury where he was spending the final weeks of his captivity. 'I intend following Leo to Germany,' she told a newspaperman. 'As soon as permission comes through I shall spend my savings on getting there as quickly as possible, maybe by air. We shall live at his parents' home at Herbolzheim in the French zone for a while. I feel that my case has helped in the granting of permission for POWs to marry British girls,' she added. 'That's worth a lot.' Apparently, her wish to go and live with Leo in Germany was fulfilled, but rumour has it that the marriage did not last for very long and that Monica returned to Britain alone.

From the start of 1947, the monthly repatriation quota of 15,000 men was consistently achieved and sometimes exceeded. 'It caused me a lot of problems at North Mundham because I kept losing labour,' Theo Dengel remembers. 'From 500-odd we lost 100 and had to close another camp at West Hampnett and move the chaps.'

The plan was that the European Volunteer Workers and the Polish Resettlement Corps would fill the vacuum left by the departing German prisoners. But the EVWs, on whom so much depended, were still living in camps in Germany, Belgium and elsewhere, and it was taking longer than expected to transfer them all over to Britain. When they did arrive, certain unexpected cultural difficulties were encountered. Polish men, for example, did not know how to milk cows, and were not prepared to learn: in their culture this was considered to be exclusively women's work. And farmers complained that they had trained 'their' German and didn't want to start all over again with a new EVW.

As the 1947 harvest drew near, the government suddenly realised that there would again be a labour shortage. As a panic measure, they would permit POWs to stay in Britain until the end of the year if they wished. In April, Ness Edwards MP presented the scheme to Parliament:

> If the farmer feels that he can continue to employ a German prisoner of war and can provide him with accommodation, and the German prisoner is prepared to stay, in those cases the farmer will be asked to communicate with the Agricultural Executive Committees who will institute the arrangements for the transfer of the man from

prisoner of war status to civilian status for an experimental period. Between the prisoner and the farmer there is a fairly regularised and intimate relationship. If the farmer thinks the prisoner is a good fellow he will want to keep him.

A selection committee comprising the camp commandant, a representative of the WAEC and a representative of the War Office decided which prisoners could be considered as potential civilian workers.

Hans Teske reflects:

Before being eligible we had to be declassified. There came another one from Whitehall in mufti but this time not in a darkened room – this time I could speak to him and see him. And he looked quite human – not like the other monster. He asked me a question and I said, 'I will give the answers exactly as your superiors would like to hear them because I want to stay here.' And I was reclassified as 'B' which was the correct procedure to do it.

Hans had earlier discovered that his father had been murdered by the Russians in 1945, and that his mother and his sisters had been expelled from Eastern Germany. He claims:

I couldn't go home. My home was 'ethnically cleansed' – so I couldn't go there. I had to look for a job with somebody who would employ me as a civilian. And a nursery was prepared to do it, so I signed a contract and I was one of the first four to be released in England.

Arno Christiansen remembers being called into the farmhouse one day. 'You're going to be sent home!' the farmer told him. Christiansen cast his mind back to the years of 'living rough, belonging nowhere, an unwelcome alien in a foreign land, being rapidly despatched from one camp to another like a mislaid parcel … The Nissen huts, the cold, the endless boiled vegetables! The smell of other people's clothing!'

But he says he heard a voice in his head that said, 'I don't want to go back' – and realised it was his own.

Eberhard Wendler recalls that he continued to go to the base camp every Saturday to collect his pay until shortly before his release from POW status. Then the War Agricultural Executive Committee made the farmers responsible for paying out the wages and gave them the money to pass on to POWs. However, Eberhard says that he never received any of this cash because the farmer always took it all in the form of deductions – 'for soap, toothpaste, and so on.'

Eventually, he received notice from the camp that he would be freed on a certain date. When that day finally came, Eberhard opened his diary and ended his day-by-day account of almost four years as a soldier and POW. In a narrative which amounts to some 5,500 words, it is the only comment in English:

23 September 1947: *became a free man.*

He recalls:

> All I had was one blanket, which I had to buy from the camp, and one set of the prisoner of war uniform – trousers, jacket, boots, shirt and underwear – that's all. Then, gradually, I had to buy myself clothes on coupons. There was an Army & Navy stores and I bought ex-army clothes there.

To overcome objections from the farming unions, the prisoners of war on this scheme had to sign a fixed-term contract with a farmer, and from this point on were paid the going rate for their work. 'As a farmworker I got £4 weekly – on that I had to pay income tax, insurance, and £2 for lodgings,' Eberhard says. Henceforth, he never went back to the camp, which was filling up with EVWs. But after having been released from POW status there was almost no difference in the daily routine of his life: he took his meals with the foreman, but lived separately. He had to work and, when the farmer needed it, was required to do overtime, which he agreed to with reluctance. 'There was no freedom, and I had to work in all weathers, still wearing POW clothes.'

Outside the rigid structure of life in the army and as prisoners of war, the men quickly had to learn how to stand on their own two feet in a new and bewildering environment. *Lagerecho* (the camp magazine of Hardwick Heath, Bury St Edmunds, Suffolk) warned prisoners who were considering becoming civilians that 'the POW will be liable for all medical and dental fees, etc. exactly the same as a civilian':

> There was no one to look after our welfare [writes Theo Dengel], the canteen had closed, if we wanted cigarettes, soap, or razor blades we had to find a shop that stocked what we needed. The medical centre had closed, if we wanted to see a doctor we had to travel to the far side of Chichester; for minor ailments we had to pluck up courage to ask the dispenser or a shop assistant at the chemist's in Chichester. If we wanted to send letters to Germany, we had to buy our own notepaper and envelopes and find out the cost of postage of our letters.
>
> We were issued with a special identity card classifying us as 'Enemy Aliens' … The description … brutally defined our status. We had no rights, we had no expectations of being accepted into English society, or being regarded as equal with the people in the village … When we were Prisoners of War, our status was clearly defined … now, each one of us had to learn to be independent in a strange, and partly hostile environment and try to earn the acceptance and respect of the English people who were, by and large, not bothered.

Anticipating protests that the ex-POWs would take up much-needed housing in rural areas, the government included in the contract a provision that the farmer must provide lodgings for the former prisoner. The reasoning behind this was that the available accommodation was usually of such low standard that a British worker would have refused to stay there anyway.

Arno Christiansen made a home for himself in 'an empty loose box in the stable yard that had not been used for livestock for some time … scrubbed the accumulated muck of years from the floor, walls and roof, and used gallons of boiling water, and a great deal of elbow grease … [and] moved his camp bed into his new quarters and took up residence.'

But when Hans Behrens was billeted at a Sussex farm, he found that the conditions exceeded all expectations. 'I was very lucky – I stayed with the Norwoods who looked after me extremely well. They treated me as their son in all respects. To this day I call them "my English parents",' he told an interviewer in 1994. 'I had lodgings there and they paid me £2 10s a week. Their daughter, Pamela, was studying catering in Paris, so I had her pink bedroom, would you believe?' He continues:

> I thought about going back to Germany all the time. I wanted to go home, but the more I got to know England the less I wanted to go back. By the time I moved in with my English parents the draw of home became less. There was a very nice family in Rodmell, the neighbouring village to Southease. They were Quakers and they used to invite five of us every other Saturday. It was there that I was introduced for the first time to afternoon English tea, cucumber sandwiches and listening to 'Greensleeves'. Very, very English! Another family would fetch us in their car, take us to Lewes for afternoon tea and then a run around the country. And I remember so well one time on the north side of the Downs, and I thought how lovely the countryside looked – lovely houses, big gardens and nice hedges and fences – it was wonderful, really wonderful.
>
> When the time came for me to be repatriated to Germany, a decree came out here to say that if an English farmer were to apply to the commandant of the area, the prisoner could be released in this country and not shipped to Germany. So Mr Norwood and I agreed and we signed a contract across a sixpenny stamp of King George to say that he would look after me and I would be his servant for a twelve-month period, renewable by mutual agreement.

Some former prisoners attach great importance to these documents, since they represent such a significant milestone in their lives. Many years later, Hans asked Mrs Norwood whether she still had the contract, but sadly it had been lost. One such document which has survived, though, was issued by the Lincolnshire War Agricultural Executive Committee. It shows signs of having been prepared in considerable haste, presumably in response to the government's rapid about-turn. It is in German but has evidently been typed by someone unfamiliar with the language: in places it is virtually incomprehensible. Under the agreement, the 'worker' (the term 'prisoner' is studiously avoided) committed himself to working for the farmer, and no other employer. He was not to do any work except agricultural work.

In exchange, the farmer was obliged to pay £4 10s per week, less deductions for food and lodgings which were, in this case, £1 10s weekly.

There was something reminiscent of a slave auction in the way that POWs were transferred to their new 'owners'. Not that the prisoner himself was sold to the farmer.

But the clothes he stood up in were. There and then, the farmer had to refund the cost of the prisoner's uniform to the authorities: he could, if he wished, recoup this expense afterwards from the ex-POW's wages.

By October 1947, the initiative had been extended until the end of the following year. POWs could also apply officially to work for the War Agricultural Committees direct (as Theo Dengel had done on an unofficial basis several months previously). A concession was also introduced under which men already repatriated to Germany could apply to return to Britain and resume work. This brought fresh hope to Bruno Liebich, who had returned to Germany to be reunited with his family, and had found employment there before fully realising that his place was in Britain with his sweetheart, Audrey.

'I had a good job there and I could have stayed. But I only had one single room which they "graciously" let you have. So I came back, which was *very* rare in those days. They didn't want people to leave Germany, they wanted them to stay and help rebuild the country.' Bruno returned in June 1948: within two weeks he and Audrey were married. 'I had no transport, no phone, no means of communication,' Bruno confesses. He borrowed a suit from Audrey's brother. The woman he had visited at Christmas, Mrs Herbert, lent him £5 to buy a ring and gave the couple a picture to hang on the wall of their new home, as – in Bruno's words – 'We had nothing'.

While working on the Norwoods' farm, Hans Behrens decided to bend the rules by taking a part-time job that was unconnected with agriculture. He says:

> I started working as a projectionist at a cinema at Burgess Hill, just to get my fingers in, because I knew that, in the long term, farming wasn't my trade. I got £1 for Saturday and Sunday work from 2.00 to 10.00. And I remember one time taking the whole projector to pieces – and the manager came up and said, 'What are you doing?' and I told him I was cleaning and oiling it, and he said, 'We've got a show starting at three o'clock!' and I told him not to worry, it'll be ready. And of course it was. At least I had my hands on again, using tools, doing something mechanical.
>
> Mr Norwood, the farmer, told me he couldn't pay me higher wages. He couldn't give me work that was any more interesting and he couldn't further my education as far as my long-term trade was concerned. But he knew somebody who could.

Norwood's acquaintance was a local dignitary. Hans recalls:

> We drove up to this big house. I was introduced to the lord and master of the house and was shown up to my little room. And there comes a young woman in, wearing a blue dress and a white apron with pillows in her hand – her name was Ivy. As time developed, we got very fond of each other and in due course we got married.

19

'The Germans Were All Right'

On 12 July 1948, the last troopship taking newly released prisoners home to Germany left the docks at Harwich. There was little fuss or ceremony and *The Times* allotted only a few lines to the event. But for the prisoners, it must have been a moment tinged with emotion:

> As the ship pulled away from the quayside, the men lined the rails waving, and from an accordion came the strains of 'Lili Marlene', the German *Afrika Korps* song.

'The Germans were all right,' a *Sunday Express* report gushed. 'At first we thought them all things, lately we have pitied them as slave labour,' the journalist wrote (in contrast to the vehement anti-German tone adopted by his newspaper during the war years). The public had found the Germans to be 'mild, reasonable young men', he declared, and people had been 'surprised'.

Those who had signed up to stay on as agricultural workers until the end of the year looked on as their comrades left Britain for good. Close friendships had formed but now had to end. Bruno Liebich has remained in St Albans, not far from the camp where he was a prisoner, while his comrade, Alfred Mertens, returned to Germany. They have stayed in contact ever since, but they were probably the exceptions.

'If anybody had told me I'd finish up in England I'd have said they needed a brain test,' exclaims Peter Roth. But events conspired to change his mind. 'I hadn't got a good home. When my mother died, my stepmother was good to me. But my father – he would never talk to me like father and son. And then he went one step further; he got too friendly with a woman, one of the neighbours. He thought I was blind, but when you're 13 or 14 years old you know what's going on.' He says, 'In a Catholic village the people talk – and then some of the boys weren't allowed to come and see me any more. I finished up with only one friend – and in a Catholic community he and I were outsiders.'

Peter has never got over this conflict with his father but meeting his future wife, Margaret, gave him a new perspective. 'Margaret's father had died in 1930,' Peter says. 'Her mother was a cook for the wealthiest farmer in March, Mr Johnson. He had 1,000 acres of land. The first time I visited her home – there was a massive walk-in kitchen – I went in and her mother said to me, "Peter, what is here isn't 'mine' or 'yours' – everything here is *ours*. If you want anything, help yourself." This was the attitude.' Peter immediately sensed a kindness that he had seldom experienced before. This was all it took to convince him that Britain would be his future home.

After his unfavourable first impressions of Britain, Henry Metelmann also came to see things in a different light. The turning point came when he was being moved to a camp near Romsey, Hampshire, and watched the countryside rolling by as he gazed out of the train window:

> In many ways England was a strange country. That narrow channel of water seemed to have made much difference over the centuries. Most things seemed small and old-fashioned. The rows and rows of houses in the towns, with their small backyards and gardens, seemed cramped. The people were friendly enough, but strangely reserved, and life generally had an unhurried flow, so very different from America and the Continent of Europe. And yet, there was something likeable about it all ... Those [prisoners] who lived out on the farms had very good relations with the farming people, and on the whole were treated very well ... I was transferred to an out-camp in a beautiful old country house called Hazelhurst, near the village of Corhampton. It did me much psychological good, as it gave me a feeling of freedom which I had not had for many years.

Eberhard Wendler's mind was virtually made up much earlier, the day he saw the film of the concentration camps. 'I felt ashamed to be German. I didn't want anything to do with them – I didn't want to go home. I couldn't go to the East and I knew nobody in West Germany. Mum kept writing, "Come home, come home," but I thought, "*Never!*"'

Since the spring of 1946, Eberhard had been on a farm with two other prisoners of war. One at a time, the others moved elsewhere:

> And so I lived alone in the empty cottage, next door to the farm manager. The farmer himself was very old – he was somewhere in Newfoundland on government work. The manager had two unmarried daughters in their 60s. These were the only civilians I knew. I lived on the farm over a mile from the road at Bocking – the farm was remote and I never saw anyone else. I had nobody to talk to and never saw any Germans any more.

Finally, towards the end of 1948, the POWs still in Britain were offered a chance to stay permanently in the country. Thirty thousand applied and just under 25,000 were allowed to do so. The government feared that those who wanted to stay but were not accepted on the scheme might cause difficulties: the Home Secretary consulted with police forces around the country to discuss ways of removing the men forcibly if necessary. He was, however, advised that 'In the absence of individual deportation orders no such power exists ... the police will not have any power to withhold or restrain individual ex-prisoners-of-war as such or to compel them to join a repatriation party.' In the event, it seems, most or all of the prisoners being sent home left without a fuss.

When it came to the prisoners who had elected to stay in Britain, the government still feared accusations of slave labour. The Russians, in particular, would grasp any opportunity to divert attention away from the thousands of Germans they themselves were still holding. The problem was eventually solved in a most ingenious way. All prisoners who applied to stay on would be sent on a four-week 'holiday' in Germany. They could visit friends and relatives and see for themselves what life there was really like now. Most importantly, the scheme ensured that those who did decide to return to Britain were quite patently doing so of their own free will. The government would avoid any hint of forced labour; and in addition the section of the Geneva Convention which dictates that prisoners should be repatriated *to their own country* would be followed to the letter.

Each POW was required to pay £5 in advance for the return fare. Those who went back to Britain after the four-week period got their money back; those who remained in Germany did not. Thus, despite the government's attempt to be scrupulously fair, there was in practice a small incentive, whether intended or not, to return to Britain.

The decision over whether to stay in Germany or return to Britain was not an easy one. Often, it was only during this 'holiday' that the final choice was made. Says Heinz Czieselsky:

> After three years my mother and I had found each other again through the Red Cross, and I found out that my father was killed in Holland, and my mother had escaped from Upper Silesia and it took her a long time to get to Bavaria. The Russians came in and the Germans moved out. When I was released … I went down to Bavaria to visit my mother and sister, but they only had two rooms – a bedroom and a living room, and I couldn't stay there. There was no living accommodation because all the people from East Germany came to West Germany then, mainly Bavaria because they arrived via Czechoslovakia. There was no work there, nothing, so I came back to England. Then I met my wife, who's German too – she'd come over as a domestic help – and we got married. And we stayed another year, and another year. We were always half and half. 'Shall we go back to Germany?' But I got so used to working here … and finally I got a job in an industry outside agriculture.

Dieter Hahn, on the other hand, had already made up his mind:

> We had a choice of either staying in England or going home. I was married by then so of course I decided to stay. I was in love with my wife – I suppose I *could* have taken her back to Germany, but I didn't. I knew jolly well what the conditions were like in Germany. I knew it was more or less a complete wasteland – bombed cities, destroyed houses – everything just flattened. So I decided to stay.

Fritz Jeltsch says:

> My brother and sister were in East Germany already. But I couldn't have gone back
> to East Germany; they would have kept me there. The only place I could go was to
> my brother-in-law in Bavaria, who had his own farm. So I went there to get my
> discharge papers. But the British government had already given us a return ticket
> and the farmer wanted me back. I was already working on a farm near Northampton
> looking after cows and pigs and doing everything. We Germans were all young and
> good workers. All the farmers wanted to keep us. In Britain I had my room on the
> farm – I had my work on the farm, although I got paid very little, about £4 a week –
> but I knew I had a place here. But there I was a stranger because my home was taken
> by the Poles. I didn't have a home any more.

Karl-Heinz Decker made his way to the area where his family had resettled:

> I'd been reported missing and my father didn't recognise me when I got there. My
> father had been released from a British POW camp not long before me and he was
> just skin and bones. He said they'd been on an island in the North Sea and all they
> had to live on was nettles. Nettle soup, nettle tea and all that.
>   Seeing the plight of my family and the state of the country I decided to Britain
> and start a new life. I returned to my old job with Mr and Mrs Roberts at Cefn Farm.

Henry Metelmann recalls:

> A prisoner transport took me back to Germany. My parents were now both dead;
> everything we had [was] destroyed in the bombings. The clothes I stood up in and
> the blue American kitbag on my shoulder were my only possessions. … Germany
> irritated me. There was no attempt even to talk about the war and what had
> happened and why. I had no home, there was much unemployment and I felt lost
> and alone. And when a close relative told me that the defeat of Germany was the
> fault of people like me who had no faith in the Führer and who had not given their
> all in the struggle, I had had enough. I took my kitbag and went back to England,
> after only four weeks.

On the ferry, Eberhard Wendler looked at the other prisoners around him:

> Most of them were from the western part of Germany, and were going home to see
> their loved ones. My family were in the East and it was impossible for me to visit
> them. But I had relations by marriage in Wilhelmshafen. When I arrived there the
> station was all dark and there was destruction all around. I saw lights which seemed
> to come from under the ground, and when I looked more closely I realised that

people were living in what had once been the cellars of the houses. The lights were coming from the people's candles.

While I was at my relation's house the doorbell rang. And there at the door were my uncle and my mum. I was *so* surprised! Mum looked so small and thin and shrivelled up. She was nearly starving. They weren't supposed to leave the East and so they bribed someone to take them to a place near the East–West border, and then bribed another person to take them across. It was December – freezing cold. At one point they waded across a river and they were soaked in icy water. The man insisted on another payment – they had no money and paid him by giving him some of their clothes.

The reunion didn't go well. Eberhard says:

I don't often talk about it because they'd risked their lives to come and see me and I hurt mum's feelings. I wasn't the little boy she'd said goodbye to. Instead I'd grown up into a man and I was hardened. The world had been unkind – I was living as a POW with a lot of other men, older men, and you get as hard as they are. And my mum and my uncle had to smuggle themselves back into the East again. When the trip was over I was glad to be back in England.

It would be years before he saw his family again.

Theo Dengel says:

'When it came to the final discharge everybody who wanted to stay behind had to go to the base camp at Billingshurst, where it took three days to do all the paperwork. I had applied to stay behind and it was refused at Billingshurst – not once but twice. Ted Page said, "I need this chap, he's important in our work. He wants to stay and I want him in the office." It took another week before they consented to my staying on.'

Although Theo had originally been quoted a date of 1949 for his repatriation, events turned out somewhat differently. The pace of repatriation speeded up. Theo now believes that if he had not contracted to stay on he would have been sent home anyway by February or March 1948, which was the case with many of his fellow prisoners. He says:

It was a funny set-up because, whereas the British had discharged me as a POW and given me papers as an enemy alien, I was still in the German army!

Shortly afterwards it was announced that all other Germans on a one-year contract would be repatriated by the end of November 1948 … All this added an element of insecurity to my own situation although, to some extent, I was relieved that my forthcoming marriage would allow me to remain in England until we had saved up sufficiently to enable us to apply for an immigration visa to the United States.

Theo and Joan were married at the beginning of October. 'The wedding was in the Register Office with a few friends and my parents – that was it,' says Joan:

> Straight after the wedding, before we could go on honeymoon, Theo had to go to the police station and register that he was now married, to make it all legal. My best friend got married soon after I did and said, 'I'm sorry, my father won't let Theo come to the wedding.' I could understand that – her father was gassed in the First World War. I'm not stupid, I could understand where this was coming from, but it upset me a little bit. And I said, 'Unless my husband is welcome I don't intend to come.' There was a certain amount of being snubbed because most of the girls who worked there were either married to – or very friendly with – a serviceman. Marrying a German was looked down on. And the vicar came round and told my mother he disapproved. But I'd realised that life wasn't going to be easy.

North Mundham hardly resembled a POW camp any longer. The German *Lagerführer* had married an English girl and they had a little flat in the camp. Ted Page had been moved to head office in Chichester, leaving Theo in charge of the Labour Office and directing the work done by no fewer than nine separate camps.

'Ted Page eventually became our best man when we got married,' Theo says. 'But he was terribly lonely, because nobody would make friends with him, and he was such a lovely man. Just after I was married to Joan she said she would take him to dances to find a girlfriend. And she tried to introduce him to girls at the telephone exchange but "conscientious objector" – dirty word. That prejudice! I couldn't understand it. It must have been so hurtful.'

But Theo remembered the people who'd invited him to spend Christmas with them in 1947 – the Wellcome family. Since that first meeting he had seen them regularly and received frequent invitations to tea. Their eldest daughter, Mary, taught at a local primary school where a Christmas carol concert had been arranged for the children. Theo and Joan were invited and Joan asked if she could bring a friend – Ted. And six months later Ted and Mary were married, with Theo as best man.

A few weeks later, Theo received a conciliatory letter from his mother, and at the same time he was offered a chance to take the 'holiday' in Germany:

> Having just got married, that wasn't really on because we were having problems finding accommodation and so on. Just before Christmas 1948 – by that time we'd found a flat in Chichester – Joan said, "You ought to go and see your parents." And I said, "Well … yeah, sort of."
>
> I spoke to Ted Page about it and he offered to ring the War Office about it, but they told him there were no places left on that scheme. [The original deadline for applications was 30 September] Lo and behold, after about three days a chap came in to see Ted about a problem. He'd asked to go to Germany but since then his marriage had broken up – his wife had gone with someone else and he no longer

wanted to go. But he'd been told he couldn't cancel. And Ted told me there was a vacancy – and I said "Yes, please!" It was at very short notice.'

Theo travelled to Munsterlager to be formally discharged, and then to his home town, Kaiserslautern, where he arrived just before Christmas. 'My parents' joy to see me again was overwhelming. Somehow or other, we did not have any unpleasantness or recriminations. There was a lot to talk about, but much was left unsaid.'

While in Kaiserslautern he was required to report to the police and be issued with a ration card.

The thing that stuck in my throat was that there was an unpleasant-looking woman in her 40s. I told her I only wanted ration cards for one month. 'Why is that? You just got your discharge.' I told her I was going back to England. 'Why do you want to go back there?' I told her I'd married an English girl. And she exploded. In front of a room full of people, clerks and so on, she screamed at me, 'You traitor! You married an *Engländerin* and there's all these German girls who have no husband and haven't a chance of getting married. You're a traitor.' It was so embarrassing in front of about fifty people. I felt like belting her, but I didn't reply, and I kept my calm and walked out.

After this incident, Theo writes, 'I was even more pleased that I had decided to make my home elsewhere.'

Werner Völkner was discharged on 23 December 1948. 'If I'd saluted in a different way and been a bit more forthcoming with the interpreter I probably wouldn't have finished up with a 'C-minus',' he says with a good-natured laugh:

When I was discharged I had one battledress – a proper one without markings – a pair of trousers, a pair of boots, a pair of socks, a towel, a spoon, my old [German army] mess-tin. Those were my worldly possessions. And since then I've become a hoarder. I had the chance of going back to Germany but the Russians occupied that part of Berlin where my home was. I was talking to George, my employer's son, and he said, 'You don't want to go back to Germany under the Russians, you stay here. You can have a job with me as long as you like.' And I wondered what would happen if I went back to the Russian zone of Berlin, and anybody realised I'd been with the *Waffen-SS* in Russia. Plus the fact that my father wrote, 'If you can stay another year – *or so* [his emphasis] – do so by all means.' Some of the earlier releases, people I'd been to school with and done my apprenticeship with, the Russians took them away to the Soviet Union. So one year went into another and another and I became acclimatised to living in Britain. I started reading the newspaper with a dictionary and learned English.

The contract which prisoners had to sign in order to stay behind in Britain made it clear that they were not allowed to engage in any occupation other than agriculture. This presented difficulties for those who would have preferred the profession they had originally trained for. In civilian life, Robert Frettlöhr had been an electrician at the Thyssen steelworks in Duisburg. 'The only way to stay was working on farms. I couldn't work in *my* trade – no way. That wasn't allowed if you were an alien. I actually sent a letter to King George [he laughs] asking if I could pursue my own trade.'

Hans Teske fell foul of the same regulation. He had been wounded and considered himself unfit to continue in farming. He applied for an exemption, but the authorities – probably fearing that many other ex-POWs would have the same thought – insisted that Hans should see an officially approved doctor in London.

'I see you were wounded,' the doctor said. 'Where were you in action?'

'Bou Arada in Tunisia,' Hans replied.

'So you were one of the buggers who fought against us?'

'Yes I was one of the buggers,' Hans admitted.

They then enjoyed a long, animated conversation about old times. At length the doctor called his nurse into the surgery and sent her out for fish and chips.

'So we ate the fish and chips and the doctor sent the nurse home,' Hans says. The doctor enquired about his injuries. 'You're not fit for agriculture,' he pronounced without examining Hans, and he wrote out a certificate. Subsequently, Hans met the Minister who, for some reason, chose to give him a lecture in democracy and then told him he could work in any occupation – *except* printing, which was Hans's own trade.

'He wanted to be nasty,' Hans says. Hans asked him to put his decision in writing, and took the letter to his Member of Parliament, Norman Dodds. 'He was lost for words. He said, "He gave you a lesson in democracy, but *we'll* show you the *real* democracy." The next day he said, "I've obtained permission for you to return to your vocation. We have a great shortage of compositors but not so great a need for people growing cabbages. I've found an excellent job for you locally in Crayford. The man is not only prepared to employ you – he does jobs in foreign languages and he's prepared to pay you 25 per cent above the rate." That was nothing to sneeze at.'

Hans Behrens recalls:

I was still officially restricted to working on the land, but the family I was working for needed some help in the house and asked me to be their butler. Well, anything to get off the farm, because they had turkeys and pigs and there was all this muck and dirt and I had a skin infection on my hands. So I got on to the local MP, Colonel Clarke, and asked for his help. And he wrote to me, 'Dear Mr Behrens —.' It was the first time I'd been addressed as '*Mister* Behrens'. He told me there were only three ways I could be released from the state I was in: One: if you're a nuclear scientist. Two: if you marry a British woman – I wanted to, but not on £2 10s a week. Three: for medical reasons. I went to my doctor in Cuckfield, and he agreed that my hands were bad. I applied to the Home Office for release from this status.

A further medical examination followed, as it had for Hans Teske. As luck would have it, the government-approved medic was an old friend of Behrens's own doctor – 'and within eight weeks I was released'.

The 1948 Summer Olympics were dubbed 'the Austerity Games'. The elaborate and expensive preparations typical of previous and subsequent Games alike were absent. Instead, existing buildings and facilities were used to save the cost of building new ones, although a new road, Wembley Way, was laid to link Wembley Park Station with the stadium. Prisoner of war labour was used in the construction of this road: a press photograph shows a smiling POW – still wearing his German uniform cap – apparently discussing the work with a British engineer. Early plans for the Games had toyed with the idea of using German POWs to pick up cigarette ends and other litter left by the spectators. But the authorities, fearing yet more accusations of slave labour, eventually shied away from this proposal.

The world's premier athletes would be housed at former army barracks: some of the British competitors prepared by training at a Butlin's holiday camp, others at a recently closed prisoner of war camp. The defeated nations, Germany and Japan, were excluded from the event, but pre-war German gymnastics champion Helmut Bantz played a vital role in Britain's quest for medals.

Bantz was the prisoner of war who had arranged an athletics championship in the camp where he was held, which had so impressed the guards. After approaching the British gymnastics trainers, he attended a practice session in Leicester. 'It later transpired that Britain had been waiting for one of the German POWs to come forward and help their gymnastic team. As it happens, some had presented themselves, but hadn't shown them anything useful – perhaps they were just people who saw this as an excuse to get away from the camp.'

Bantz became a trainer to the British squad. He lived with the athletes, and proudly wore the team's Olympic uniform. 'Everyone knew I was a prisoner of war and yet, on the opening day, I was offered the chance to march into the stadium with the British team at the opening ceremony. I'd have been the only German participant in 1948!' Bantz, however, declined this invitation, considering that 'it wasn't right' for him to take part in this way. (He subsequently competed as a member of the German Olympic team in the 1952 and 1956 Games.)

As Bantz stood on the sidelines watching his protégés march around the arena at the opening ceremony, the last of Britain's POWs to be repatriated to Germany had left the country less than three weeks earlier. The only ones remaining were those who had chosen to stay on, plus a very small group of suspected war criminals and the like.

20

Britain's Last POW

Bruno Liebich went on to work as a milkman, a gardener and then a window cleaner. He and Audrey had five children – three girls and two boys. Later, after taking a correspondence course, he set up his own company selling electrical goods all over the country. 'Business was doing very well and I had a bit of spare money. And I wanted a nice classic car. A man in Lincolnshire told me he had a car for sale which was due to be sent to auction in America and he expected to get £50,000 for it – in 1973! And I was determined to buy it.' The vehicle in question was Hermann Göring's Mercedes – one of only a handful manufactured to that design.*

Bruno is at pains to emphasise that his decision to buy the vehicle was motivated only by the opportunity to own a piece of history and not by any admiration for the Nazis. With three others, he formed a consortium to buy the car, but to his dismay the others eventually got cold feet and backed out:

> And then the oil crisis started. The car was armour-plated and it did 5 miles per gallon. And I was stuck with it! I'd paid a 50 per cent deposit. It was still standing where I'd seen it in Lincolnshire but they'd cancelled the auction and the owner was worried. The best offer they'd had was £25,000 and I'd paid a deposit of more than that. Nobody wanted to insure it. It only fitted into my garage with a couple of inches to spare either end. I was really getting worried. Finally an American buyer was found, and I had to take it back to Peterborough. I was so nervous I couldn't drive it – my son had to drive. And when we got there it was discovered that one of the pistons had broken. They were going to give me £33,000 but because of this mechanical problem they only offered £25,000. I just broke even. But it was a nice experience.

Bruno's beloved wife, Audrey, died from breast cancer in 1975 at the age of 45. Their youngest child was only 6 years old. In later years Bruno ran a wine bar and – after the fall of the Iron Curtain – went back to Germany where he set up a wholesale business. Then in 1993 he returned to Britain and sold glassware imported from Europe.

---

* Bruno Liebich states that one of these cars was allocated to Adolf Hitler, and Heinrich Himmler and Martin Bormann each had one. Göring used the car in question, and potentates in Portugal, Finland and Norway who were sympathetic to the Nazi cause received the others.

In 1994 Bruno finally discovered the fate of his brother who had been 'missing' since the war: he had died while a prisoner in Russia, as Bruno had always feared.

Since retiring from business Bruno has travelled the world. A Saga cruise turned out to be less sedate than one might expect. Off the coast of Madagascar, the ship was threatened by pirates, but Bruno's past life as a soldier and a POW stood him in good stead. 'I tried to remain calm because whatever is going to happen will happen and there's little you can do to prevent it,' he told a reporter. Quick thinking on the part of the cruise liner's captain saved the day and the liner sped away from the suspected pirate boat.

'I've been to India, Vietnam, Peru,' he says. 'When I go on trips abroad if I can enter a home I feel I've really *been* there.' And it all began when Bruno and a friend were invited as POWs to visit a British family for Christmas many, many years ago. He has appeared on several television programmes about D-Day and POWs. And he has recently finished the life story he was writing when this author first went to interview him.

Joan Dengel says that it was not until the mid-1950s that people accepted her and Theo as a couple. 'But I didn't shut myself away, and I've always been friendly … I wouldn't say it didn't hurt at times, when people snubbed me, because it did. And I used to hurt for Theo when people snubbed him.'

For his part, Theo felt that his life had been on hold while he was a prisoner of war: afterwards, he simply wanted to make a fresh start. He went to work as a clerk for a local firm of wool merchants who operated from rather Dickensian offices in Chichester. 'The business had been founded in Victorian times by Ebenezer Prior. Now it was run by five of his sons, all in their 60s and 70s. After about eight or nine years I was on £12 a week. By then, we had four kids and it was a struggle. Joan sewed curtains to get some extra money.'

Joan picks up the story here. 'He kept saying, "I'm not getting anywhere – I've asked for a pay rise of half a crown and they refused." So I got quite cross and told him to stop moaning. "If you want to change your job go and get some certificates at night school." ' Theo diligently signed up for no fewer than three nights a week of evening classes and was successful in gaining the qualifications he needed. Joan says, 'I used to take the three children round and round the park in all weathers at weekends so that he could have time for studying. And my stepmother and my father said, "I *always* knew he would do it – I always knew he'd make something of himself." '

'This is going to sound really stupid,' Joan adds, 'and perhaps Theo won't want me to say this. When we moved to Chichester, Theo used to go to the bank every Friday morning, and I used to walk down – with a baby in the pram usually – meet him outside the office, walk to the bank with him, wait outside, and walk back to the office – just to *be* with him. This sounds a bit silly, doesn't it, when you're 80-odd? But it's the truth. It's how we felt about each other – we still do.'

Theo's parents still had their doubts about him marrying an *Engländerin:*

In 1952 I took Joan there for the first time. My parents had been very 'anti', but when they met her they just fell in love with her and they couldn't do enough for her; they really worshipped her.

My parents came to England in 1956 – my father was very anti-English and had weird ideas. My boss lent me his chauffeur and his big, posh car and we took my father and mother all around West Sussex. And we visited London – I've got a picture of them standing in front of 10 Downing Street. They loved that – it really opened their eyes.

Joan adds:

Theo's father took our son, Stephen, who was 3, to the park, and he didn't speak a word of English. It started to rain as they walked back, and they were getting absolutely drenched and somebody came out of their house and shouted to Theo's father. They made signs to ask whether he wanted a raincoat and umbrella. And they gave him a raincoat and umbrella and he came back with a piece of paper with the people's address written on it. And he could not believe that somebody would come out, shout to him, and give him a raincoat and umbrella. And it impressed him no end, knowing he was a German.

Theo qualified as a chartered accountant and specialised in cost accounting. He turned around the financial fortunes of more than one large company before buying a business of his own in the late 1970s. The company was performing poorly when Theo purchased it but with Joan's help he turned it into a highly successful and profitable concern, which they finally sold for a handsome sum.

His career, he acknowledges, was 'very satisfying'. The wartime hardships were pushed more and more to the back of his mind as new challenges constantly presented themselves:

When I was discharged and started building my career, I tried hard to forget all of that, and I was fortunate because it wasn't the routine jobs that I got – it was changing systems, introducing new systems. It wasn't until I retired that all of a sudden there was this vacuum. Bit by bit, as I went for walks with the dogs, it started flooding back and I started talking about it. Previously I could never ever talk about it when people asked me. But after retiring I started digging all the old notebooks out. There are some experiences in life which you never forget.

And, as he says, his entire life could have turned out very differently if he had not been taken prisoner. And if his name had not begun with the letter D.

For a long time, Eberhard Wendler lived alone in the old cottage at the farm where he was employed. The work was hard and he was out in all weathers:

> Eventually I became the main tractor driver on the farm. The farm manager would just tell me what had to be done, and most of the time I was working alone. The tractors had no cab like they do now. You sat high up and the wind blew across the fields and you're ploughing up and down, frozen. The tractors were monsters made of cast iron, and in winter you had to drain all the water out of the radiator into 5-gallon drums to stop it freezing overnight. Next morning it was so cold if you touched anything metal with your fingers the skin stuck to it and you lost it. You had to take the cover off the 5-gallon drums and break the ice a bit – then you had to lift up these heavy drums and pour the water back into the radiator. Then you had to crank the engine by hand. Sometimes it would kick backwards and nearly take your arm off. Then ploughing – up and down, up and down – in rain you had an old sack over yourself, not all the gear they have now.

Eberhard bought a motorcycle and travelled to far-flung parts of Britain, learning about his newly adopted country, and taking many beautiful photographs. But he missed his parents. He hadn't seen his mother since that traumatic reunion in late 1948 at a relative's house in Wilhelmshafen. And so, in about 1954, he went to East Germany, aware of the consequences if he was caught.

'My mother always wanted me to come home, she kept on and on. So I thought I'd risk it. I applied for a visa but it was refused totally. They didn't let anybody in. They'd have been glad to have me live there, but I'd never have been able to leave again. I asked the Foreign Office and they told me if I got stopped they wouldn't be able to do anything to help.'

With the assistance of a relative who worked in local government in West Germany, Eberhard managed – quite unofficially – to obtain suitable documents and using these he smuggled himself into the East:

> At border control they looked at all our papers, and I was afraid they'd find out. I was terrified. Eventually I arrived at night in my town. When I came out of the station a young woman came over and said 'Eberhard?' It was my brother's wife. I'd never seen her before. When I left home my young brother was still going to school and now here he was, married with a child. His wife went back into the station and called him. He'd walked past me and I'd walked past him. We didn't know each other – hadn't seen each other for eleven years. They took me home to my parents. And, of course, *they were overjoyed!* But all the time I was there I was terrified.

On his return to Britain, his life seemed even lonelier than before: only on Sundays did he ever come into contact with other people. 'The old ladies who lived in the next cottage retired and I moved into their cottage. They were *very* strict. They used to go to the Congregational Chapel, and I went with them although I could hardly speak English.' But one day Eberhard was stunned to learn that the minister had been heard to say, 'The only good German is a dead one.' Even now, as he recalls the event, his expression reflects the shock and betrayal he felt at the time.

He started attending another chapel, and one day in the early 1960s he met another member of the congregation in the hall after the service. Her name was Kathleen Shelley. She had noticed Eberhard before but they had never spoken. 'I knew he came from Germany, and I knew he'd been a prisoner of war, and I knew he had lodgings in Bocking. But that's all I knew about him. I liked the look of him – he had lovely black curly hair.'

'We started talking,' says Eberhard, 'and then every Sunday after the service we just chatted.'

Kathleen remembers:

There was a young man at the church who had the idea of organising outings. Every August Bank Holiday he arranged a trip. Some of us were discussing these outings and wondering why people didn't go on them. And somebody said, 'Why doesn't that Eberhard come?' and I said I'd ask him. I had no idea what was in *his* mind, but I asked him if he'd come with us. And to my amazement he said, 'I will if I can sit with you.' I had no idea that he'd had his eye on me for some time. But when we sat together that was it. I knew how he felt for me and there was a spark between us and we went from there.

As children we were taught to hate the Germans. There were all the songs about Germans. But after the war a friend of mine married a German prisoner of war when she was seventeen. I got to know him through her and what they'd said about Germans just didn't add up. They were just as good as we are. I had no anti-German feelings in me at all. And my parents were OK about it. I think they were glad I'd found someone at last. Mother despaired, and said, 'There's no one good enough for you, is there?' I was in my thirties before I married.

'And I was 37,' Eberhard adds. Until then, he says, there was still the remote possibility that he might have returned to Germany: but his marriage to Kathleen determined that Britain would be his permanent home. He had left the farm by now and was employed by an engineering firm. The work consisted of repairing heavy farm machinery and the like – far from the precision engineering he had trained for. And his employer neglected to provide him with proper eye protection when he was welding. Throughout his life he has experienced problems with his back and with his eyes, the legacy of the jobs he had in those days.

In the hope of finding a position where his training could be put to better use, and with more pleasant surroundings, Eberhard approached the Marconi Company. 'They told me, "We'd love to have you but the unions wouldn't."' The problem was that Eberhard was not a British national. He applied for naturalisation, which was granted in

February 1964, and soon afterwards went to work for Crompton Parkinson, who had opened a new factory nearby specialising in electrical instruments. 'I went straight into that because of my certificate. They had a unit which was cordoned off and only certain employees could go in. We did stuff for the Royal Navy – power factor meters – and eventually I was the only one doing it. Everything had to be just so. The products were exported to other countries – including Japan and Germany. It was very interesting.' And working indoors in a warm environment was a bonus. Whenever something special had to be made, Eberhard was called upon to do it. Sometimes he came up with ways to improve productivity and received a cash bonus for his ideas.

During this time, he and Kathleen visited Eberhard's parents in East Germany, and finally his mother and father were permitted to leave the East to visit them in England, a trip they made three times in all. 'The first time Mum came to see us I took her into Tesco's in Braintree and she wept. "You've got all this to choose from," she said.'

Eberhard stayed at Crompton Parkinson for twenty-three-and-a-half years until the time came for his retirement. 'I've always been reticent about meeting people,' he says, 'in case they hold it against me for being German.' But he admits that such attitudes are much less common than they once were. 'We've got on well with our neighbours – always stop and have a chat. We've been very, very happy ever since.'

For several years Werner Völkner remained on the farm where he had been employed as a POW. Sometimes his employer's young son, Richard, would say to him, 'There's a good film on at the cinema but I can't go. Mum and Dad won't go. Have you seen that film? – it's supposed to be very good.'

'You see, he had to have somebody grown-up go with him,' says Werner. 'I used to go to what they used to call the fleapit, buy a ticket for 9d and sit in a 1s 3d seat because the usherette let me. Seeing the films and seeing the action that went with the speech helped me improve my English.'

Werner was married in 1949, but the couple split up after a relatively short time. When, in 1958, he was married for the second time to his present wife, Iris, a local newspaper showed a picture of the happy couple as they left Kingston Register Office. The paper described Werner's extraordinary military background as if it were an everyday occurrence. 'Mr Völkner served in the Death's Head Division of the Panzers and was awarded the Iron Cross, first class.'

But Werner's army career was far from over. At the end of the 1950s, he took the remarkable step of joining the British army, and signed up with the Westminster Dragoons, a Territorial Unit linked to the 2nd Royal Tank Regiment. 'We were in the depths of the Cold War and needed every man we could get,' a former comrade explains. 'Werner had experience so he was an ideal recruit. The other lads got on very well with him. His experience really shone through on occasion. He would notice things others missed, such as the broken branches at the side of a road where a vehicle had passed previously and its aerial had snapped them.'

Years later, Werner was invited to the wedding of his former boss's son, Richard. 'His father hired top hats and tails for us and there were seven of us including the best man, the ushers, and Richard. And the strange thing is – I've thought about it many times – I was invited to the wedding with Iris and the boys. I went to the weddings of all his children but none of the other farmworkers were invited' – an example, perhaps, of the 'regularised and intimate relationship' between farmer and prisoner mentioned previously.

Werner may be the only former SS member ever to have joined the British army. Two of his children have also served in the nation's armed forces. He is a member of the Royal British Legion, and he supports the charity *Help for Heroes*, which assists wounded war veterans.

Having met at a dance in 1949, Karl-Heinz Decker and Gladys were married the following year. He continued to work in agriculture for many years, but in the late 1960s he sustained a serious back injury while rescuing a sheep which had fallen into a hollow. Forced to change occupation, he became a postal worker. But his lifelong love of horses never left him, and soon he was – in his own words – 'back in the saddle again'. The Riding for the Disabled Association has enjoyed the benefit of his skills as a qualified rider and carriage driver, and during his thirty years with the charity he has met its president, Princess Anne, on two separate occasions.

Karl-Heinz's wife, Gladys, became seriously ill. 'She had bowel cancer and then she had the operation and did well, then she started smoking again. And one day she said, "I'm not getting up any more."' He says, 'I knew she was dying. She just sat and watched TV all day and smoked. And she wouldn't go back to hospital. And in the end she passed away. I said to the nurse, "I'll do it myself," and I closed her eyes and laid her out.'

He spent the next thirteen years becoming increasingly lonely. 'I enjoy conversation. I needed to speak to people [so] I decided to join a computer class.' Here he was reacquainted with an old friend, Dorothy Masterman, and they 'got together as a couple'. They now live together happily in Nottinghamshire.

After his release in 1948, Peter Roth married his sweetheart, Margaret. Crowds of curious onlookers lined the streets of March, Cambridgeshire, to see them on their wedding day. 'She was a well-respected person in the town. People couldn't believe that Margaret Stratton was marrying a German … *and a Catholic as well*! They couldn't *believe* it,' he repeats with a laugh:

> On a Sunday afternoon we'd go sometimes with my mother-in-law for a walk through the town. Now, you wouldn't see many married men go for a walk in the town with the mother-in-law, would you? People used to look. But mother-in-law

didn't care. In Manea I was called Peter the Painter, because I used to do all the decorating for Crouch – he was the biggest employer there. He had acres of crops being cultivated under glass. Everybody who wanted a job went to Crouch's. For me as a prisoner of war who'd just been discharged, I could go in any shop in March and buy anything in Crouch's name without paying. In all the time I worked for him – it was about six years – he never queried anything, a bill or anything like that.

Eventually, Peter wanted to start a nursery business of his own. But first he needed to buy a piece of land, and he had very little money. Margaret's mother, as a widow, couldn't help either. So Peter asked Charlie Johnson, the farmer for whom his mother-in-law worked, for a loan. Johnson advanced the money without hesitation. Peter declares:

> The estate agent couldn't believe it. 'Doesn't he want any *security*?' Of course he didn't want security. If I said I'd pay him the money back on that particular day, I'll pay it back. 'He doesn't want anything in writing?' No. People trusted me for one reason or the other. Individual people are all different – not everybody is good, and everybody takes a different view of things. I tried not to set anybody against us – against Germany. The only way I could do that was to show the best side of me so that they had no reason to go against me.

As a boy, Hans Behrens had not excelled at academic studies and he found schoolwork to be hard. When he left school at 14 he persuaded his father to let him go to an engineering college. Here he did much better, and enjoyed every minute. He took an apprenticeship and gained the equivalent of a City and Guilds certificate. One day a week they practised their precision engineering skills by repairing Leica cameras. As he says, his part-time job as a cinema projectionist signalled a welcome return to working with optical machinery. And after obtaining his exemption from agricultural work he was offered a job at a leading camera shop in London's Bond Street.

'Wallace Heaton was *the* company in those days. While I was there I had the opportunity to repair the Queen's camera – a Leica which was given to King George as a personal gift from Herr Leitz himself. And I also worked on Princess Margaret's Rolleiflex.'

After a time, though, the daily commute to London began to take its toll on Hans and he started working for a German engineering company which was keen to open a British branch. The business grew and he opened a small office above a dentist's surgery in Burgess Hill, Sussex, and took on staff. 'For twenty-seven years I built up the British end of the company. We had offices in Sussex and in Leicester. So in all I'd started from nothing in 1964 [and] when I retired in 1991 we had a staff of thirty-four people and a turnover of about £6 million. When I think back to when I stood at the station at Haywards Heath in my POW outfit, my kitbag with my few belongings and 5 shillings – and then the 5 shillings went on the taxi fare, so I had nothing …'

His voice tails off and after a few moments he speaks again. 'I suppose I've worked for it – so here we are.'

Robert Frettlöhr took a job with a Dewsbury building firm. His workmates found him to be a genial companion and from them he picked up the local dialect, completely losing his German accent. He was given the job of operating a digger, one of the first JCB excavators in the country:

> It were pretty easy. The machine did all the damn work. And I started playing again as a musician. And in them days you were treated like a little tin god because you did the excavation and the lads said, 'Right, have a rest now while we lay the drains, and then you can back-fill it again.' So I used to lie there and have a little sleep, you see, because as a musician I'd been playing till ten, eleven or twelve o'clock at night.

He joined a local jazz band, The White Eagles, as the bass player and discovered that he had much in common with the other musicians. Drummer Gordon Tilburn was a former RAF pilot, and trumpeter John Cook had been a Royal Marines Commando. In 1956, they were playing in Liverpool when local jazz enthusiast Alan Sytner invited them to look at a place he thought would make an ideal music venue. They accompanied Sytner to Mathew Street and made their way down eighteen stone steps into a former air-raid shelter 'in filthy condition, full of the usual bricks and rubbish. There was a single light bulb at the bottom of the stairs which provided the only illumination,' John Cook recalls. But the acoustics were perfect.

Sytner wondered what to call the new venue: crucially, it was the White Eagles themselves who came up with an answer – 'It looks like a bloody cavern,' one of them muttered.

The band went on to play at The Cavern once a month, and on 14 July 1961 they shared the bill with the Beatles, who were giving their first evening performance at the club since returning from Hamburg. 'We've often considered the consequences if we had not approved The Cavern – there may never have been the opportunity for the Beatles to become so legendary,' Cook told a journalist.

Hans Teske settled in Bexleyheath (then a town in Kent, now a London suburb). In a 1999 interview he said:

> I moved in there just before Ted Heath became the local MP and I was impressed with his views, especially on Europe, even in 1949. We got to know each other and in 1953 I joined his constituency party. I helped him with his next general election campaign, for which he was grateful because his majority increased considerably. I've attended joint functions with him on many occasions: on Europe Day a few years

ago wreaths were laid at the tomb of the Unknown Warrior in Westminster Abbey. Edward Heath laid the British wreath and I laid the German one.

Hans became vice-chairman of the Confederation of European Ex-Combatants. 'I was the first German to become a life member of the British Parachute Association,' he explained. 'They had to change their constitution for the purpose.'

But that wasn't his only claim to fame. A clerical error meant that he was never formally discharged from POW status. On several occasions he asked Ted Heath to intervene; he contacted Dr Konrad Adenauer and a string of German Ambassadors to Great Britain – all without success. In 1970, he informed Winston Ramsey, editor of *After the Battle* magazine, that he was going to give up trying.

Technically, he remained Britain's last POW of the Second World War until his death in 2000.

Ulrich Steinhilper, the pilot who fought against the RAF in the Battle of Britain, became a typewriter salesman with IBM in Germany and is credited by some sources with inventing the concept of word processing. His crashed aircraft – 'Yellow 2' – was rediscovered by a team of aviation archaeologists and excavated in 1980, almost exactly forty years after his crash. He returned to Britain on several occasions to see it on display at the Battle of Britain Museum, Hawkinge, before his death in 2009.

Harry Wappler – the one who *nearly* got away by stealing a plane with Heinz Schnabel – returned to Newport after the war and was reconciled with the Phillips family, two of whom died when his crippled aircraft crashed on to their house in September 1940. He is understood to have died in 1986.

Rolf von Bargen, who had edited the camp magazine *die Zeit am Tyne* at Featherstone Camp, became the original editor-in-chief of *Bild* – Germany's best-selling tabloid newspaper – when it started in 1952. Many other prisoners used skills they had acquired in the camps as a springboard for their civilian careers. Some repaid the British people's hospitality in their own individual ways. Günther Anton, a former rear gunner in the Luftwaffe, returned in the early 1960s to the village where he had been a POW and installed in the local church a stained-glass window which he had made. Over a thirty-year period, he went on to replace all of the remaining windows with new ones from his own workshop.

Monica Ganter – whose 'illegal' marriage to a POW in early 1947 made headline news – returned to her home town of Liverpool. Some accounts say that she worked in journalism for a time. She never remarried. While still in her mid-sixties her health deteriorated and she was admitted to a care home in Crosby. 'We understood that her husband had died very young,[*] and she didn't speak about him much,' one of her

---

[*]   There is no evidence to suggest that he actually did die young.

carers says. 'She never mentioned how she met him. She was very studious, always reading, and she could be quite pedantic. Everything had a place and had to be in its place. She was very nice and quiet but when she wanted something she let you know.' Until the end of her life, Monica kept up the office skills she had practised during the war. 'She kept a journal every single day in shorthand,' her carer recalled. 'We had a gentleman resident and she almost literally became his secretary. She used to do letters for him and looked after him. We've still got her old typewriter somewhere.' Monica died around 2007.

Werner Vetter, who married Olive Reynolds after being convicted for 'consorting' with her, stayed on in Britain – but not for very long. His name crops up again in March 1949 when he was found guilty of stealing £218 worth of property from a private house. 'The 23-year-old German ex-POW for whom the law was altered to allow him to marry an English girl while he was a prisoner, has been deported,' a newspaper revealed with a barely concealed note of disapproval at the way he had betrayed Britain's trust in him.

Ted Page, the former Labour Officer at North Mundham Camp, trained as a teacher after the war. A teaching aid which he devised with colleague Bernard Sadler – *Blackwell's Spelling Workshop* – received great acclaim and sold around the world for some thirty years. However, Ted did not live to see its success: he died in 1975 in the very same week that the book was published.

Harry Grenville, the former Interpreter Officer, also became a teacher after the war. He still gives talks to schoolchildren about the Holocaust. In 2013, at the age of 85, he finally obtained positive proof that his family had perished in Auschwitz, as he had suspected all along.

Postscript

The Americans fed us well but treated us badly.
The British fed us badly but treated us well.

The statement above is a sweeping generalisation, of course, and a tad unfair to the Americans, who tried to make their POWs as comfortable as possible. What is relevant, though, is that many prisoners saw things in this way. In 1957, the West German government commissioned a comprehensive history of German prisoners during the Second World War. After fifteen years of research, the Maschke Commission (named after its chairman, Erich Maschke) published its findings in twenty-two volumes. No other country, it concluded, had made so determined an effort as Britain, especially where the POWs were concerned, in easing Germany's re-entry into a community of free and democratic countries. 'In this respect,' the report claims, 'the prisoners of war from Britain were head and shoulders above their compatriots in Germany.'

Another German report found that with few exceptions the prisoners held in Britain were humanely treated, and were fed and clothed to an adequate – in fact, mainly very good – standard. Sanitary conditions were almost always satisfactory. Consequently, the overwhelming majority of the prisoners had returned home 'healthy and capable of working'.

A comparison between the experiences of prisoners in British hands and those held by other powers puts these findings in perspective.

France held around 900,000 German prisoners in total, 740,000 of whom were transferred there from the United States in 1945 and 1946.* As many as 50,000 are believed to have been put to work clearing the millions of landmines around France's coastline and tons of other dangerous materials left from the war. Others were sent to work in coal mining and similar hazardous occupations. Deaths and injuries among the prisoners reached such high proportions that the United States – which considered itself responsible, at least in part, for the men's welfare – made urgent representations to France over the treatment of the prisoners.

---

* At roughly the same time, 127,000 men were sent from America to Britain, as we have seen, but the two 'transactions' were subtly different. Whereas those sent to Britain were designated 'British-owned', those shipped to France were simply made available as a 'loan'.

Approximately 23,000 German POWs died in French captivity between 1944 and 1946, a death rate of 2.5 per cent.

The situation in the East was much worse, with as many as a million German servicemen dying while prisoners of the Russians. Guenther Wulff is the former POW who was urged by the Americans, 'Be in Linz by three o'clock if you want to be our prisoner.' He says:

> My father was called up near the end of the war and he didn't have the luck that I had. He got there *after* three o'clock and he was handed over to the Russians. He was a prisoner of war in Russia for five years. He did very little work because he was ill when he got there. He was too weak to work but he was too strong to die.

Tens of thousands of German prisoners were held in the USSR until as late as 1955 – ten years after the end of the war. They were finally released after a long and tireless campaign by Dr Konrad Adenauer, the first West German Chancellor. In addition, no fewer than 1.3 million German servicemen were listed as 'missing' and have never been accounted for. Russia is likely to have been responsible for a significant number of these men.

The death rate among prisoners in British hands was only 0.03 per cent – a minuscule figure in comparison – and 'while the number of deaths in American captivity is small in comparison with other states, it should be observed that the holding power with the highest level of resources was by no means the one with the lowest death rate'.

A comparison would be incomplete without mentioning the fate of Allied servicemen in German hands. In the main, Allied military personnel who were captured by the Germans were treated with an appropriate degree of respect, although severe shortages of food, fuel and clothing meant that conditions in the camps could be extremely uncomfortable. There were, however, instances of brutality: two atrocities which stand out are the slaughter by a *Waffen-SS* unit of eighty British prisoners captured at Dunkirk in 1940, and the execution of fifty RAF officers who escaped from the Sagan POW camp in 1944, the episode known as the Great Escape. These incidents must, however, be seen against a backdrop of many thousands of British servicemen who were, for the most part, treated reasonably by the Germans, even though the Geneva Convention was seldom strictly adhered to.

Britain's re-education programme was an ambitious and high-minded attempt to prepare Germans for the post-war world. 'The de-nazification process at every level led to a free, democratic Germany which still functions as such today,' says Harry Brook, an interrogator of German Jewish descent. 'Anti-Semitism and discrimination against Jews is now outlawed in Germany. That's what I fought to achieve.' But, as one observer remarked at the time, 'Those who need re-education most do not want it and those that are interested do not need it as much.' Some historians have labelled the initiative as 'very idealistic'.

Only when the decision was taken to hold men as a labour force for an indefinite period after the war was it even feasible for re-education to take place: paradoxically, Britain held the men against their will and against the spirit of the Geneva Convention but used the opportunity to teach them about democracy. But no matter what commentators say about the re-education scheme in general, most agree that Wilton Park achieved impressive results. No longer located at Beaconsfield, it has survived as an institution and is now situated in Sussex, its original goal unchanged: 'to turn ignorance into understanding, prejudice into appreciation, suspicion and hatred into respect and trust'.

As writer J.A. Hellen concludes, 'The main *raison d'être* of the camps, the political re-education of the Germans in Britain, had the unintended and long-term effect of re-educating the British themselves in their perceptions of and attitudes towards the German enemy in particular, and to Europeans in general.'

While conditions in British camps as a whole outshone those in other territories, Britain's treatment of the POWs was by no means flawless. The most regrettable incident, in this author's opinion, was the Repatriation Deceit.* At a time when Britain was extolling the virtues of democracy, this mean-spirited trick doubtless undermined the prisoners' trust. Better information – more 'transparency', as we would say today – would not have made the hardships go away but it might have made them easier for the prisoners to bear. 'Blood, toil, tears and sweat' are a lighter burden when one has been forewarned that they are coming and when the reasons for them have been explained.

Britain's continued detention of the German POWs after the war is another matter for concern. The country justified its actions by claiming to be technically within the provisions of the Geneva Convention, which subsequently 'was found to be lacking in precision and offered many loopholes to those who wished to evade their obligation'.

In 1949, a new and revised version of the Geneva Convention attempted to close the loopholes. The amended text states:

Prisoners of war shall be released and repatriated *without delay after the cessation of active hostilities.* In the absence of stipulations to the above effect in any agreement concluded between the parties to the conflict … *or failing any such agreement,* each of the Detaining Powers shall itself establish and execute *without delay* a plan of repatriation. [Author's emphasis.]

* As reviewed in Chapter 10.

Had this version of the Convention been in force at the time, Britain's continued detention of POWs long after the war would clearly have been in breach of the rules.

The use of POWs to clear unexploded mines and bombs also contravened the Geneva Convention, which specifically prohibited such employment. The best that can be said is that far fewer prisoners were engaged in this deadly work in Britain than in France, for example, where hundreds if not thousands of untrained Germans were used, many of them being killed or maimed in the process. According to Henry Faulk, only three Germans met their deaths while engaged in this work in Britain, and three others were wounded.*

It would be no exaggeration to say that the German prisoners played a pivotal role in saving Britain from economic collapse and famine. Arguably Britain's darkest hour came not during the war, when her Empire and her allies stood ready to support her in her time of need: the most critical point came immediately afterwards, when the country, alone, weakened by her wartime exertions and battered by cataclysmic weather, came perilously close to the abyss.

That is when thousands of Britain's former enemies helped fill the breach.

Perhaps the nation could have rounded up a labour force elsewhere: but, in practical terms, where in the world would a near-bankrupt nation have found 400,000 fit, strong and reasonably willing workers for a shilling a day per head? It was suggested in early 1946 that the POWs were a burden on the nation. Deputy Prime Minister Herbert Morrison immediately refuted the accusation, saying: 'The great majority of these prisoners, both Germans and Italians, are engaged on *work of the highest importance*, for which British labour is not available.' [Author's emphasis.] The events of the following few months were to prove their value beyond any doubt.

For the most part, the former prisoners of war who stayed on have blended quietly into society: Britain has now been their home for three-quarters of their lives. A surprising number have lived for decades within just a few miles of the camp where they were detained. They have absorbed the language and customs of their adopted country – and for many it hasn't been the easiest task.

'After I got married, I went on the bus for the first time on my own,' says Dieter Hahn. 'I didn't know how to ask for a return ticket. The conductor asked, "Single?" And I said, "No, married."' He laughs.

A proper knowledge of English only came with time:

There was a road sign which said, 'Dead Slow'. It puzzled me. Do you die if you go slow, or do you die a slow death, or what? And that wasn't the end of it. One day my

---

* A total of 185 British bomb disposal men were injured in this way, 139 of them fatally. The difference was that, unlike the German prisoners, the British genuinely had volunteered.

foreman persuaded me to back a horse, and I bet a shilling – a lot of money for me. Two days later he came to me and gave me 2 shillings. I said, 'Horse win?' He said, 'No it was a dead heat.' 'Horse dead with heat?' Eventually I got him to talk in the same pidgin English that I did!

Eduard Winkler says, 'I took every opportunity to listen to English people talking and gain the melody of the language, the tone of it. I got hold of a dictionary so I could find out what every word meant. And now my knowledge of English is quite extensive.'

They have subliminally taken on the local dialect of the area they have settled in, though in many cases their accents still reveal their German origins. Their sayings sometimes seem reminiscent of the Second World War era: both former comrades and enemies alike may be referred to as 'chaps' or 'chappies', and vaguely military expressions such as 'This is the drill' may still heard. Most of the former POWs speak English all the time, even when conversing with each other. Some find that German no longer comes spontaneously. 'I went to Germany on a business trip,' Theo Dengel remembers with a grin. 'They asked me if I really was German. "You speak a funny kind of German," they said.' If one of today's teenagers were to be magically transported seventy years into the future it would very likely be the same.

'I haven't spoken any German for a long time,' says Eberhard Wendler. 'I don't know any Germans here. If I met one today I doubt whether he'd understand me at all.' His links with Germany are tenuous now, but he hasn't severed them entirely. 'I've got a satellite dish and I get German music – I don't listen to the news or the politics, but the lovely songs – Strauss, Lehar.'

About one-third of the former POWs who stayed in Britain eventually became British citizens. Others didn't think it was worthwhile. 'I've still got my German citizenship,' Guenter Wulff told an interviewer. 'When I applied for citizenship they wanted £500, and I told myself, the work I did all those years I earned that. I'm doing all right, and I knew I'd get a pension, so what's a sheet of paper? The people next door took British citizenship but they're still the "bloody foreigners" in British eyes – so you might just as well *be* a bloody foreigner!'

Only a scattering survive out of the original 25,000 who elected to stay. All are, at the time of writing, in their mid- to late 80s or in some cases their 90s. In certain villages and towns there were once small communities of ex-POWs, but many have since died. 'There were quite a few of us locally, but we didn't keep in touch on a regular basis,' Dieter Hahn says. 'We didn't have regular meetings. It was more a case of meeting them by accident and having a bit of a chat about things, that's all. But there was a POW reunion organised by the Red Cross. It wasn't only German POWs but British as well. It was excellent – I made a lot of friends.'

'There's actually another former POW here in Burgess Hill,' Hans Behrens said in a 1994 interview. 'His name's Wally. He was with me at Southease camp – a jolly fellow.

He was in the German navy, and after the war he did quite a bit of minesweeping under British command. He's now a taxi driver. We see each other occasionally, but we have different interests now.'

Many of the Germans achieved success and distinction in their local communities and in their own professions, but probably the only one to become a household name was footballer Bert Trautmann. Upon being released from POW status, he played in goal for a local football team in Lancashire, and was recruited by Manchester City the following year. In 1956, he received the Footballer of the Year Award. In that year's Cup Final the tough former paratrooper broke his neck while tackling Peter Murphy. Yet despite his injury he continued to play until the final whistle. Between 1949 and 1964 he played in 545 league matches. He received the Order of the British Empire in 2004 for promoting Anglo-German understanding through football. 'I'm more English than German,' he told one interviewer. Bert Trautmann died in 2013 at the age of 89.

In 1997, with the end of the twentieth century not far away, Bruno Liebich decided to make contact with as many of the survivors as he could. With no special clubs or associations for German ex-servicemen, it would be no easy task. After 1948, as civilians, they had all blended into the population at large, and were no longer separately enumerated in the statistics. A flash of inspiration led Bruno to realise that many of them might still have connections with agriculture. He placed advertisements in a farming magazine, and a number of former POWs answered. Often, one of the men knew of other ex-prisoners in the locality. Eventually he found 'well over 100' and made an effort to visit as many of them as possible, even though they were widely scattered around the country. When asked in 1999 to estimate how many were still in Britain, he estimated that 25 per cent had died and a further 15 per cent had returned to Germany or emigrated to destinations such as the United States or Australia.

Bruno kept in touch with the former POWs by sending out an occasional newsletter. The December issue always brought forth many Christmas cards, letters or phone calls in reply. But by 2011 only twenty-five survivors remained on the mailing list.

And this time only six replied.

As one might expect, there is no monument in Britain to the hundreds of thousands of Germans POWs who were held in the country, with the exception of the German Military Cemetery at Cannock Chase, the last resting place of some of those who died on British soil while prisoners. For many years now, the cemetery has been carefully tended by the Commonwealth Graves Commission.

Karl-Heinz Decker has been a visitor there for some years:

A comrade in Germany asked me to find out, on behalf of a neighbour, what had happened to the remains of her husband, a German pilot who was shot down in the war. She'd never found out where he was buried. So I went to Cannock Chase, found his grave, and sent a photograph back to Germany. And the old lady was absolutely over the moon – she knows where he is now. Nearly 5,000 from the First World War and the Second World War are buried there, and it's beautifully laid out. And from then on I went once a year to lay a wreath there. I've done that now for about twenty-odd years. There's hardly any of us still going there now. The German ambassador is there, German and British military people. The last time I went I had to have a chair to sit on. I was so cold I wore coats and two pairs of trousers.

The only other tangible memorials are the remains of the camps themselves. After the last POWs had left, some camps housed EVWs; others were used by the military, in certain cases right into the twenty-first century. A few were used as temporary accommodation for civilians until more permanent homes could be built. Harperley Camp – described as 'a site of national significance that must be protected for future generations' – has in recent years been given a listing by English Heritage and will be preserved as a piece of living history.

Naturally, no formation of German ex-POWs is invited to march along Whitehall on Remembrance Day. But there are exceptions to every rule. 'I'm a member of the British Para Association,' Robert Frettlöhr told an Imperial War Museum researcher in 1999. 'Nowadays you have the same maroon beret but it's just with a different badge. I do my parades here at the Cenotaph or whatever. And some of the lads from here come with me and we go over there.'

Others are content just to remember these special events and to watch the ceremonies on television. 'I rejoice with the British on occasions such as this,' Eberhard Wendler says. At Meopham, Kent, Guenther Duebel tended the village war memorial for over twenty years until ill health prevented him from continuing. 'The man who looked after it before died, and I took over from him as a matter of course. I was a soldier, too. I've been here since 1950 and never encountered any animosity.' In 2003, Duebel was awarded a silver plaque by the local branch of the Royal British Legion as a sign of their appreciation for his work.

Hans Behrens, whose job in the German army was to encode and transmit messages, has been to Bletchley Park, and speaks of the 'wonderful job' that was done there, breaking the German ciphers. He says:

My number-one home is here in Britain. It's where my family is, plus my friends, and our home that we've built. My roots are here now but there's still a very strong link to Germany. When I cross the border from Holland or Belgium into Germany I think, 'That's the Fatherland.' I don't compare so much now between there and here. But I'm all for retaining one's individuality both as people and as countries. Once, the film *The Battle of the Bulge* was on at the local cinema. I wouldn't go – I was in the real thing. I didn't want to know anything about Germany, anything about the military; it was a part of history I wanted to forget. Now I'm older I have more time and it's less stressful. And one of my principles is, 'You don't know where you're going unless you know where you come from.' I visited Dachau – did a lot of thinking. And, yes, it *is* good to think back.

Georg Kotzyba has always kept his German passport, despite having lived in Dumfries for many years. 'I always support Scotland when they're playing another team. Except for when it's Germany,' he adds with a laugh.

The British public, for their part, treated the Germans with remarkable compassion and understanding. Lifelong friendships were forged between former enemies. One farmer left his farm to the prisoner who had worked for him. An ex-POW literally helped to carry 'his' farmer to his grave.

In the 1960s, a former soldier claimed:

Looking back, one must confess that captivity was no waste of time for any of us, even for the worst fanatics. In every case, the POW was the gainer and so much of it stuck that … one notices constantly, in every serious conversation, who had the luck to be a prisoner of war in Britain. I write the word 'luck' quite intentionally, because, believe it or not, it is today here in West Germany considered an advantage to have been a prisoner of war in Britain.

June 2005. More than sixty years have passed since the war between Britain and Germany came to an end. A 70-year-old woman is at home in the farmhouse where she has lived all her life. She hears a sound; glances out of the window.

A Mercedes car has pulled up in the farmyard. Two people get out. One of them is a lad of about 19 with striking blond hair. The other is a much older man:

As soon as he got out of the car [the woman says] I knew who it was – *Heinz!* One of the two POWs who used to come for tea on Sundays and who made the little carved sewing box for me. It was a shock. And he wasn't expecting to find anyone from the same family still at the farm. He was amazed. He remembered it all very well – the old black kitchen range we had with the boiler and the oven and the fire in the middle. He went in the stack yard and looked everywhere and he was telling his grandson all about it. I thought, 'How funny him coming back' – because I've *never* forgotten them. It was like a childhood memory. And I think it was of sentimental importance to *him*. He was over 80 and he probably wanted to do it before …

She pauses, leaving the sentence unfinished. 'It was sad. As he was leaving, he said he wouldn't ever see England again.'

Notes

Prologue

p.8 'a powerful, stocky woman, very strong'. General background on hop-picking and Bodiam. Heffernan, p.17

p.8 'The prisoners were wonderful.' *Daily Herald*, 13 September 1947, p.1

p.9 'The entire POW experience ... here at all.' Reuters

1 'Let's Go, Let's Go!'

p.11 Vierville. *Guide du Pneu Michelin*, 1939

p.12 By this stage ... carts or bicycles. 'Sieg um Jeden Preis', Der Spiegel, 29 May 2004, p.61

p.13 The largest combined ... just beginning. 'Sieg um Jeden Preis', Der Spiegel, 29 May 2004, p.53

p.13 Before them an armada ... as far as the horizon. D-Day Museum

p.13 'gigantic town on the sea'. Beevor, A., p.92

p.14 'apt in going along ... make up for it'. TNA, FO 916/913 (quoted in Scheipers, p.119)

p.14 'What's going to happen to me? ... That was all.' *Soldaten Hinter Stacheldraht*, episode 2

p.14 'What you have to ... but a dead one.' *Soldaten Hinter Stacheldraht*, episode 2

p.14 'A strange new existence ... whatever the future held.' Christiansen, p.17

p.18 'They drove like devils ... war alive!' Metelmann p.187

p.18 'There were sixty ... he was finished.' *Soldaten Hinter Stacheldraht*, episode 2

2 In the Land of the Enemy

p.19 65,000 copies ... printed. 'Sieg um Jeden Preis', *Der Spiegel*, 29 May 2004, p.60

p.19 The Channel crossing ... twenty-four hours. TNA WO 199/2432

p.19 in bad weather ... four days. Beevor, p.216

p.19 'like gigantic whales' Knopp, p.109

p.19–20 'an enormous square ... fitfully among the POWs'. Christiansen, pp.34-5

p.20 'cruisers, destroyers, ...' ... untangle it. Andrews

p.20 'Every second ... couldn't influence.' *Soldaten Hinter Stacheldraht*, episode 2

p.23 From previous information ... maps before us. Hare, p.153

p.23 'a long hall ... in a line'. Hare, p.106

p.23 'The interrogator was a Norwegian ... is dead.' Holewa

p.23 'They knew more ... did ourselves.' *The Germans We Kept*

p.23 Staff-sergeant Deutsch TNA WO 199/2432

p.24 'They used to gather ... little blighters.' Wilson, p.71

p.24 DDT and Lauseto. Wikipedia (Germany)

p.24 'The cavernous areas ... squirted with DDT.' Sullivan, p.43

p.24 'A British soldier … fold of skin.' Christiansen, p.40

p.24 'Trestle tables … dressed in something.' Christiansen, p.42

p.26 'Our lessons comprised … any exams.' Damm, BBC People's War, Ref: A 3673208

p.26 Details of journey from London to Camp 16. Wendler

p.26 Gosford Camp description East Lothian at War

p.27 Every new arrival … sign for it. Wendler

p.27 Bread-making; apprentice bakers. Hellen, I., p.65

p.27 Bakery supplies POW camps and British barracks Kochan, p.203

p.27–8 'There was nothing to read … seriously' and 'The question of … horribly beaten up.' Kochan, pp.24-5

p.28 'Death Valley.' Sullivan, p.191

p.29 Automatic 'C' grade for paratroopers, SS-men etc. Sullivan, p.123

3 The Darkest Day

p.31 'They gave us spades … by the battalion.' Wilson, p.80

p.32 'We were told … and so on.' *Soldaten Hinter Stacheldraht*, episode 2

p.32 'We must try … carry on their work.' *Hansard*, 18 July 1944 (HC)

p.32 'We were stopped … brought him some water.' Kochan, p.9

p.32 'The first French … of their spit.' Sullivan, p.13

p.33 'At the end of October … railway lines inside.' Holewa

p.33 The Twickenham Ferry and similar vessels. Mullay, p.100

p.33 'looked healthy … helping in the galley'. Andrews, J.; IWM documents; and personal communication with the author

p.33 LCTs unsuitable as POW transports. TNA WO 199/2432

p.33 'Civilians stood on the pavement … on the Continent.' Knopp, p.117

p.33–4 'We used to follow … they were going into.' French TV documentary

p.34 'In spite of their unkempt … slightly.' Christiansen, pp.39-40

p.34 'the end of a link … belonged to the past'. Christiansen, p.40

p.34 'The English civilians … Hitler's last army!' Knopp, p.117

p.34–5 'Sunday, 10 September … areas I have been through.' Hildemann (diary entries)

p.35 'The soldiers were retreating … English dictionary.' Riegel, pp.72, 82

p.35 'a submariner's dream'. Blair, p.87

p.36 Account of sinking of U-39. uboatarchive.net

p.36 For general information on the U-boat war see Blair and uboat.net

p.36 3.5 million German servicemen. Knopp, p.77

p.36 Korvettenkapitän Glattes, length of detention, etc. *Sunday Express*, 13/6/48 p.6

p.36 'the requisitioned home of a margarine millionaire.' After the Battle, ed. 17, p.48

p.37 'The cost is … at the Ritz?' *Hansard*, 21/11/1939 (HC)

p.37 'the last in a row … above the camp.' Sullivan, p.98

p.37 'Well everybody … the prisoner's way.' Völkner, p.217

p.37 'I've seen Colditz … excitement we had.' Kochan, pp.41–2

p.37 More general information on Glen Mill Camp may be found in After the Battle, ed. 17, pp.50–3

p.37 See also Glen Mill

p.37 'miracle of deliverance'. Winston S. Churchill, speech of 4 June 1940

p.38 'evacuated to depots … danger.' Geneva Convention, 1929, Article 7

4 The Ones That Got Away

p.39 Now I had to accept … now in custody. Steinhilper & Osborne, pp.25-6

p.40 Flying, as I did … started. Steinhilper & Osborne, p.32

p.40 I, and the majority … of peace again. Steinhilper & Osborne, p.27

p.40 Franz von Werra. Burt & Leasor; see also Wikipedia

p.41 Walter Kurt Reich's escape. New York Times, 3/8/1940, p.7

p.41 A detailed account of the shipments of gold to Canada may be found in 'Operation Fish'. Curiously, however, this book makes no mention of prisoners of war being carried on the Sobieski. Draper

p.42 'It all then happened … were killed.' Goss, pp.332-3

p.42 The exploits of Wappler and Schnabel are detailed in Jackson, R., pp.49-67

p.42 Description of the Woolwich hospital where they met. After the Battle, ed. 70, p.40

p.43 'These fellows … jolly good show.' Jackson, R., p.67

p.43 The Max Probst incident is detailed in Steinhilper & Osborne, pp.60-1

p.43 Probst's aircraft shot down: see Ramsey (ed.), pp.228, 229, 251.

p.45 Messerschmitt pilot's interrogation. Saunders, pp.153-6

p.45 Electrification of Berlin-Hamburg railway line. uboatarchive.net (Interrogation Report: crew of U-15. 570)

p.46 'The end was inevitable … very friendly.' Schenkel

p.46 North Africa: sources vary somewhat as to the numbers of prisoners. Wolff, H., (p.103) quotes a figure of 125,000 Germans

p.46 Italians to Britain to work. Hansard, 3/12/41 (HL)

p.46 Arrangement to 'share' POWs. Jung, pp.11-12 and p.243

p.46–7 Difficulty providing for POWs, North Africa. USA assumes responsibility. Wolff, H., p.243

p.47 'We haven't measured … in the country!' TNA WO 199/405 (quoted in Hellen, J.A., Temporary Settlements …), p.203

p.47 Featherstone Camp at 'dead centre' of Britain: Wikipedia states 'Haltwhistle … sports banners stating that it is the "Centre of Britain."'.

p.47 'When it was opened … fishing was better.' Maiden Newton at War

p.47 'We think it would be almost … War Office could either.' Hellen, J.A., (Temporary Settlements …), p.205; see also English Heritage (web)

5 All Walks of Life

p.49–50 'The other German POWs … as the other.' Christiansen, p.53

p.50 'How long … to your lot?' Christiansen, p.49

p.50 Arno Christiansen's friend, Erwin. Christiansen, p.48

p.50 Werner Reinhold's acquaintance. Hull Daily Mail, 27/9/46, p.1

p.50 Typical camp sizes and populations. Jung, p.33; Hellen, J.A., (Temporary Settlements …), p.198

p.50 'worked out the hut allocation before they even arrived'. Faulk, (Group Captives), p.25

p.50 'surrounded by a morass of mud … disappeared'. Camp 179

p.50 'Every hut had a garden … our camp.' The Germans We Kept

p.50 'Anyone who sees … worthy gardeners.' Lagerecho, 31 August 1947, p.5

p.51 Rabbits as pets. Hansard, 4 March 1947 (HC)

p.51 'We were shown how … placed on it.' Hettwer, p.10

p.51 'Apart from the beds … two-tiered bunks.' Paper presented to Herbert Sulzbach by POWs, quoted in Kochan, p.105

p.51 'Sometimes it glows … deserving edge.' Kochan, p.161

p.52–3 Diary entries. Wendler

p.53 'There was nothing … craftsmen in camp'. Wolkenhauer interview (Youtube)

p.53 Diary entries. Wendler

p.54 'They came from all walks … manicured.' Christiansen, p.94

p.54 'a 14-year-old Nazi … part of Britain'. Hansard, 29 September 1944 (HC)

p.54 'an old man … remarkable?' Jackson, R., p.12

p.54 Nationalities in Camp 179. Camp 179

p.54 pressed into German service against their will'. Hansard, 18 February 1947 (HC)

p.55 'In general the prisoners … meagre indeed.' Arcumes, J.S. & Helvet, J.F., p.42
p.55 Percentage with full uniform. Jung, p.35
p.55 Diary entry. Wendler
p.55 'One parachutist … useful situation.' Kochan, p.54
p.56 Romulus and Remus statue at High Garrett. Wendler interview
p.56 'The rubbish dump … Italians.' Kochan, p.32
p.56 Notices in Italian. Christiansen p.61
p.56 'Germans and Italians … likely to meet.' *Daily Express*, 26 April 1945
p.56 'We felt the Italians stabbed … for them.' Wendler interview
p.56 'I am very sorry … German custom!' Sullivan, pp.210-11
p.56 Stoberry Park, Wells, Somerset.
p.57 Stoberry Park, Wells, Somerset. 'He was a lovely person … to our homes.' Riegel, p.88
p.57 'Lord Mayor and Town Clerk.' Sulzbach, p.42
p.57 'Sergeant … threw me out.' Sulzbach, p.8
p.57 'Every postman … or himself.' Sulzbach, p.5
p.58 Ratio of interpreters to POWs. Kochan, p.60
p.58 Interpreter's office details. Arcumes & Helvet, p.49
p.58 Duties of Polish soldiers. Dunham POW Camp
p.58 POWs shot by Poles. Jackson, S., pp.65-8
p.58 'One of our paratroopers … ding-dong!' Winkler
p.58 Numbers of staff. Kochan, p.146
p.58 Staff numbers country-wide were quoted as: 2,246 guards; 11,594 camp administration staff; 254 'other' administration staff. *Hansard*, 25 March 1947 (HC)
p.59 'an elderly soldier … both of us'. Steinhilper & Osborne, p.38
p.59 'My personal recollection … Geneva Convention.' Funk, p.10

6 Nazis Rule the Roost

p.61 Diary entry. Wendler
p.61 The purpose of the meeting … prisoners of war.' Arcumes & Helvet, p.58
p.61 Loudspeaker system. Arcumes & Helvet, p.62
p.61 'Everyone was surprised … camp inmates.' Kochan, p.44
p.61-2 'The camp commandants … hitherto served.' *Hansard*, 17 May 1944 (HL)
p.62 'The *Lagerführer* is chosen … Nazi régime.' *Hansard*, 15 March 1945 (HC)
p.63 'whether German prisoners … rest of the war?' *Hansard*, 21 February 1940 (HC)
p.63 'Does not my honourable … our own country?' *Hansard*, 29 June 1943 (HC)
p.63 'Why not employ German prisoners of war?' *Hansard*, 14 February 1945 (HC)
p.63 'Where are those men … German prisoners!' *Hansard*, 20 October 1943 (HC)
p.64 Women's Land Army: for background, see. Porter, V.; see also Kramer, A.
p.64 'might well be a critical … final victory'. *Hansard*, 18 March 1942 (HC)
p.64 'That summer … hens disappeared.' Barnes (Mary), BBC People's War, Ref: A2895834
p.64 'human, happy band … as their brother'. Page, (diary) pp.69, 73
p.65 Germans replace Italians. Held, pp.148-50
p.65 '969 specially selected … and 103'. Hellen, J.A., (*Temporary Settlements*), p.198
p.65 Labour scheme with Germans extended. Held, p.88
p.65 'the idleness of Italian … proper discipline'. *Hansard*, 16 November 1944 (HC)
p.65 'because if they are kept … more of them in that area'. *Hansard*, 16 November 1944 (HC)
p.65 'If selected German … people in general.' Minutes of meeting, 6 October 1943, TNA FO371-34474, quoted in Held, p.149 (n)
p.65 National Farmers' Union. *Hansard*, 17 December 1945 (HC)
p.66 'Opinions as to … discussions took place.' Kochan, p.35
p.66 Rettig murder. *The Times*, 8 August 1945, p.2; 9 August 1945, p.8; 14 August 1945, p.2

p.66 'utterly decrepit … for scrap'. Christiansen, p.127

p.67 'After a long journey … the shoulders.' Kochan, pp.34, 35

p.67 Parliament was told that 'German prisoners of war in this country are forbidden to fraternise with members of the public or to hold any conversation with them except in so far as may be strictly necessary for the efficient performance of the work allotted to them'. *Hansard*, 19 March 1946 (HC)

p.68 POWs take sugar beet to camp. West Sussex County Council – Wartime West Sussex

p.68 Production of syrup. Wendler

p.68 Mike Arron: sweet tea. Dunham POW Camp

p.68 'abject, cowed, spiritless … such an ordeal'. Page, (diary) p.73

7 The Final Battle

p.70 'the healthy kind of tired … a good day'. Christiansen, p.99

p.70–1 Rations, Camp 54. Wolff, H., pp.36-9

p.71 'There was not a single … same environment.' Quoted in Kochan, p.105

p.71 'Day after day went by … one another.' (The reference is to captivity in Belgium prior to being taken to Britain, but is representative nonetheless). Völkner, p.211

p.71 'concentrated imbecility … naked woman'. Kochan, p.161

p.71 'Talking to friends … in this way.' Kochan, p.111

p.71 'Huge squadrons … the camp.' Wendler

p.72 'The situation in the scenes … to victory.' Hildemann (diary, 6-7 January 1945)

p.72 Christmas 1944 … our loved ones.' Wendler

p.73 Ours was second … German Christmas. Wendler

p.73 On 23 September … peaceful island. Kochan, pp.33-4

p.73 Eberhard Wendler's record of V-2 missiles. Wendler

p.73 'whether, in providing … our own prisoners.' *Hansard*, 17 October 1944 (HC)

p.73 Hartmann incident. After the Battle, ed. 17, pp.51-2

p.73 Numbers of deaths to January 1947. *Hansard*, 24 January 1947 (HC)

p.75–6 We were required … no alternative. Dengel, pp.26-7

p.76 Whilst I was dashing … also got through. Dengel, pp.29-30

p.76 An episode … for a long time. Dengel, p.31

p.77 'I remember the day … near the sea.' Metelmann, pp.14-15

p.77 'We were an odd collection … from France.' Metelmann, p.181

p.77 'From leaflets … sounded good.' Metelmann, p.185

p.77 'They carried no weapons … end of the street.' Metelmann, p.186

p.77 Transfer of POWs and camps on Continent. Jung, p.13

p.78 *Queen Elizabeth* and *Ile de France* as POW transports. Knopp, p.88

p.78 Prisoners' belief that the *Queen Mary* had been sunk. World War II Front Line Nurse

p.79 'a fabulous luxury … marvellous facilities'. Kuhn, BBC People's War, Ref: A 4347597

p.79 'It was an unforgettable experience'. *Soldaten Hinter Stacheldraht*, episode 2

p.79 'In our entire … food like this.' Knopp, p.225

p.79 'When I was captured … see my eyes.' Wikipedia: German Prisoners of War in the United States

p.79 Picking cotton, 80 cents per day. Jung, p.120

8 An Eternal Yesterday

p.80 'The other day a neighbour … prison camp.' *Aberdeen Journal*, 5 December 1946, p.4

p.81 'Three names appeared … their contents.' Kochan, p.63

p.82 Planned escape from Le Marchant Camp, Devizes. Jackson, R., pp.9-39 p.83 Escape from Island Farm Camp, Bridgend. Jackson, R., pp.113–41; Island Farm website

p.83–4 'Before the bulletin … marched out.' Countryfile, 27 January 2013 (BBC)

p.84 'Hut 16 acquired … prisoners assembled below.' Christiansen, p.114

p.85 Hitler's death dismissed as 'propaganda'. Sullivan, p.65

p.85 'islands of men … Hitler's Empire'. Sacher-Masoch, (von) (quoted in Faulk, [Group Captives], p.191)

p.85 'Until the end of April … POWs free.' Sulzbach, p.7

p.85 Recruitment of POWs 'to fight Japanese'. TNA WO 32/1132 (quoted in Held, p.150)

p.86 'I cannot help recalling … this village, yesterday!' Hansard, 28 September 1944 (HC)

p.86 'Profumo? … giving in.' Profumo, p.96

p.87 'The British HQ … as a POW.' Elfner

p.88 'as far as Denmark if it was ever possible'. Völkner, p.188

p.88 'from most of the upstairs … almost non-existent'. Völkner, p.189

p.88 'Red Army crosses the Elbe'. Daily Mirror, 26 April 1945, p.1

p.88 'An Entire Nation … Pincer Move'. The Times, 28 April 1945, p.4

p.88 'Half a Million … in 24 Hours'. Daily Worker, 4 May 1945, p.1

p.89 'My young comrades … lost ourselves.' Quoted in Mayne, p.1

p.89 'Germany has been defeated … all go home!' Christiansen, p.115

p.90 'Though we have not recognised … similar treatment.' Hansard, 17 June 1947 (HC)

9 The POWs Are Guarding The Camp

p.91 Diary entry. Wendler

p.92 'Having no idea … dead now, anyway.' Metelmann, p.192

p.92 It's 3 p.m. … turned into reality. Hildemann (diary, 8 May 1945)

p.92 'On 8 May … their lives.' After the Battle, ed. 76, p.41

p.93 Surrender of U-boats. Derby Daily Telegraph, 14 May 1945, p.8; Western Gazette, 14 September 1945, p.8

p.93 Red Cross takes over role held by Switzerland. Held, pp.231–2

p.93 Numbers of Red Cross representatives. TNA FO 939/270

p.93 'In all the time … Red Cross.' Hettwer, p.14

p.93–4 'cases where requests … camp leaders'. Hansard, 5 June 1946 (HC)

p.94 'when belligerents … conclusion of peace'. Geneva Convention, 1929

p.94 I ask myself … since 1933. Hildemann (diary, 22 June 1945)

p.94 'thousands of German prisoners … disease and death'. The Times, 19 April 1945, p.4

p.94 Mayors of six towns taken to Belsen. The Times, 25 April 1945, p.3

p.94 Citizens of Weimar view Buchenwald. Hansard, 1 May 1945 (HL)

p.94 'What else can … going on there.' Hansard, 1 May 1945 (HL)

p.95 'It was a really crude … and yelling.' From a POW's diary, 1 August 1945, quoted in Wolff, H.

p.95 'Many didn't want to believe … dishonoured people.' Riegel, p.89

p.95 'I couldn't believe it … was terrible.' Bert Trautmann Story

p.95 'We simply could not … crumbled.' After the Battle, ed. 76, p.41

p.95 'We were all … had been shown.' Dengel, p.45

p.95 Diary entry. Wendler

p.96 'a manifesto … the people'. Sullivan, p.119

p.96 'All POWs had to stand … few prisoners.' Kochan, p.94

p.96 'Our meagre rations … not retaliate'. Hettwer, p.9

p.96 Reduced rations announced. The Times, 23 May 1945, p.2

p.96 'Non-working German … prisoners.' Hansard, 29 May 1945 (HC)

p.98 'The sort of menus … breakfast or lunch.' Hansard, 25 October 1946 (HC)

p.98 'The British guards … by the prisoners.' Wendler

p.98 'We bring no charge … law-abiding nations.' Pederson, p.429

p.99 'There must be every effort … that country.' *Hansard*, 19 December 1944 (HL)

p.99 No plan for military … '… perfected bomber.' *The Times*, 20 April 1945, p.5

p.100 'Trying to do that … with a fart.' Stanley Unwin

p.100 Template for future conduct of Germany; POWs as ambassadors. Held, p.176-7

p.101 'This sympathetic … chance of his life.' Sullivan, p.74

p.101 'Mr. K— was very … was happening.' TNA FO 939/310

p.101 'the impression was so profound … happened before'. TNA FO 939/310

p.101 'while the content … to attend'. Held, p.216

p.101 Camp magazines and newspapers: these are described in impressive detail in 'The Boy's Own Papers,'. Hellen, I.

p.101–2 *Mein Kampf* and *Hansard*. *The Times*, 21 February 1948, p.2

p.102 Training Advisers etc. Sullivan, p.150

p.102 'the Foreign Office … their bodies'. Mayne, p.45

p.102 'I was received … much as possible.' TNA FO 939/310

p.102 'The Commanding Officer's … and behaves.' Brainin (quoted in Fry, p.157)

p.102 44. 'The commandants themselves … resentment.' Held, p.176

p.102 'patchy and qualified'. *The Times*, 8 January 1973, p.8

p.103 'The education scheme … these courses.' *Hansard*, 5 February 1947 (HC)

p.103 'I was a Nazi … changed my life.' Wilton Park

p.103 'I was suspicious at first … to move forward.' Elfner

10 Sold Like Slaves

p.104 Reconversion in USA. Harry S. Truman

p.104 Repatriation deadline fixed for late June 1946. Lewis & Mewha, p.91

p.104 US War Department wanted to keep POWs but they were repatriated to achieve prompt reconversion. *New York Times*, 13 September 1945, p.5

p.104 Mauretania – war brides. Liverpool Ships

p.105 'On board the ship … would be punished.' Jung, p.251

p.106 'When we arrived at Liverpool … down the gangway.' Metelmann, p.200

p.106 Background: Britain 'imports' prisoners from USA to replace Italians who are being sent home. Held, p.170

p.106 Statistics on repatriation of Italians. Hellen, J.A., *Temporary Settlements*, p.194

p.106 'would have been spoiled … in America.' Sullivan, p.171

p.107 Number of POWs transferred from USA (127,000). Sullivan, pp.170-1

p.107 'Wherever possible … to the farmer'. *Hansard*, 8 April 1946 (HC)

p.108 All POWs repatriated from USA, except 141 individuals. Lewis & Mewha, p.91 (note to table)

p.108 'The war had been over … slaves to the British.' Metelmann, p.200

p.108 'When we arrived … forced labour.' *The Germans We Kept*

p.108 'We were greeted … was going on.' Schenkel

p.109 'The prisoners repatriated … of imprisonment.. International Red Cross Report No. 4381, 15 May 1946, (quoted in Jung, p.251)

p.109–10 'one step nearer to Germany'. Funk, p.8

p.111 'The other POWs were envious … handsome young boy!' Wolkenhauer interview (Youtube)

p.111 Diary entries (purchases). Wendler

p.111 Arthur Riegel meets old friend. Riegel, p.95

p.111 'Generally the people in camp … barbed wire in England.' POW's diary (22 February 1946), quoted in Wolff, H.

p.112 Metelmann's complaint and the subsequent inquiry. Metelmann, pp.201-2

p.112 Sullivan's analysis. Sullivan, p.172-3

p.112 'the treatment … of prisoners of war'. *Hansard*, 27 March 1946 (HC) p.112 Biographical details of Richard Stokes . *The Times*, 5 August 1957, p.9 (obituary)

p.112–13 Sir Frederick Stokes and the Stokes Mortar. Wikipedia

p.113 'our MP'. Sullivan, p. 196

p.113 'It becomes all the more important … from America'. *Hansard*, 27 March 1946 (HC)

p.113 'May I ask my right honourable Friend … was provoked.' *Hansard*, 6 November 1945 (HC)

p.113 'Is the right honourable Gentleman … should stop?' *Hansard*, 30 July 1946 (HC)

p.114 'actually importing them … under a Labour Government'. *Manchester Guardian*, 28 August 1946, p.4

p.114 'It may be that … to be good democrats?' *Hansard*, 24 March 1947 (HC)

p.114 'Under National Socialism … anything at all?' POWD report quoted in Faulk, *Group Captives*, p.177

11 Shilling a Day

p.115 Belgium. See also Wolff, H., pp.70-5

p.115 beatings and kickings. *Daily Express*, 20 May 1946, p.1

p.115 'filled with horror'. Wolff, H., p.75

p.116 'As recently as the beginning of April … starvation.' *Hansard*, 21 May 1946 (HC)

p.116 Closure of camps and transfer of men to Britain. Wolff, H., p.75; *Hansard*, 30 July 1946 (HC)

p.116 Deaths in camps in Belgium. *Hansard*, 12 August 1947 (HC)

p.117 'My turn to be repatriated … with the harvest!' Elfner

p.117 'The first snow fell … circumstances permit.' Hildemann (diary 19-20 January 1946)

p.118 '9 April 1946 … happy as a child.' POW's diary (9 April 1946) (quoted in Wolff, H.)

p.118 Cake, *Linzertorte*. Christiansen, p.101

p.119 'Applications for rubber boots … Serial No. 1600.' TNA MAF 47/54

p.119 'to help in gardens … unless we use them?' *Hansard*, 12 October 1944 (HC)

p.119 'Why not employ German prisoners?' *Hansard*, 22 March 1945 (HC)

p.120 'the first day a German … a Britisher goes down'. *Tamworth Herald*, 10 November 1945, p.5

p.120 'possible Nazis underground … objective'. *Tamworth Herald*, 10 November 1945, p.5

p.120 Brick production. *The Times*, 23 April 1946, p.2

p.120–21 Shortage of building materials. *Hansard*, 26 September 1944 (HC)

p.121 Statistics on building. *The Times*, 27 February 1946, p.4

p.121 Housing, Greenwich and Bromley. *The Times*, 23 May 1945, p.6

p.121 'Eighty German prisoners … since Saturday.' *Folkestone Herald*, 9 March 1946, p.1

p.121 'We were down to our last bit of bread and margarine'. *Folkestone Herald*, 9 March 1946, p.1

p.121 Mine clearance: 'loss of beach plans'. *Daily Express*, 10 May 1946, p.3

p.121 Bert Trautmann. Clay, pp.248-9

p.121 men with suitable experience. Faulk, (*Group Captives*), pp.42-3

p.122 'There were so many unexploded …' … home soon. Elfner

p.122 After all we were fed … '… in squalor.' Elfner: BBC People's War, Ref: A8595200

p.122 Selsey mine clearance death. The victim's name is shown as Heinz Lenz in Hansard, 28 October 1947 (HC); and as Heinz Lentz in the records of the General Register Office (3rd quarter, 1947).

p.122 Bridlington accident. *The Times*, 18 September 1947, p. 2; *Hull Daily Mail*, 29 November 1947, p.3

p.122 Compensation for injured POWs. *Hansard*, 1 July 1947 (HC)

p.123 'washed the Bramall Lane benches … football stand'. Rowe, p.99

p.123 Victory Parade. *The Times*, 6 April 1946, p.4

p.123 Victory Parade clean-up. *The Times*, 12 June 1946, p.3

p.123 Newsreel: Victory Parade preparations. British Pathé: film ID Nos. 2309.05; and 2197.03

p.123 8 June 1946 … victory celebration. Wendler

p.123 It is a rather awkward situation … like so much. Page (correspondence) p.123 'many of whom … created by the jet engine'. *The Times*, 7 May 1946, p.2

p.124 We all know … remain in this country.' *Hansard*, 17 October 1946 (HC)

p.125 Is that all … seems incredible.' *Hansard*, 25 May 1943 (HL)

p.125 Lack of agreement on pay for 'other ranks'. *Hansard*, 27 March 1946 (HC)

p.125 Basis of pay awarded to POWs for work. *Royal Warrant*, pp.241, 272-3

p.125 'Prisoners of war are paid … their own homes.' *Hansard*, 27 March 1946 (HC)

p.126 Camp money 'valueless' in other camps. Kochan, p.36

p.126 Disparity between amount paid by farmer to WAEC and portion of this received by prisoner. *Hansard*, 25 June 1946 (HC)

12 Britain Switched Off

p.127 General information of Britain's postwar economy. Clarke (especially pp.510-12)

p.127 'the psychology of a victor … defeated country'. Wasting of Marshall Aid

p.127 'broad sunlit uplands'. Winston S. Churchill, speech of 18 June 1940

p.127 Damage to houses. TNA CAB 129/55 [C(53) 24 22 January 1953] (quoted in Hennessy, p.21)

p.127 Shipping losses. *Lloyd's War Losses*

p.127 'We had not anticipated … serious financial situation.' *Hansard*, 24 August 1945 (HC)

p.127 'I found out years later … unnecessary aggravation.' Kochan, p.182

p.128 'Some prisoners express … Germany down.' TNA FO 939/310

p.128 'Many people wonder … been impoverished.' *Lagerecho*, 12 October 1947, p.1

p.128 'The position created … world famine.'. *The Times*, 16 February 1946, p.4

p.128 'Britain Switched Off … been disastrous.' *Daily Express*, 8 February 1947, p.1

p.129 'Pits have been blocked … week or ten days.' *Hansard*, 7 February 1947 (HC)

p.129 'Intensive efforts are being made … for this work.' *The Times*, 10 February 1947, p.4

p.129 '2,610 British troops … of coal.' *The Times*, 18 February 1947, p.4

p.129 Prisoners switched to snow clearing. *Hansard*, 17 February 1947 (HC)

p.129 Coldest day since 1843. *The Times*, 18 February, 1947, p.4

p.129 Train at Crick dug out. *The Times*, 8 March 1947, p.4

p.129 Lost shovels. Barnoldswick (web)

p.129 Gas Supply Critical … About Food.' *Daily Express*, 23 February 1947, p.1

p.130 two hundred men … '… terrible conditions'. *The Times*, 1 March 1947, p.4

p.130 'You take the Jerries … shoot some pigeons.' Völkner, p.232

p.130 'When the thaw came … was flooding out.' Ray Rudolf, BBC People's War, Ref: A3323215

p.130 Germans arrived at 9.00 and left at 4.30. *Hansard*, 25 February 1946 (HC)

p.131 John Profumo MP: question about small groups. *Hansard*, 15 June 1945 (HC)

p.131 'Prisoners will be taken … of the day.' TNA MAF 47/54

p.131 'When asked who could speak English … chewing gum.' Hettwer, p.11

p.131 'picked up one potato … into the ground'. Christiansen, p.132

p.132 'When driving my car around a bend … in this country.' *The Times*, 30 April 1946, p.8

p.132 'Selected men are permitted … a particular journey.' *Hansard*, 6 May 1946 (HC)

p.132 New bicycles. Wolff, H., p.59

p.132 'To prisoners who had been … shifting of a weight.' Christiansen, p.167

p.132 'reduces the availability … British citizens'. TNA MAF 47/54

p.132 'were asked to stay … cigarettes as well'. Christiansen, p.168

p.133 'I thought all the German … play with me.' Patrick Barrett, BBC People's War, Ref: A8080102

p.133 'I was only about nine or ten … out of wood.' Anonymous contributor, Derbyshire

p.133 'I remember so well … to be let down.' Roger Clark, BBC People's War

p.133 'swore at our planes … never came back'. Whitaker

p.133 'Although our backs … words of encouragement. Kochan, p.34

p.134 'Some farmers report … they have had'. *Daily Express*, 26 April 1945

p.134 One German 'equal to' 3.77 Italians. *Hansard*, 8 April 1946 (HC) p.134 'We didn't mind the farm work … we worked hard.' *The Germans We Kept*

p.134 70 per cent of diet grown on home soil. *The Times*, 2 January 1945, p.14

p.134 'Voluntary workers … pride in their work.' *The Times*, 9 July 1945 p.8

p.134 'I have seen a good many Italians … without them.' *Hansard*, 15 February 1946 (HC)

p.134–5 'If it were not for a few prisoners … penny or two.' *The Times*, 6 August 1945, p.6

p.135 German POWs responsible for one third of all agricultural labour (entire country). *Hansard*, 6 December 1945 (HL)

p.135 German POWs responsible for half of all agricultural labour (Leicestershire). *Hansard*, 4 December 1945 (HC)

p.135 'How long are we going to … without them now.' *Hansard*, 5 March 1946 (HL)

p.135 'The quarry workers … fine for him and us.' Hettwer, p.15

p.135–6 Billeting of POWs. *Hansard*, 26 March 1946 (HC)

p.136 'We have sent all the Italians … to return.' *Hansard*, 12 February 1947 (HL)

p.136 'Our farmhouse … does not.' *The Times*, 6 June 1946, p.5

p.136 Diary entries. Wendler

p.137 'How long … tomorrow we get more.' Josef Kox, BBC People's War, Ref: A7564548

p.137 'unsatisfactory behaviour … the prisoners'. *Hansard*, 13 February 1947 (HL)

p.137 'We worked for our food … sons.' Weber-Newth & Steinert, p.65

13 An Affair of the Heart

p.138 Nurses fined for fraternisation. *The Times*, 2 March 1945, p.2

p.138 Gifts to POWs. *The Times*, 5 September 1946, p.2

p.139 Gift of cake, Chatham. *The Times*, 7 May 1946, p.2

p.139 Commons debate on fraternisation. *Hansard*, 14 March 1946 (HC)

p.139 'I see in today's … it was stopped. *Hansard*, 11 July 1946 (HL)

p.140 Margaret Stone waves to POWs. Email communication: Stephen Walton (Imperial War Museum) to author

p.140 Doris Blake and Alexander Todt escape in yacht Lalun. *The Times*, 26 August 1946, p.2; *Dover*
p.140 *Express*, 30 August 1946, p.5

p.140 Fritz Todt reportedly had three daughters, and a son who was killed in action in 1944. Fritz Todt

p.141 Relaxation of regulations for Christmas. 'I do not at present contemplate … answer I have given.' *Hansard*, 26 November 1946 (HC)

p.142 Pay and bonus: comparison between initial and revised systems. *Hansard*, 24 June 1947 (HC)

p.142 'Arrangements are being made … considerable advance.' *Hansard*, 10 December 1946 (HC)

p.142 Camps more than 5 miles from town. Kochan, p.149

p.142 'queues of cars'. Sullivan, p.187

p.143 'one live body'. Sullivan, p.187

p.143 'Prisoners will share … will be held.' *Daily Mail*, 21 December 1946, p.3

p.143 Diary entry. Wendler

p.144 'You're going to have … of the family.' Kox, BBC People's War, Ref: A7564548

p.144 'It was a wonderful … my dying days.' Elfner

p.144 'As we entered … kissed us.' After the Battle, ed. 76, p.45

p.144 Colchester POWs make toys for children. *The Times*, 27 December 1946, p.2

p.144–5 I am one of the German … fairy dream. *The Times*, 30 December 1947, p.5

p.145 'The tunes … Holy Night.' *Morpeth Herald*, 9 January 1948, p.3

p.145 'Hunger and despair … could buy anything.' *The Times*, 24 December 1946, p.4

p.145 Revised restrictions. Hansard, 18 March 1947 (HC)

p.145 Commandant places mirror near exit. Arcumes & Helvet, pp.39–40

p.147 Prisoners refused transport on buses. *Sunday Express*, 13 June 1948, p.6

14 Brush Up Your English

p.148 'After Stalingrad … just for entertainment.' Doerfel

p.148 Diary entry. Wendler

p.149 The excellent facilities … appreciative write-up. Dengel, p.76

p.149 'The members … from civilians!' Wolkenhauer interview (Youtube)

p.150 Recycling materials to make toys and rabbit cages. Funk, p.9

p.151 'Free distribution … affect the toy industry.' *Hansard*, 3 December 1946 (HC)

p.151 'Many of these men … benefit of the camp.' *Hansard*, 24 March 1947 (HC)

p.151 8. Quality of facilities for sport and games. Wolff, H., p.44

p.151 'We played a lot … thrilled'. Bantz, p.44

p.151–2 'The civilian Camp Labour … faltered.' Dengel: Personal communication with author

p.152 German POWs teach English. Faulk, (*Group Captives*) p.113

p.152 Diary entry. Wendler

p.153 'Norton offered me … as a POW.' Riegel, p.90

p.153 Medical academy. *Hansard*, 11 July 1946 (HL)

p.153 Request for books on paediatrics and other subjects. Camp 179

p.153 Lack of chaplains in Wehrmacht. Sullivan, p.33

p.153 Diary entries. Wendler

p.153 'Glorious Things of Thee are Spoken'. Sullivan, p.175

p.154 'We arrived at the church … the same race.' BBC People's War, Julian Barrett, Ref: A2033209

p.154 'a thanksgiving service … worked splendidly'. *The Times*, 28 October 1946, p.2

p.154 Dr Bell, Bishop of Chichester. Sullivan, pp.80-1

p.154 Interest in religion fades. Faulk, (*Group Captives*), pp.162-3

p.154 Learning Chinese. Kochan, p.42

p.154 Hadrian's Wall. Sullivan, p.203

p.154 'About fourteen or fifteen … in our country.' *Hansard*, 12 February 1947 (HL)

p.155 Improved pay. Relaxation of discipline. *Hansard*, 24 June 1947 (HC)

p.155 It was somewhat ironic … by the Council. Dengel, p.77

p.155 Removal of patches. *Hansard*, 20 May 1947 (HC)

p.156 'Of course, while we are not … very little use.' *Hansard*, 2 December 1947 (HC)

p.156 Permission to visit cinemas etc. *Hansard*, 24 June 1947 (HC)

p.156 'Some shops … had also disappeared.' Dengel, p.77

p.156 POWs in Spalding cinema queue. *Sunday Express*, 13 June 1948, p.6

p.156 'of what tobacco … and nothing else'. *Hansard*, 1 July 1947 (HC)

p.157 'were anxious to please … go easily'. Page (diary) p. 89

p.159–60 Only a few weeks after … be so wrong. Dengel, p.84

p.160 'You have brought great joy … and understanding.' Page (correspondence)

p.160 Gift parcels. *Hansard*, 28 November 1947 (HC)

p.160 Prohibited articles. TNA FO 939/270

p.160 Someone sold me a dozen … for another parcel. Dengel, p.105

p.160 'after many years … one's family.' Page (correspondence)

p.161 Heinz Kroll rescues girl. *Evening Telegraph*, 19 July 1947, p.5

p.161 'This feeling is different … changed to friendliness.' *Sussex Express*, 27 October 1947, p.7

15 'What Are You Doing with a German?'

p.162 'I tried to placate … my protestations.' Riegel, p.97

p.163 Misinterpretation of 'public house'. Herzog, p.91; see also *Duden German Dictionary* (online)

p.163 'a couple of females … shilling a time'. Kochan, p.147

p.163 'It is an almost universal … in one area.' *Manchester Guardian*, 30 August 1946, (quoted in

Weber-Newth & Steinert, p.60)

p.163 We grew up … what they're like. 1947 report quoted in Faulk, (*Group Captives*), p.169

p.164 'The lads back in camp … always correct.' Wilson, p.97

p.164 'And we used to go to Chester … silly things.' Decker interview

p.165 ATS girl under bed. *Evening Telegraph*, 21 January 1947, p.6

p.165 'we have very rightly … and utterly wrong'. *Hansard*, 5 February 1947 (HC)

p.165–6 Monica Cann marriage to Hermann Ganter: 'ATS girl … disclosed everything.' *Sunday Express*, 18 May 1947, p.1; *The Times*, 5 June 1947, p.2

p.166 'Her punishment was not too grave … without frontiers!' *Pflugschar*, (camp magazine of Camp 250, Old Malton, Yorkshire), (quoted in Kochan, pp.177-9)

p.166 Commons debate on POW marriages. *Hansard*, 10 June 1947 (HC)

p.166 Commons debate on Vetter. *Hansard*, 8 July 1947 (HC)

p.167 'no disciplinary action … inquiry received'. *Hansard*, 10 June 1947 (HC)

p.167 Werner Vetter case reported in Germany. *Der Spiegel*, 12 July 1947, p.19

p.167 POWs to be allowed to marry British women. Pitfalls. *Hansard*, 8 July 1947 (HC)

p.167 'The woman, if British … become an alien.' TNA RG 48/2009

p.167 'would not be entitled … provided for aliens'. TNA RG 48/2009

p.167 Vetter and 24 others have sentences overturned. *Hansard*, 5 August 1947 (written answer)

p.167 The British Nationality Act 1948 came into force on 1 January 1948. Women who had lost their British nationality upon marrying a German then regained it with retrospective effect. *Hansard*, 8 July 1947 (HC); and 21 June 1948 (HL); see also Weber-Newth & Steinert, p.61

p.167 'When he realised … systems could work.' Phil Fairclough letter to author

p.167 'A couple of my girlfriends … between us.' General details of Fellbrich marriage. *Southern Daily Echo*, 15 August 1947

p.168–9 Nicholas Gold and Frances Russell. *Daily Mirror*, 19 January 1949, p.1; *Daily Express*, 19 January 1949, p.5; and 9 February 1949, p.3; *Evening Telegraph*, 8 February, 1949, p.7; *Gloucestershire Echo*, 8 February 1949, p.6; *Western Daily Press*, 9 February 1949, p.4

p.169 Bruno Liebich meets Audrey. Liebich interview; see also *St Albans Observer*, 31 December 1999

p.171 POWs directly employed by WAECs to be compulsorily repatriated. WAECs to be abolished. *Hansard*, 1 November 1948 (HC)

p.172 Fritz Zimmermann meets Lilian and they marry. Zimmermann, F.H.

16 Home in Time for Christmas

p.173 'Repatriation: … the POW thinks about.' Die Zeit am Tyne, (camp magazine of Camp 18, Featherstone Park), quoted in Hellen, I., p. 77

p.173 'They needed farm workers … is right.' *The Germans We Kept*

p.173 Farm conditions. Hansard, 1 May 1946 (written answers, HC);

p.173 Farmers Weekly, 30 August 1946 p. 22

p.174 'We conquered Germany … fell into chaos.' *Hansard*, 29 July 1946 (HC)

p.174 'say that they would give … conditions there are.' *Hansard,* 11 July 1946 (HL)

p.174 'It is not unreasonable … reparation was required.' *Hansard*, 29 July 1946 (HC)

p.174 'If there is to be slave labour … hostilities ceased.' *Hansard*, 24 March 1947 (HC)

p.174 'When belligerents conclude … conclusion of peace.' Geneva Convention 1929, Article 75

p.175 'We have, with more adroitness … international law.' *The Times*, 23 September 1946, p. 7

p.175 Whatever his faults … co-operative one. *The Times*, 19 August 1946, p. 5

p.175 'doing some of the very things … they are here.' *Hansard*, 27 March 1946 (HC);

p.175 see also *The Times*, 19 August 1946, p. 5

p.175 'Give us something … ten years.' Faulk, (Group Captives), p. 46

p.175 'A British officer was appointed … three years.' Hettwer, p. 13

p.175 Men over sixty repatriated. Kochan, p. 54

p.175 Wounded prisoner exchange. *The Times*, 16 January 1945, p. 2

p.175 Operation Oberon. Kochan, p. 116

p.176 900 prominent people. *The Times*, 22 August 1946, p. 4

p.176 10 million German women sign petition. *Hansard*, 12 November 1946 (HL)

p.176 'Criminals at least … and behave themselves.' *Daily Mirror*, 9 August 1946, p. 2

p.177 Cabinet decision on repatriation:'As regards the form … ardent Nazis.'TNA CAB128/6 (Meeting of 4 September 1946)

p.177 Repatriation scheme. *The Times*, 13 September 1946 p. 4

p.177 No priority for married men. *Hansard*, 24 March 1947 (HC)

p.177 Compassionate repatriation was announced in the Cabinet statement of September 1946, and a full explanation was given to Parliament in October. *Hansard*, 8 October 1946 (HC)

p.178 Paul Becker case. *Hansard*, 5 February 1947 (HC)

p.178 'rough and ready'. *Hansard*, 24 March 1947 (HC)

p.178 'It has been announced … wife's bad conduct.' *Lagerecho*, 31 August 1947, p. 8

p.178 Make up of repatriation groups.Wolff, H., p. 67

p.179 The position of the Government … greatest respect.' *Hansard*, 8 October 1946 (HC)

p.179 Mosquito crash:Wolf Oeder and Schönsteiner attempt rescue of crew. 'I heard a roar … they were dead.' TNA ATA 5/28 (Accident report No.W2364)

p.179 Spiegel report. *Der Spiegel*, 4 January 1947, p. 6

p.179 Bellenger promises early repatriation. *Hansard*, 3 December 1946 (HC)

17 Please Come Back!

p.180 Schulte escape attempt. *Daily Mirror*, 5 September 1946, p.8

p.180 Escapers locked in lavatory. *The Times*, 12 September 1946, p.2

p.180–1 Rehaag escape. *Evening Telegraph*, 20 October 1945, p.1

p.181 Gehrke escape attempt. *Dover Express*, 13 September 1946, p.5

p.181 Bartsch and Spindler escape. *Daily Mail*, 21 August 1946

p.181 Müller escape. Scotland, A.P., (quoted in Jackson, R., pp.202-3)

p.181 Escape West Malling - POWs steal boat. *The Times*, 19 September 1946, p.3

p.181 'nestling only a few yards … the shingle'. *Dover Express*, 28 October 1955

p.181 George Arnold biographical details. *Dover Express*, 28 October 1955

p.181 The Victory public house. *Dover Mercury*, 18 August 2011

p.182 Rescue by French trawler skipper; returned to Britain. *Dover Express*, 20 September 1946, p.4; and 27 September 1946, p.6; and *The Times*, 26 September 1946, p.2

p.182 Background on screening. Held, p. 173; Knopp, p.110

p.183 'not too nice (cat-lover!)'. (quoted in Sullivan, p.198)

p.183 'How could a man … what you were?' Kochan, p.138

p.183 Issel suicide. *Cheltenham Chronicle*, 26 October 1946, p.3

p.184 Twenty-seven interviewers. Sullivan, p.125

p.184 Fifteen-minute interview. *Hansard*, 12 February 1947 (HL)

p.184 'I would urge … at worst minor offenders.' *Hansard*, 12 February 1947 (HL)

p.184 'Every prisoner … if he thinks fit.' *Hansard*, 25 October 1946 (HC)

p.185 General criticisms of screening. See also Held, pp.171-2

p.185 'to separate the strong … by the others'. *Hansard*, 12 February 1947 (HL)

p.185 'inevitably been rather hasty'. *Hansard*, 12 February 1947 (HL)

p.185 Prospect of repatriation for prisoners graded C. *Hansard*, 18 February 1947 (HC)

p.185 Suicide at Surrey camp. *The Times*, 21 August 1946, p.2

p.185 'There were no reported … 'C' grading.' Faulk, (*Group Captives*), p.86

p.185 'Grade up the blacks … get them home.' Kochan, p.139

p.185 Screening abandoned. *Hansard*, 30 June 1947 (HC)

p.185 Bruno Liebich re-graded. Personal communication with the author

p.185 Choice of repatriation zone. *Hansard*, 8 December 1947 (HC)

18 Next Stop Germany

p.187 Moscow Conference: agreement to repatriate POWs. Sullivan, p.186 (n.)

p.187 Britain demands release of prisoners in USSR. Weber-Newth & Steinert, p.25

p.187 Gollancz petition. *The Times*, 9 September 1947, p.2

p.187 PM Attlee: reasons for slowness. *The Times*, 9 September 1947, p.2

p.187 'Although the forces … of human society.' *The Times*, 27 December 1947, p.3

p.187 35,000 repatriated, December 1947. Wolff, H., p.67

p.189 International Olympic Committee did not impose conditions on Britain. Email communication from International Olympic Committee Press Office to the author, 4 April 2012

p.189 Three hours' notice. Kochan, p.174

p.189 Cigarette lighter flints. Wolkenhauer interview (Youtube)

p.189 'Rationed goods … if legally obtained.' *Wochenpost*, 17 October 1947, p.7

p.189 Larger goods by parcel post. *Hansard*, 18 November 1947 (HC)

p.190 'Military Government … Dates?' TNA FO 939/460

p.190 Convoluted journey to Germany. Page (correspondence)

p.190–1 'Next Stop – Germany … 500 POWs go home.' *Daily Express*, 27 September 1946, p.5

p.191 'sorry to leave … after they married'. *Daily Mirror*, 27 September 1946, p.3

p.191 'Light-hearted German prisoners … own land again.' *Hull Daily Mail*, 27 September 1946, p.1

p.191 Battle-dress in many colours. *Hull Daily Mail*, 27 September 1946, p.1

p.191 Heinz Lothe. *Hull Daily Mail*, 27 September 1946, p.1

p.191 Taking tea home. *Hull Daily Mail*, 27 September 1946, p.1

p.191 'We were on deck … unknown future.' After the Battle, ed. 76, p.48

p.191 'Germany is still my home … so many people'. Page (correspondence – Engelhard to Page)

p.191 'My wife and young daughter … that trade again'. *Wochenpost*, 4 October 1946, p.11

p.192 Hull–Cuxhaven crossing takes 24 hours. Page (correspondence)

p.192 'Very good quality and sufficient in quantity'. Mainrad memoir

p.192 Greeted with flowers. Riegel, p.98

p.192 'None of us feels like shouting or cheering now'. Mainrad memoir

p.192 'The sun-tanned men … taciturn and shy.' *Die Zeit*, ed. no. 30, 1948

p.192 'We met ex-POWs … night and day.' Page (correspondence)

p.192 'We arrived at 2 A.m. … when you get here.' Mainrad memoir

p.192 'We heard a rumour … throughout the camps.' Riegel, p.98

p.193 Money paid to officers. Mainrad memoir

p.193 Accusation of 'sweating' and 'swindling'. *Hansard*, 11 February 1947 (HC)

p.193 'I do not think … and the German Government.' *Hansard*, 11 February 1947 (HC)

p.193 'May I ask what German Government … notice?' *Hansard*, 11 February 1947 (HC)

p.193 'Most of them … their former Government.' *Hansard*, 12 February 1947 (HL)

p.194 'Black-marketeers were thriving … cheat us.' Kochan, p.243

p.194 'We were taken in a cattle truck … food mediocre.' Mainrad memoir

p.194 I was a free man again … in front of her.' Page (correspondence)

p.194 'I arrived safely … and Captain Brill.' Page (correspondence)

p.194 'go back to the broken … return to it'. *Eltham & Kentish Times*, 19 September 1947, p.3

p.195 'Lately they have been escaping to avoid repatriation.' *Sunday Express*, 13 June 1948, p.6

p.195 'It is bitter to feel … all over again.' *Aberdeen Journal*, 28 February 1948, p.1

p.195 'I intend following Leo … worth a lot.' *Derby Daily Telegraph*, 10 July 1947, p.7

p.195–6 'If the farmer feels … want to keep him.' *Hansard*, 22 April 1947 (HC) p.196   Composition of selection committee. *Hansard*, 3 February 1948 (HC)

p.196   'You're going to be sent … want to go back.' Christiansen, pp.224-5

p.197   'the POW will be liable … as a civilian'. *Lagerecho*, 17 August 1947, p.9

p.197   'There was no one to look after … not bothered.' Dengel, p.111

p.198   'an empty loose box … took up residence'. Christiansen, pp.213-14

p.198   Contract terms; clothes charged. Christiansen

p.199   Civilianisation. *Hansard*, 27 October 1947 (HC); The Times, 12 May 1947, p.8

19 'The Germans Were All Right'

p.200   'As the ship pulled away … Afrika Korps song.' *The Times*, 13 July 1948, p.3

p.200   'The Germans were all right … surprised'. *Sunday Express*, 13 June 1948, p.6

p.201   'In many ways … not had for many years.' Metelmann, pp.202-3

p.201-2 'In the absence of individual … a repatriation party.' TNA HO 45/22522

p.202   Staying-on permanently. *Hansard*, 22 April 1947 (HC)

p.203   'Seeing the plight … at Cefn Farm.' Wilson, p.101

p.203   'A prisoner transport … after only four weeks.' Metelmann, p.203

p.204   'Shortly afterwards … to the United States.' Dengel, p.120

p.205   'My parents' joy to see me … was left unsaid.' Dengel, p.124

p.206   'I was even more pleased … my home elsewhere.' Dengel, p.125

p.208   Helmut Bantz trains British Olympic gymnasts. Bantz, pp.44-8

20 Britain's Last POW

p.210   Bruno Liebich's cruise. *Eastern Daily Press* – posted 27 January 2011)

p.214   'We were in the depths … snapped them.' *The Telegraph* – posted 5 May 2002)

p.217   The White Eagles and The Cavern. *Yorkshire Evening Post*, 24 February 2007 and 19 January 2009; Lewisohn, p.75; *The Beatles Encyclopedia*, p.240; see also Leigh.

p.217   Wappler returns to UK, visits Phillips family. Barrage Balloon Reunion Club

p.218   Rolf von Bargen. See Bild

p.218   Günter Anton. Howe-Taylor, pp.12-21

p.218-9 'We understood that her … typewriter somewhere.' Parker

p.219   'The 23-year-old German … has been deported.' *Gloucestershire Echo*, 2 February 1949, p.6

p.219   Ted Page : school course. Personal communication with Mr Page's daughter, Anne Smith

p.219   Harry Grenville: proof that parents died in Auschwitz. Mailonline (*Daily Mail*)

Postscript

p.220   'The Americans fed us … treated us well.' Devizes Heritage

p.220   'In this respect … in Germany.' Wolff, H., p.47

p.220   'healthy and capable of working'. Report of Stuttgart Regional Assembly, quoted in Wolff, H., p.32

p.220-1 French captivity. Overmans & Bischof (*Kriegsgefangenschaft*) pp.103-4

p.221   'while the number of deaths … lowest death rate'. Overmans, *Ende des Dritten…*, p.278 [table]; p.279

p.221   'The denazification process … to achieve'. Fry, p.166

p.221-2 'Those who need re-education … as much.' TNA FO 939/310

p.222   'very idealistic'. Smith, A.L., p.70

p.222   'to turn ignorance … respect and trust'. Mayne, p.146 (see also Wilton Park website)

p.222   'the main *raison d'etre* … in general'. Hellen, J.A., *Revisiting …*, p.12

p.222   'Blood, toil, tears and sweat'. Winston S. Churchill, speech 13 May 1940 p.222 'was found to be lacking … their obligations.' *The Times*, 21 April 1949 p.5

p.222 'Prisoners of war shall be released … repatriation.' Geneva Convention 1949, Article 118

p.223 Dead and wounded while clearing explosives. Faulk, (*Group Captives*) p.43; Wolff, H., p.61

p.223 British casualties. *Hansard*, 8 October 1946 (HC)

p.223 'The great majority … available.' *Hansard*, 7 February 1946 (HC)

p.224 One-third of POWs become naturalised British citizens. Weber-Newth & Steinert, p.160

p.225 25 per cent have died; 15 per cent emigrated. Hellen, J.A., (*Temporary Settlements*), p.217

p.226 'a site of national significance … future generations'. English Heritage website

p.226 Guenther Duebel. Personal communication with the author

p.227 Carried to grave etc. Weber-Newth & Steinert, p.66

p.227 'looking back … prisoner of war in Britain'. Faulk, (Re-education), p.196

p.227 Events of June 2005: Heinz returns. Anonymous contributor, Derbyshire

References

Every attempt has been made to contact copyright owners, where possible. Owners of any material not acknowledged here are requested to contact the author/publisher, and due acknowledgment will be made in any future edition of this work.

Translations of original German-language material are by the author.

SECTION I: Interviews

Unless otherwise indicated, all quotations by or about the persons named below are taken from these interviews.

Anonymous female contributor (Derbyshire) – Author's interview
Behrens, Hans – Imperial War Museum, Ref: 14228
Blackman, Raymond – Author's interview
Churchill, Karin (née Busch) – Imperial War Museum, Ref: 16585
Czieselsky – Imperial War Museum, Ref: 20517
Decker, Karl-Heinz – Author's interview
Dengel, Joan – Author's interview
Dengel, Theo – Author's interview
Doerfel, Nora – Imperial War Museum, Ref: 10400
Frettlöhr, Robert – Imperial War Museum, Ref: 19590
Grenville, Harry – Author's interview
Hahn, Dieter – Imperial War Museum, Ref: 27497
Holewa – Imperial War Museum, Ref: 12340
Jeltsch, Fritz – Imperial War Museum, Ref: 20598
Liebich, Bruno – Author's interview
Miles, Reg – see West Sussex County Council under 'Websites' below
Parker, Veronica – Author's interview
Rall, Gunther – Imperial War Museum, Ref: 10934
Roth, Peter – Authorv
Small, Maureen (née Blackman) – Author's interview
Teske, Hans – Imperial War Museum, Ref: 19101
Völkner, Werner – Author's interview
Wendler, Eberhard – Author's interview
Wendler, Kathleen – Author's interview
Winkler – Imperial War Museum, Ref: 18523
Wolff, George (interpreter) – Imperial War Museum, Ref: 27068
Wulff, Günter – Imperial War Museum, Ref: 23201
Zimmermann, Johannes – Imperial War Museum, Ref: 13275

SECTION II: German Official Publications

Report of the Maschke Commission (*Wissenschaftliche Kommission für deutsche
    Kriegsgefangenengeschichte* - Scientific Commission for the History of German Prisoners of War)
    Published: Bielefeld: Ernst & Werner Gieseking (various authors and dates as indicated below).
This work consists of 22 volumes – only those relevant to this book are listed here.

    Jung, Hermann, Vol. X/1, *Die deutschen Kriegsgefangenen in amerikanischer Hand – USA. (1972)*
    Böhme, Kurt W., Vol. X/2, *Die deutschen Kriegsgefangenen in amerikanischer Hand – Europa. (1973)*
    Wolff, Helmut, Vol. XI/1, *Die deutschen Kriegsgefangenen in britischer Hand. Ein Überblick. (1974)*
    Faulk, Henry Vol. XI/2, *Die deutschen Kriegsgefangenen in Großbritannien – Re-education. (1970)*
    See also *Group Captives*

SECTION III: Other Books and Published Papers

—, *Guide du pneu Michelin* (Paris: Services de Tourisme Michelin, 1939)
—, *Lloyd's War Losses: The Second World War, 3 September 1939 – 14 August 1945. Vol 1* (London: Lloyd's
    of London Press, 1989)
—, *Royal Warrant for the Pay, Appointment, and Promotion and Non Effective Pay of the Army, 1940.*
    Reprint (1945) incorporating amendments nos. 1-127 (H.M.S.O., 1945)
Arcumes, J.S. & Helvet, J.F., *Prisoner of War Camps in County Durham* (Durham: County Durham
    Books, 2002)
Bacque, James, *Crimes and Mercies: the Fate of German Civilians Under Allied occupation 1944–1950*
    (London: Little, Brown & Co., 1997)
Bantz, Helmut, *So Weit war mein Weg* (Frankfurt a.M.: Wilhelm Limpert, 1959)
Beevor, Anthony, *D-Day London* (Penguin, 2012)
Bischof, G. & Ambrose, S.E., *Eisenhower and the German POWs: Facts Against Falsehood* (Baton
    Rouge; London: Louisiana State University Press, 1992)
Blair, C., *Hitler's U-boat War* (London: Cassell, 2000)
Burt, K. & Leasor, J., *The One That Got Away* (London: Companion Book Club, date?)
Clarke, Peter, *Last 1,000 Days of the British Empire* (London: Penguin, 2007)
Clay, Catrine, *Trautmann's Journey* (London: Yellow Jersey Press, 2011)
Draper, Alfred, *Operation Fish* (London: Cassell, 1979)
Faulk, Henry, *Group Captives* (London: Chatto & Windus, 1977)
Fry, Helen, *Denazification* (Stroud: The History Press, 2010)
Goss, Christopher H., Luftwaffe *Fighters and Bombers – The Battle of Britain* (Mechanicsburg, PA,
    USA: Stackpole, 2011)
Hare, Tony, *Spanning the Century* (Spennymoor: Memoir Club, 2002)
Harry, Bill, *Beatles Encyclopedia* (London: Virgin, 2000)
Heffernan, Hilary, *Voices of Kent and East Sussex Hop Pickers* (Stroud: Tempus, 2004)
Held, Renate, *Kriegsgefangenschaft in Großbritannien* (Munich: R. Oldenbourg Verlag, 2008)
Hellen, Ingeborg, 'The Boys' Own Papers', *Bulletin of the German Historical Institute London,*
    vol XXX, no. 2 (date?) pp. 38-79
Hellen, J.A.H., 'Temporary Settlements and Transient Populations – The Legacy of Britain's
    Prisoner of War Camps: 1940-1948', *Erdkunde*, ed. 53, 1999
Hellen, J.A.H., 'Revisiting the Past: German Prisoners of War and their legacy in Britain,' in *Rozvoj
    české společnosti v Evropské unii*, ed. Koncelik J. et al., (Charles University, Prague, date?), pp. 218-30
Hennessy, Peter, *Having It So Good: Britain in the Fifties* (London: Allen Lane, 2006)
Herzog, Dagmar (ed.), *Sexuality and German Fascism* (USA : Berghahn, 2005)
Howe Taylor, Pamela, *The Germans We Trusted* (Cambridge: Lutterworth, 2003)
Jackson, Robert, *A Taste of Freedom* (London: Arthur Barker, 1964)

Jackson, Sophie, *Churchill's Unexpected Guests* (Stroud: The History Press, 2010)

Knopp, Guido, *Die Gefangenen* (Munich: Goldmann, 2005)

Kochan, Myriam, *Prisoners of England* (London: Macmillan, 1980)

Kramer, Ann, *Land Girls and Their Impact* (Barnsley: Remember When, 2008)

Lewis, George G. & Mewha, John, *History of Prisoner of War Utilization by the United States Army 1776–1945* (USA: Department of the Army, 1955)

Lewisohn, Mark, *The Beatles Live!* (London: Pavilion in association with Joseph, 1986)

Mayne, Richard, *In Victory, Magnanimity, In Peace, Goodwill: A History of Wilton Park* (London: Frank Cass, 2003)

Metelmann, Henry, *Through Hell for Hitler* (Staplehurst: Spellmount, 2003)

Mullay, A.J., *Railway Ships at War* (York: Pendragon, 2008)

Neitzel, Sönke & Welzer, Harald, *Soldaten* (London: Simon & Schuster, 2013)

Overmans, Rüdiger, 'Die Rheinwiesenlager 1945', in *Ende des Dritten Reiches – Ende des Zweiten Weltkrieges. Eine Perspektivische Rundschau*, Hans-Erich Volkmann, ed., (Munich: Piper, 1995)

Overmans, Rüdiger & Bischof, Günter, *Kriegsgefangenschaft im Zweiten Weltkrieg: eine vergleichende Perspektive* (Ternitz-Pottschach: Gerhard Höller, 1999)

Pederson, William D., *The FDR Years* (London: Eurospan, 2006)

Porter, Valerie, *Yesterday's Farm* (Newton Abbott: David & Charles, 2006)

Profumo, David, *Bringing the House Down* (London: John Murray, 2006)

Ramsey, Winston G. (ed.), *The Blitz Then and Now, Vol. 2* (London: After the Battle, 1988)

Rowe, Mark, *The Victory Tests* (Australia: Sportsbooks, 2010)

Sacher-Masoch, (von), A., 'Die Insel der Gestrigen' in *Der Bund*, No. 576, December 1946

Saunders, Andy, *Bader's Last Fight* (London: Grub Street, 2007)

Scheipers, Sibylle (ed.), *Prisoners in War* (Oxford: OUP, 2010)

Scotland, A. P., *The London Cage* (Maidstone: George Mann Ltd., 1973)

Smith, Arthur L., *The War for the German Mind* (Oxford: Berghahn, 1996)

Steinhilper, Ulrich & Osborne, Peter, *Ten Minutes to Buffalo* (Bromley: Independent Books, 1991)

Sullivan, Matthew Barry, *Thresholds of Peace* (London: Hamish Hamilton, 1979)

Völkner, Werner, *Many Rivers I Crossed* (St Austell: W.Völkner, date?)

Weber-Newth, Inge, & Steinert, Johannes-Dieter, *German Migrants in Post-War Britain* (Abingdon: Routledge, 2006)

Wilson, James, *Hitler's Teenage Warriors* (Exeter: Short Run Press, date?)

SECTION IV: Newspapers, Periodicals etc.

Aberdeen Journal

After the Battle

Cheltenham Chronicle

Daily Express

Daily Herald

Derby Daily Telegraph

Dover Express

Eltham and Kentish Times

Evening Telegraph (Angus)

Farmers Weekly

Gloucestershire Echo

Hansard

Hull Daily Mail

Lagerecho

Manchester Guardian

New York Times
Spiegel (der)
St Albans Observer
Sunday Express
Tamworth Herald
Times, The (London)
Western Gazette
Wochenpost
Die Zeit

SECTION V: Unpublished Manuscripts etc.

Andrews, John, IWM Ref: 13302
Brainin, Julius, IWM Ref. 19080
Christiansen, Arno J., IWM Ref: 05/3/1
Dengel, Theo, *D for Destiny* (manuscript for book – unpublished at time of writing this work)
Elfner, Heinz, Memoirs (by kind permission of Phil Fairclough)
Funk, Otto, IWM ref: 99/3/1
'Mainrad', Memoir by POW (identified by first name only)
Page, E.G. (Ted), IWM ref: 17224 (Items quoted are identified as either 'diary' or 'correspondence')
Riegel, Arthur, IWM Ref: 95/30/1
TNA, The National Archives: see individual references.
Wendler, Eberhard, Diary
Whitaker, M., IWM ref: 09/31/1
Zimmermann, Fritz H., IWM Ref: 05/68/1

SECTION VI: Television and Video

Soldaten hinter Stacheldraht, TV documentary, *Das Erste*, first broadcast 16 November 2000
Germans We Kept, (The), Timewatch
Bert Trautmann Story, (The), Testimony Films for 'Yesterday' Channel
Countryfile, BBC 1

SECTION VII: Websites

Barnoldswick ('Barlick') Lancashire: oneguyfrombarlick.co.uk
Barrage Balloon Reunion Clup: www.bbrc.org
BBC People's War: www.bbc.co.uk
Bild (German newspaper): de.wikipedia.org
Camp 179: http://www.pegasusarchive.org/pow/cB_Hayes_History1.htm
D-Day Museum: www.ddaymuseum.co.uk
Devizes Heritage : www.devizesheritage.org.uk/pow_memories.html
Duden German Dictionary: http://www.duden.de
Dunham POW Camp: www.communigate.co.uk/chesh/altrincham/page6.phtml
East Lothian at War: eastlothianatwar.co.uk
Eastern Daily Press: www.edp24.co.uk/news/st_albans_pensioner_s_pirate_peril
English Heritage (general): http://www.english-heritage.org.uk

English Heritage (POW camps list): http://www.english-heritage.org.uk/publications/prisoner-of-war-camps/prisoner-of-war-camps.pdf

German Prisoners of War in the United States: Wikipedia

Glen Mill: www.mcrh.mmu.ac.uk/pubs/pdf/mrhr_10_moore.pdf

Gunther Wolkenhauer interview: See Youtube

Hettwer, Erwin (memoir) (by kind permission of Mark Hickman): www.pegasusarchive.org/pow/frames.htm

Hildemann memoir: http://www.dhm.de/lemo/forum/kollektives_gedaechtnis/376/index.html

International Committee of the Red Cross Geneva Convention 1929: http://www.icrc.org/ihl/INTRO/305

International Committee of the Red Cross Geneva Convention 1949: http://www.icrc.org/applic/ihl/ihl.nsf/Treaty.xsp?documentId=77CB9983BE01D004C12563CD002D6B3E&action=openDocument

Island Farm: www.islandfarm.fsnet.co.uk

Liverpool Ships: liverpoolships.org

Maiden Newton at War: http://www.maidennewton.info/page/maiden+newton+at+war

Mailonline (Daily Mail): www.dailymail.co.uk

Mainrad memoir: Home.arcor.de/kr/kriegsgefangen/deutsch/uk/gb/camp_18/mayer1.html

British Pathé: www.britishpathe.com

Pegasus Archive: www.pegasusarchive.org/pow/frames.htm

Reuters: www.uk.mobile.reuters.com

Schenkel, Martin (memoir): home.arcor.de/kriegsgefangene/memoirs/siebenbrot.html

Stanley Unwin: www.stanleyunwin.com

Stoberry Park, Somerset: www.adkinshistory.com/newsletter21.aspx

The (Daily) Telegraph : www.telegraph.co.uk

The U-Boat war: uboat.net; and uboatarchive.net

Todt, Fritz: www.leo-bw.de

Truman, Harry S.: Millercenter.org/president/Truman/essays/biography/4

Wasting of Marshall Aid: BBC

West Sussex County Council – Wartime West Sussex: https://www.westsussex.gov.uk/learning/learning_resources/wartime_west_sussex_1939-45/memories/memories_by_theme/prisoners_of_war_pows.aspx

Wikipedia (English): en.wikipedia.org

Wikipedia (German): de.wikipedia.org

Wilton Park: www.wiltonpark.org.uk

World War II Front Line Nurse: www.press.umich.edu/pdf/9780472033317-ch1.pdf

Index

If you enjoyed this book, you may also be interested in…

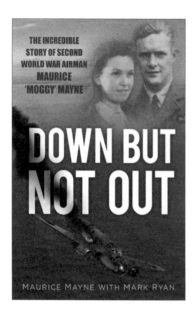

Down But Not Out: The Incredible Story of Second World War Airman Maurice 'Moggy' Mayne

MAURICE MAYNE AND MARK RYAN

978 0 7509 5206 4

Maurice 'Moggy' Mayne was a cricket-loving air gunner in the Second World War, with a pretty girlfriend back home in rural England. His turret was in a Bristol Beaufort and his pilot had to fly with almost suicidal bravery at giant German warships before releasing the torpedo. No wonder Moggy's first pilot cracked up and his second liked to drink. When he was shot down, Moggy miraculously survived – unlike his best friend Stan. Moggy was sent to Stalag Luft VIIIB, an infamous German POW camp near the Polish border, where he was badly treated. Fearing losing his beloved girlfriend Sylvia forever, and risking recapture and execution, he saw the chance to escape alone, thus beginning an epic journey through Nazi-occupied Germany. As the Gestapo shot other escaped British servicemen, Moggy Mayne came agonisingly close to lasting freedom. Instead, as the war neared its end, he had to face the horrors of the 'long march' west – and he felt his life slipping away. Would he ever see his Sylvia again?

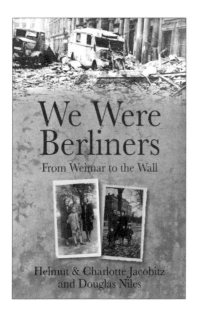

We Were Berliners:From Weimar to the Wall

DOUGLAS NILES, CHARLOTTE JACOBITZ
AND HELMUT JACOBITZ

978 0 7524 6461 9

Helmut and Charlotte Jacobitz were born in Berlin during the mid-1920s. They experienced depression and inflation, and witnessed violence as fascists and communists vied for control of Germany. When the Nazis prevailed, they survived the 12 years of the Third Reich. Drafted in 1943, Helmut was wounded fighting in Normandy. Charlotte, meanwhile, worked at the Reichsbank and took shelter against frequent bombing raids. After the Russians surrounded Berlin in April 1945, she witnessed firsthand the brutal battle for the city. The two young Germans met each other after the war, Charlotte joining Helmut to smuggle food into Berlin through the Russian blockade. The family finally immigrated to America, barely escaping before the Berlin Wall sliced the city in half. We Were Berliners combines the personal reminiscences of the Jacobitzs with a lively, detailed overview of historical events as they related to the family, to Germany, and to Europe.

The Reluctant Nazi: Searching for my Grandfather

GABRIELLE ROBINSON

978 0 7524 6447 3

After her father, a fighter pilot in the Luftwaffe, was killed during a mission over the south coast of England, Gabrielle Robinson was mainly brought up by her grandparents. Her grandfather, known to her as Api, was an opthalmologist: a kind, gentle man who helped her with her schoolwork and told her bedtime stories. Forty years after his death, she discovered a diary that he had kept during the darkest of dark days, beginning in April 1945, when he had left her and her grandmother in the countryside and returned to Berlin. Api had been an army doctor, stationed in the centre of the city, and as such, however reluctantly, he had had to join the Nazi Party. His diary is a heart-rending account of what it was like to live in Berlin as Hitler's Reich collapsed – the hunger, the disease, the bombing, the threat of retribution from the occupiers – and his struggle to survive, to shake off the stigma of being a Party member, to rebuild his life and to return to his beloved wife and granddaughter.

Visit our website and discover thousands of other History Press books.

www.thehistorypress.co.uk